London's Hidden Walks 2

by Stephen Millar

Volume 2

London's Hidden Walks 2

Written by Stephen Millar
Photography by Stephen Millar
Additional photography by Chris Dorney
Edited by Abigail Willis
Additional research by Tony Whyte
Book design by Lesley Gilmour and Susi Koch
Illustrations by Lesley Gilmour

2nd edition published in 2024 by Metro Publications Ltd
www.metropublications.com

Metro® is a registered trade mark of Associated Newspapers Limited. The METRO mark is under licence from Associated Newspapers Limited.

Printed and bound in India.
This book is produced using paper from registered sustainable and managed sources.

MIX
Paper | Supporting
responsible forestry
FSC® C043100
FSC www.fsc.org

© Stephen Millar
British Library Cataloguing in Publication Data. A catalogue record for this book is available from the British Library.

ISBN 978-1-902910-77-2

In memory of Bill Millar

Acknowledgements

I would like to thank the walkers who have completed volume 2 and pointed out corrections, particularly the closure of pubs, shops and other changes that have taken place over time. I would especially like to thank Michael Barrie and Stephen Magee who provided valuable comments on every chapter.

My thanks also go to Chris Dorney for his efforts in walking every route to take additional, excellent photographs. Additional (and equally superb) photographs were also taken by Tony Whyte and Neena Ullal. Once again, as with Volume 1, Tony as been a great sounding board on the content and provided valuable factual corrections.

Finally a big thank you to everyone at Metro for their continued support and enthusiasm. I look forward to working with them on London's Hidden Walks Volume 5.

Note: Larger maps of each walk are available to download and print. Just visit our website www.metropublications.com

Contents

St Saviour's Dock, see p.362

Introduction

Updating this second volume of London's Hidden Walks has made me realise both how much London has changed over the last few years but also how much stays the same. In recent years there has been an acceleration in historic pubs closing as tastes have changed. Medieval alleys I explored years ago have disappeared under office blocks, whilst parks have been built over and cemeteries moved for the sake of new transport links. However, if I walk around Camden in my 50s it doesn't seem very different to when I lived there in my early 20s. Everyone around me has just got a bit younger.

We mostly live our lives darting around a city, sticking to where we know best. However, I hope you use this book to slow things down and take the alternative route. Be the person standing still in the street looking up to see some detail on a building. It is a relatively rare sight. Look up to notice an inscription, plaque or architectural feature but also take the time to look down. There is a whole world of neglected hidden rivers, historic coal-hole covers and horse mounting stones that are easily missed but have a story to tell.

Over the years many readers have contacted me having walked most – and sometimes all – the routes across the four London volumes. They always provide useful feedback: this pub has shut, that street direction could be improved, did you know about this? It is always appreciated and as technology increases more information is available than when I first drafted the original walks. Some readers spent time in London before moving back home – often abroad. I hope the walks provided some nice memories of London to cherish. Let me know how you get on!

Stephen Millar
stephenwmillar@hotmail.com

KING'S CROSS
ST PANCRAS
& CAMDEN WAL

8

Regent's
Park

EUSTON

MARYLEBONE
WALK

2

OXFORD STREET

Kensington
Gardens

Hyde Park

3

ST JAMES
WALK

HOLLAND PARK AVE

WESTWAY

9

KENSINGTON
WALK

CROMWELL ROAD

KING'S RD

CHELSEA & BROMPTON
CEMETERY WALK

10

CHELSEA EMBANKMENT

River Thame

FULHAM RD

Battersea
Park

BATTERSEA BRIDGE

BATTERSEA PARK RD

BATTERSEA PARK RD

WANDSWORTH BRIDGE RD

River Thames

WANDSW

FINCHLEY RD

CAMDEN

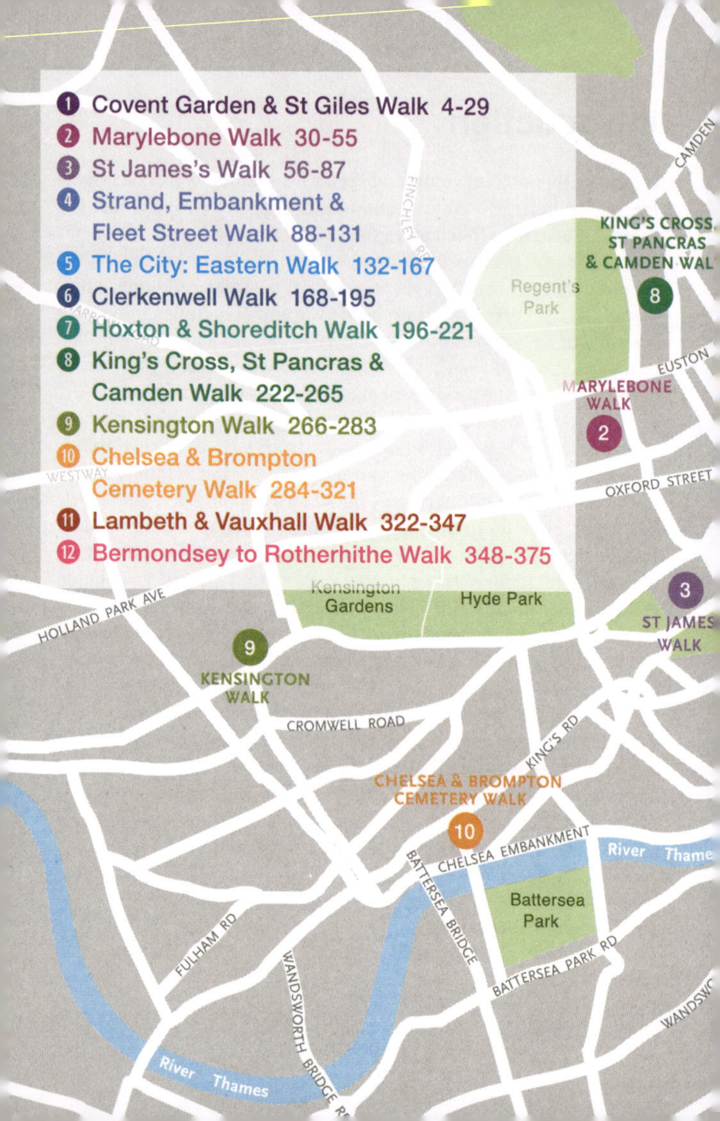

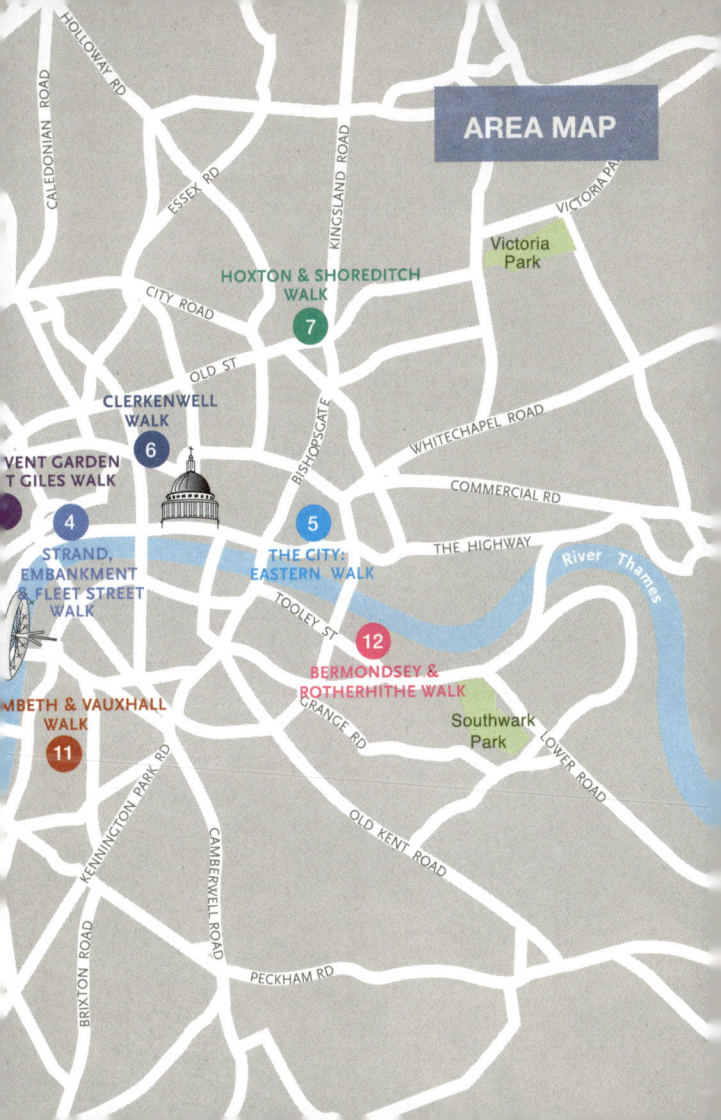

Victoria Park

HOXTON & SHOREDITCH WALK

7

CALEDONIAN ROAD

HOLLOWAY RD

ESSEX RD

KINGSLAND ROAD

VICTORIA PARK

CITY ROAD

OLD ST

CLERKENWELL WALK

6

VENT GARDEN
T GILES WALK

4

STRAND,
EMBANKMENT
& FLEET STREET
WALK

BISHOPSGATE

WHITECHAPEL ROAD

COMMERCIAL RD

THE CITY:
EASTERN WALK

5

THE HIGHWAY

River Thames

TOOLEY ST

12

BERMONDSEY &
ROTHERHITHE WALK

MBETH & VAUXHALL
WALK

11

GRANGE RD

Southwark
Park

LOWER ROAD

KENNINGTON PARK RD

CAMBERWELL ROAD

OLD KENT ROAD

BRIXTON ROAD

PECKHAM RD

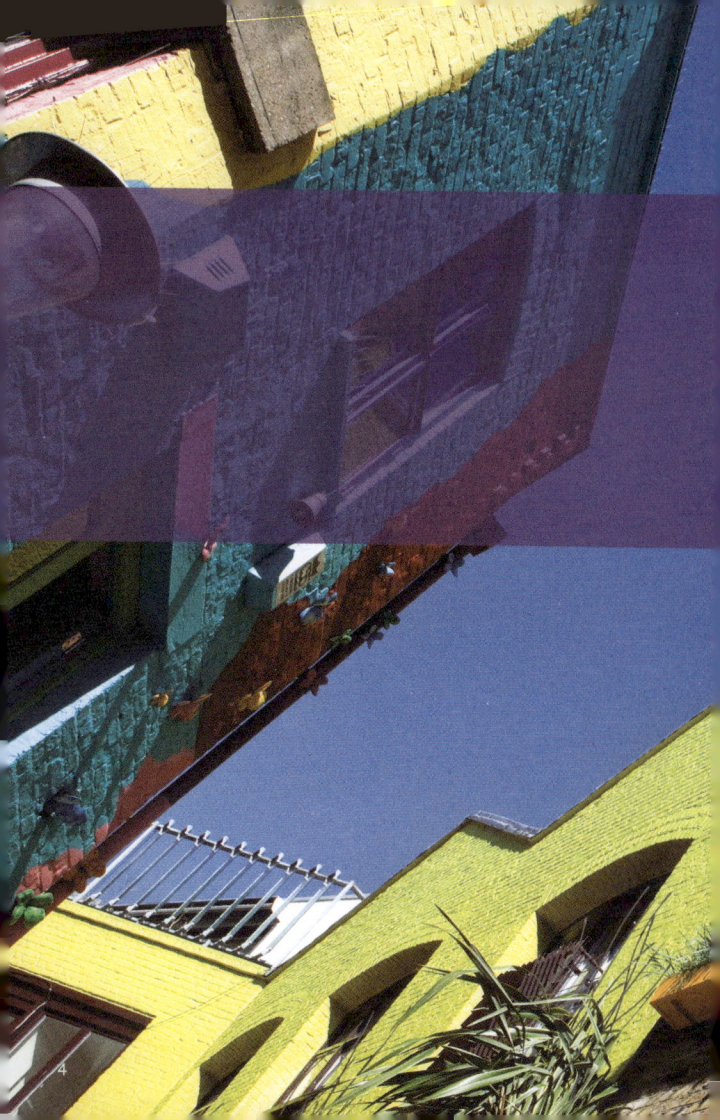

1 Covent Garden & St Giles Walk

Neal's Yard, see p.17

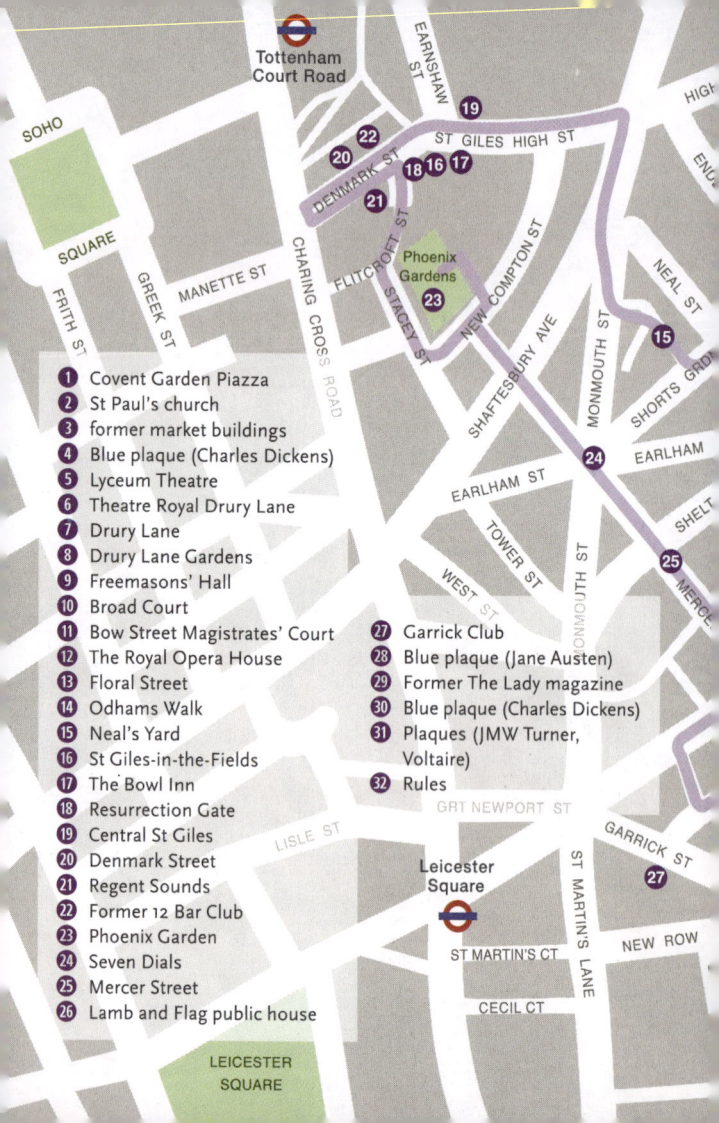

Tottenham
Court Road

SOHO

SQUARE

19

22
20
18 **16** **17**
21

St Giles High St

Phoenix
Gardens

23

15

24

25

1 Covent Garden Piazza
2 St Paul's church
3 former market buildings
4 Blue plaque (Charles Dickens)
5 Lyceum Theatre
6 Theatre Royal Drury Lane
7 Drury Lane
8 Drury Lane Gardens
9 Freemasons' Hall
10 Broad Court
11 Bow Street Magistrates' Court
12 The Royal Opera House
13 Floral Street
14 Odhams Walk
15 Neal's Yard
16 St Giles-in-the-Fields
17 The Bowl Inn
18 Resurrection Gate
19 Central St Giles
20 Denmark Street
21 Regent Sounds
22 Former 12 Bar Club
23 Phoenix Garden
24 Seven Dials
25 Mercer Street
26 Lamb and Flag public house

27 Garrick Club
28 Blue plaque (Jane Austen)
29 Former The Lady magazine
30 Blue plaque (Charles Dickens)
31 Plaques (JMW Turner, Voltaire)
32 Rules

LISLE ST

GRT NEWPORT ST

GARRICK ST

27

Leicester
Square

ST MARTIN'S CT

NEW ROW

CECIL CT

LEICESTER
SQUARE

EARNSHAM ST

DENMARK ST

CHARING CROSS ROAD

FLITCROFT ST

STACEY ST

NEW COMPTON ST

SHAFTESBURY AVE

MONMOUTH ST

NEAL ST

SHORTS GRDN

EARLHAM

EARLHAM ST

TOWER ST

WEST ST

MONMOUTH ST

MERCER

SHELT

HIGH

END

SOHO

FRITH ST

GREEK ST

MANETTE ST

Covent Garden & St Giles Walk

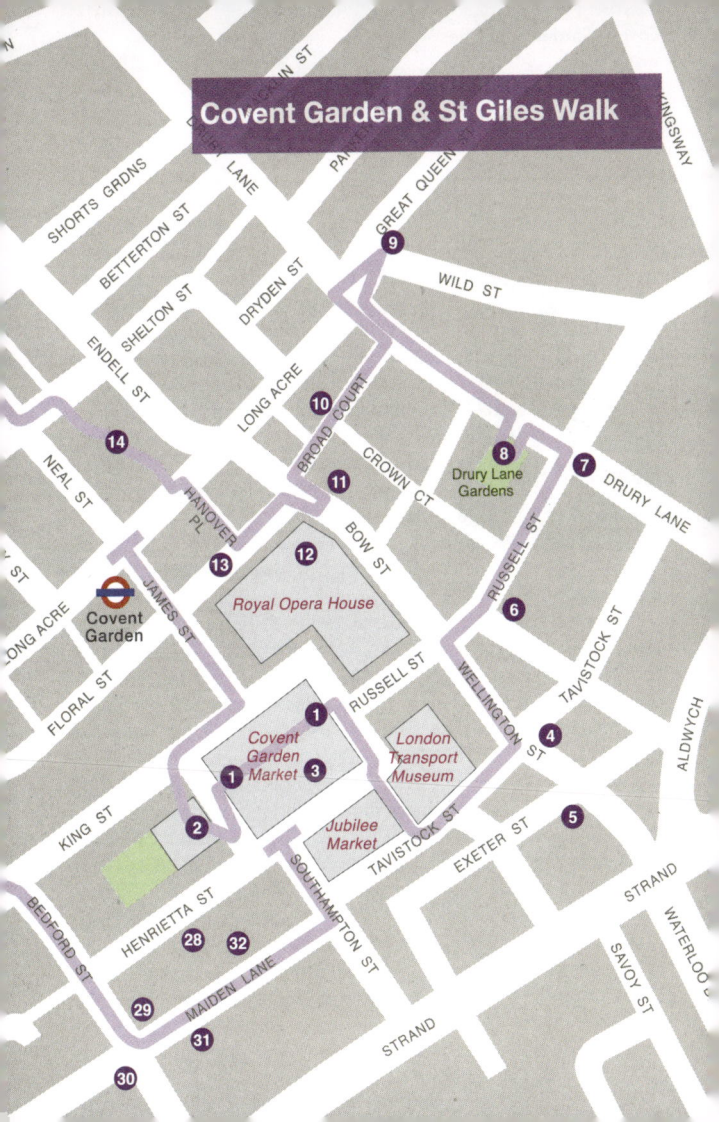

SEVEN DIALS

SHORTS GRDNS

BETTERTON ST

SHELTON ST

DRYDEN ST

ENDELL ST

LONG ACRE

NEAL ST

HANOVER PL

JAMES ST

FLORAL ST

KING ST

BEDFORD ST

HENRIETTA ST

MAIDEN LANE

BROAD COURT

BOW ST

CROWN CT

RUSSELL ST

WELLINGTON ST

TAVISTOCK ST

EXETER ST

SOUTHAMPTON ST

TAVISTOCK ST

AVENUE

GREAT QUEEN ST

WILD ST

DRURY LANE

KINGSWAY

ALDWYCH

STRAND

SAVOY ST

WATERLOO

LONG ACRE

Royal Opera House

Covent Garden Market

London Transport Museum

Jubilee Market

Drury Lane Gardens

Covent Garden

1 2 3 4 5 6 7 8 9 10 11 12 13 14

28 32 29 31 30

Covent Garden and St Giles Walk

Start/Finish: Covent Garden underground station
Distance: 2 miles

The walk begins in Covent Garden, which today is one of London's busiest shopping areas but in medieval times belonged to Westminster Abbey. The Abbey's 'convent garden' covered around 40 acres and produced fruit and vegetables for the Abbey, with surplus produce being sold to the public near the Strand.

Walk down James Street to the most famous part of Covent Garden – **❶ the piazza.** After the Dissolution of the Monasteries in the 1530s the Abbey's land fell into private hands and most of area became part of the estate of the Dukes of Bedford, whose family name is Russell.

Francis Russell, 4th Earl of Bedford, commissioned Inigo Jones, the most important English architect of the early 17th century, to develop the fields and old convent garden for residential purposes. During the early 1630s Jones laid out the piazza and built fine townhouses on all sides, the design heavily influenced by what he had seen whilst working in Italy and particularly the Piazza d'Armi in Livorno. As the first public square in the capital, the piazza's impact was huge and its novelty factor ensured that the townhouses were quickly bought up by London's wealthier residents. The craze for the 'piazza' even resulted in the term becoming a popular name for baby girls up until around 1650.

Many street names nearby recall this period, with King Street, Charles Street and Henrietta Street being named in honour of Charles I and his Queen, while Bedford Street, Russell Street, Southampton Street and Tavistock Street are all associated with the Russell family.

1 *the piazza*

During the turmoil of the Civil War in the 1640s the wealthier inhabitants of the piazza left for safer districts, many choosing new suburbs to the west such as Mayfair. The once elegant piazza slowly degenerated, dominated by a sprawling vegetable, fruit and flower market which expanded greatly after Charles II granted a market charter to the Earl of Bedford in 1670. Over the next fifty years this would develop into London's largest and most famous market, while many of Inigo Jones's elegant townhouses were converted into shops, brothels, gambling dens, Turkish baths, and coffee houses.

Start your visit to the piazza on the west side where you find ❷ **St Paul's church** with its fine Tuscan portico. It is the only substantive part of Jones's original construction still standing. Whilst it is hardly hidden, the church is often overlooked by tourists and Londoners alike as the door to the eastern entrance is sealed over. If you walk through the gate at the side you come into a very pretty and secluded garden where you can find the entrance to the church.

This was London's first classical church, and was completed in 1633. The main entrance was supposed to have been on the piazza, but William Laud, Bishop of London, insisted that the altar be located in its traditional place at the eastern end of the church and so the entrance had to be sited at the opposite end.

In building St Paul's, Inigo Jones was told by the low church Earl of Bedford not go to 'any considerable expense' and that the building should not be 'much better than a barn'. Jones responded that he would give his patron 'the handsomest barn in England' and for £5,000 built what is one of the finest and most architecturally significant churches in central London.

St Paul's is known as the 'actors' church'. Its connections with the theatrical profession began with the founding of numerous theatres in Covent Garden following the Restoration of Charles II. The church was immortalized in George Bernard Shaw's play *Pygmalion* (1913) whose opening scene depicts pedestrians sheltering from the rain beneath the portico, where later Eliza Doolittle is discovered selling violets by Henry Higgins.

Samuel Pepys (1633-1703) witnessed the first Punch and Judy show in England just outside the church, describing an 'Italian puppet play' in his diary entry of 9 May 1662. Every May an annual puppet festival and service takes place at the church in commemoration of that historic event. The artist JMW Turner and dramatist WS Gilbert (of Gilbert and Sullivan fame), were both baptised at St Paul's, and those buried here include the master woodcarver Grinling Gibbons (the pulpit is his work), Thomas Arne (composer of *Rule Britannia*) and Margaret Ponteous, the first known victim of the Great Plague of 1665. Near the church, at number 43 King Street, was the location(in the cellar) of the famous 'hippy' club *Middle Earth*, where artists such as Pink Floyd, Soft Machine and David Bowie performed and John Peel was the DJ.

Walk to the middle of the piazza and wander through the elegant ❸ **former market buildings** that today contain a wide variety of shops, stalls, restaurants and bars. The structure was built by Charles Fowler in 1830 as part of an attempt to bring some order to the area but the following century brought the market new challenges, with the Bedford family selling up its holding in 1918. An increasingly congested London traffic system made transport to and from such a centrally located market very difficult and eventually the market, re-named 'New Covent Garden', moved out to Nine Elms in Vauxhall in 1974.

Continue straight on through the market until you come onto Tavistock Court, walk right until you pass through a narrow alleyway between Jubilee Market and the London Transport Museum to enter Tavistock Street. Follow the map onto Wellington Street. If you have time you may wish to visit the excellent London Transport Museum, whose entrance faces out onto the piazza. Otherwise follow the map to the junction of Wellington Street and Tavistock Street – at the junction (above a wine bar) look out for a ❹ **blue plaque** recalling that this was once the site of Charles Dickens's magazine *All the Year Round*, and where the author lived in a little flat on the top floor on and off between 1859 and 1870 when visiting London. The weekly magazine serialised works such as Dickens's *A Tale of Two Cities* and *Great Expectations*, and Wilkie Collins's *The Woman in White*, and eager crowds would line the street outside to wait for the latest installment. Wellington Street also contains the ❺ **Lyceum Theatre**, opened in 1834, where Bram Stoker (1847-1912), author of *Dracula* (1897), worked in his day job as manager of the great 19th-century actor Sir Henry Irving.

Walk up Wellington Street then turn right into Russell Street, once notorious in Georgian London for its brothels. One such establishment, the Rose Tavern, was immortalised by Hogarth in *The Rake at the Rose Tavern*, a scene from his 1733 series *The Rakes Progress*, and it was here in 1667 that diarist Pepys recorded 'frigging with Doll Lane', one of his many lovers. The piazza itself was lined with brothels, and was described as the 'great square of Venus' by Sir John Fielding (mentioned further below).

An enterprising local waiter John Harris capitalised on Covent Garden's reputation as a red-light area by publishing from 1757 a guide to local prostitutes called *Harris's List of Covent Garden Ladies (or a Man of Pleasure's Kalendar)*. The 'Pimp General of All England's' directory contained details of each prostitute's appearance and sexual specialties and sold over a quarter of a million copies over the next 38 years. The guide was actually written by a poor Irish poet named Samuel Derrick and the fee he received from Harris helped him escape the debtor's prison.

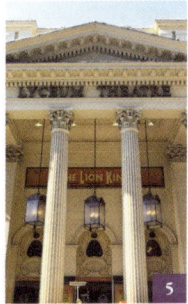

Pass the ❻ **Theatre Royal Drury Lane** on your right, noting the bust of the playwright and theatre manager Augustus Harris (1852-1896) outside. This is the oldest theatre in London, the current building being the fourth on the site. The original theatre was opened in 1663 and Charles II's mistress Nell Gywn (1650-1687) acted here, often appearing in roles penned for her by resident dramatist John Dryden (1631-1700). In May 1800 James Hadfield fired two shots at George III whilst the King sat in the Royal Box. The King was not hit and ordered the performance to continue, a famous act of bravery. The theatre has the reputation of being the most haunted in London, with the 'man in grey' in his 18th-century clothes being the most frequently seen of the half dozen apparitions recorded here.

Continue along Russell Street to meet ❼ **Drury Lane,** following in the footsteps of Samuel Pepys who came here in March 1665 and saw an 'abundance of loose women

stood at the doors, which, God forgive me, did put evil thoughts in me but proceeded no further, blessed be God'. In 1725 little had changed and one visitor counted 107 brothels along the street.

Pepys had other things on his mind three months later as the Great Plague devastated London. On that occasion he saw "two or three houses marked with a red cross upon the doors, and 'Lord have mercy upon us' writ there – which was a sad sight to me, being the first of that kind that to my remembrance I ever saw". Nearly a quarter of London's population of around 400,000 people are thought to have died in the epidemic, and Covent Garden suffered as badly as anywhere. The Sainsburys' supermarket chain began at number 173 Drury Lane, where the family's first shop opened in 1869

Turn left into Dury Lane. On the left you pass, ❽ **Drury Lane Gardens**, once the burial ground for the church of St Martin-in-the-Fields, and the buildings on either side of the entrance were originally used as a mortuary and the keeper's lodge. During the 19th century the graveyard became overcrowded as London's population increased, and in Dickens's *Bleak House* (1853) he described it as 'a hemmed-in churchyard, pestiferous and obscene, whence malignant diseases are communicated to the bodies of our dear brothers and sisters who have not departed...'.

Continue up Drury Lane, passing on the right a Peabody estate built in the 1880s and funded by the legacy of American philanthropist George Peabody. This area had many slum streets at the time, and the Peabody buildings were designed for those on low incomes. Head right into Great Queen Street. Those intrigued by the mysterious world of Freemasonry may be interested to see the vast ❾ **Freemasons' Hall** at number 60 dominating the view to the west. This serves as the headquarters of the United Grand Lodge of England and the Supreme Grand Chapter of the Arch Masons of England and is the main meeting place for Freemasons in London. The fine art-deco building is the third on the site and was built in 1927-33 as a memorial to Freemasons killed in WWI, although the Masons have been based in this street since 1775. On the first floor of the building is a Masonic shop where you can buy regalia, including a wand or apron.

Retrace your steps down Drury Lane and head right along ⑩ **Broad Court** to reach Bow Street. On your left at the junction you can see the former home of ⑪ **Bow Street Magistrates' Court and Police Station.** The court's origins on Bow Lane go back to around 1740. Early magistrates included Henry Fielding (1707-1754), author of *The History of Tom Jones*, who in the 1740s recorded that every fourth house in Covent Garden was a gin shop. At the time gin was cheap and unregulated and widely believed to be fuelling London's high levels of crime and social deprivation.

To help combat crime Fielding founded London's first police force, originally nicknamed 'the thief takers' but later more famously known as the Bow Street Runners. Numbering no more than a dozen men, this small force continued to battle against local criminals for ten years after the Metropolitan Police was founded in 1829. Fielding was succeeded upon his death by his blind brother, Sir John 'Blind Beak' Fielding (1721-1780), who could identify 3,000 individual criminals by their voices alone. In 1879 the court and its police station moved across to the western side of

the street, and remained in use until 2006. You can still see the grand but now empty Victorian building about halfway up Bow Street on the right-hand side, just opposite the main entrance to the Royal Opera House. Those who stood in the court's dock include Oscar Wilde, Lord Haw Haw, Dr Crippen, Rudolf Hess, the Kray twins, Emmeline Pankhurst, Jonathan Aitken and Lord Archer. In Dickens's *Oliver Twist* it was in the old court building that the Artful Dodger appeared charged with theft.

Giacomo Casanova (1725-1798) spent time in London in the 1760s and used to pick up prostitutes in the piazza. He appeared in the court before Sir John Fielding charged with harming a woman. In his memoirs he recalled how he 'went into the hall of justice and all eyes were at once attracted towards me; my silks and satins appeared to them the height of impertinence'. Casanova was impressed by 'Blind Beak's' excellent Italian, and was lucky to escape being punished.

General Augusto Pinochet (1915-2006) also escaped punishment on the grounds of ill health in 1998, despite

13

the District Judge at Bow Street upholding Spain's request to extradite him for his role in the deaths of Spanish nationals in Chile. The Bow Street Police Museum is based in the former police station at 28 Bow Street (see p.29 for more information).

Opposite is ⑫ **The Royal Opera House**, founded as the Theatre Royal, Covent Garden by the actor-manager John Rich (1692-1761) in 1732. The theatre became known for its music, and many of the great European operas had their English premieres here. It also hosted the first piano performance in this country in 1767.

When a second theatre was built on the site in 1809 the management tried to pass the cost on by increasing ticket prices. The audiences protested for over sixty consecutive nights in what became known as the Old Price Riots, and despite employing the famed prizefighter Daniel Mendoza to intimidate the audience, the theatre owners eventually had to back down. The Royal Opera House is a great place to visit (see p.29 for more information).

Cross over into ⑬ **Floral Street** looking up to admire the innovative 'Bridge of Aspirations' walkway, designed by Wilkinson Eyre, that links the Royal Opera House with the Royal Ballet School. Head right, down Hanover Place, you will pass the Royal Ballet School on your left (this is where the fictional Billy Elliot would have learnt his trade). Ahead, cross over Long Acre into ⑭ **Odhams Walk** to escape the crowds, this private thoroughfare is sometimes closed, in which case take the parallel Neal Street.

Walk right through to reach Shelton Street and then turn right up Neal Street, following the map through Shorts Gardens to reach ⑮ **Neal's Yard**. This pretty spot was once the hub of alternative culture in Covent Garden during the late 60s and 70s,

View of Neal Street from Odham's W...

that helped organise a successful campaign against the developers who had hoped to bulldoze the piazza after the fruit and vegetable market had moved to Nine Elms. The closure of Food for Thought (31 Neal Street) in 2015 marked the end of an era. There's a blue plaque for 'Monty Python' – in fact where Terry Gilliam and Michael Palin had studios between 1976-87. Walk through Neal's Yard and take a right on Monmouth Street and then a further right on Shaftesbury Avenue until you reach St Giles High Street.

This slightly anonymous area contrasts sharply with the prosperity and buzz of Covent Garden. It is named after the parish church of **16** **St Giles-in-the-Fields**, dedicated to the patron saint of lepers, seen on the left-hand side. The High Street was the main approach road to the City from the west until the mid-19th century. In the Middle Ages St Giles was an important site for public executions, with the gallows being located near the church.

Even after the gallows moved to Tyburn Tree (near modern-day Marble Arch), prisoners travelling from Newgate Prison would still break up their journey to have a final drink in St Giles at taverns such as **17** **The Bowl Inn** (which stood on the site of today's **Angel public house** next door to the church) or further down by the **18** 'Resurrection Gate'. The latter (dating from 1804) still stands beside the church; a relief from the earlier, 17th century, gate can be found inside the church.

The church originated in the 12th century as part of a leper hospital, and the current Grade I Palladian-style building dates from 1733. The parish of St Giles was then at the heart of a notorious slum – or 'rookery' – described by Dickens as 'a convenient asylum for the off-scourings of the night world'.

This was where Hogarth set *Gin Lane*, his famous engraving of 1751 that portrayed the rookery's outcasts and drunks wallowing in a stupor induced by cheap liquor. A real-life tragedy involving alcohol took place in 1814 when the Horseshoe Brewery near the church blew up. Ten thousand gallons of beer flooded the area, drowning eight slum-dwellers trapped in their cellars.

In 1664 a large number of deaths were recorded in the parish, the first evidence of the onset of the Great Plague. Sir Thomas Peyton later wrote 'that one parish of St Giles at London hath done us all this mischief'.

Even today the area feels unloved, perhaps unable to shake off its early association with the leper hospital, or the death of Sir John Oldcastle, the model for Shakespeare's character Falstaff. He was slowly burnt to death at the execution site in St Giles after being charged with heresy during the reign of Henry V in 1417, and died cursing the land along with the executioner and the King.

Opposite the church is a modern building complex whose multi-coloured exterior has helped to counter some of the local drabness. It is **19** **Central St Giles**, designed by the Italian architect Renzo Piano, and opened in 2010. It cost £450 million to build, and was Piano's first building in London. However it is (almost literally) overshadowed by Piano's subsequent effort – the Shard near Tower Bridge which is the tallest building in Europe. Piano was previously best known for collaborating with Richard Rogers on the Pompidou Centre in Paris. Nearby is Centre Point, one of the first skyscrapers in London when it was completed in 1967. Its fairly depressing design has not endeared it to most Londoners, and for many years it struggled to attract tenants.

Much of the rookery was planned out of existence in the mid-19th century, making way for thoroughfares such as New Oxford Street. Continue on to enter **20** **Denmark Street,** a road that

20 Denmark Street (with Centre Point in background)

gives some sense of what much of St Giles once looked like. Denmark Street was laid out in 1687 and is today best known for its guitar shops and music publishers although it is long past its hey-day in the mid-20th century when it was regarded as London's own 'Tin Pan Alley'. In the 1950s songwriters and publishers dominated the street but by the 60s, pop stars were writing much of their own material and there was less need for songwriters to produce original work for established artists. However the street continued to thrive as many bands recorded in the small studios based here, most notably at ㉑ **Regent Sounds** at number four where The Rolling Stones recorded their first two albums. Other artists who have recorded here include The Kinks, Tom Jones, Manfred Mann, Bob Marley, The Small Faces, Jimi Hendrix and Stevie Wonder.

The Kinks wrote a song entitled *Denmark Street* with the lyrics 'You go to a publisher and play him your song, he says "I hate your music, and your hair is too long, But I'll sign you up as I'd hate to be wrong..."'. Mills Music publishers, based at number 20, famously didn't follow that approach when singer-songwriter Paul Simon came to their offices in 1965, opting not to buy *The Sound of Silence* and *Homeward Bound*, later huge hits for Simon and Garfunkel.

Reg Dwight started out at Mills Music in 1965 as an office boy, later writing hits such as *Your Song* here. Eight years later – as Elton John – he was responsible for 2% of all global record sales. The influential music magazines *The Melody Maker* (number 19) and the *New Musical Express* (number 5) were based here, and in 1975 The Sex Pistols lived and rehearsed in a flat above a shop at number 6.

An impoverished David Jones, later David Bowie, lived in a camper van on the street so he could be near the trendsetters hanging out in the mod café *La Gioconda* which once occupied number 9a. The serial killer Dennis Nilsen (b.1945), responsible for the deaths of at least 15 men in the late 1970s and early 80s, used to work in the Job Centre at number one Denmark Street. During his trial in 1983 it was revealed that the saucepan he had used to make the food at the office Christmas party was the same one that he used to boil the heads of his victims.

Number 26 Denmark Street was home to the famous ㉒ **12 Bar Club**. As part of the area's redevelopment the club's lease was not renewed, and despite protests, it closed for the last time in January 2015. The building also features in the detective novels of Robert Galbraith (aka J.K. Rowlings).

Follow the map down Charing Cross Road and into the narrow Flitcroft Street which becomes Stacey Street. On the left you will find the entrance for the ㉓ **Phoenix Garden**, an award-winning community garden developed by volunteers on a former WWII bomb site. Established in 1984,

the garden is open every day and offers a pleasantly green haven amid the noise and hubbub of the inner city. The Phoenix has won numerous gardening awards and hosts planting workshops, parties and a popular annual 'agricultural show'.

On leaving the garden, continue south down Stacey Street, then walk left up New Compton Street taking a right down the narrow St Giles Passage. Cross Shaftesbury Avenue into Mercer Street to reach the conjunction of seven roads that forms **24** **Seven Dials.**

This area was first developed in the 1690s by Thomas Neale, MP. The original plan only envisaged six roads and the column at the centre only bears six sundials, although some think the column itself was supposed to be the seventh.

Neale's radial street design was intended to maximise the number of houses that could be built on the site, and he hoped the area would prove as popular with the wealthier classes of London as the nearby piazza. However, this was never the case and it became known as a rookery in its own right.

Charles Dickens (in his 1836 collection *Sketches by Boz*) writes of how a 'stranger who finds himself in the Dials for the first time ... at the entrance of seven obscure passages, uncertain which to take, will see enough around him to keep his curiosity awake for no inconsiderable time'. He was probably thinking of the prostitutes and destitute who congregated here.

Henry Mayhew (1812-1887), recorder of Victorian street life, wrote in 1860 of how he came here and found 'one of the most remarkable localities in London, inhabited by bird-fanciers, keepers of stores of old clothes and old shoes, costermongers, patterers, and a motley assemblage of others, chiefly of the lower classes. As we stood at one of the angles in the centre of the Dials we saw three young men – burglars – loitering at an opposite corner of an adjoining dial'. Thankfully, today the area is much safer.

The original column was removed in 1773, possibly by a mob that wrongly believed gold was buried underneath, but more probably by the authorities, who were concerned it was becoming a gathering point for undesirables. It ended up in Weybridge, Surrey, and in the 1980s an attempt was made to return the column to London. However Weybridge would not give it back, and the current replica was built to the original 17th-century design found in the British Museum.

Continue down **㉕ Mercer Street** to reach Long Acre. Turn right along Long Acre, then left down Rose Street onto Floral Street and then a right down Lazenby Court to reach **㉖ The Lamb and Flag public house**. It was in this alleyway in 1679 that John Dryden (1631-1700), then Poet Laureate, was beaten by thugs hired by the Earl of Rochester after the Earl mistakenly thought Dryden had written a disparaging piece alluding to him and his

Royal associates. At over 300 years old, this is the oldest pub in the area and used to be known as the *Bucket of Blood* on account of the bare-knuckle prize fights once held here. Dickens is among the famous authors who have enjoyed a pint here and the atmospheric Dryden Room upstairs does a decent lunch.

The pub faces onto Garrick Street, where on the right at number 15 is **27** **the Garrick Club.** This gentlemen's club was founded in 1831 by a group of literary figures as a place where 'actors and men of refinement and education might meet on equal terms'. It was named after the great 18th-century actor David Garrick (1717-1779), and was based at nearby 35 King Street until 1864.

The Garrick Club Affair of 1858 took place at the King Street premises, and gave rise to a long-running feud between William Makepeace Thackeray and Charles Dickens. Both members, they fell out after Edmund Yates, a friend of Dickens, made critical remarks about Thackeray. Thackeray complained and Yates was blackballed, with Dickens

26

resigning in protest. However, it is thought the real reason for the animosity originated a few months earlier after Thackeray was heard speculating openly to other members of the Club about Dickens's affair with an actress. The two men were only reconciled a few days before Thackeray's death in 1863.

Past members of the Garrick have included writers Anthony Trollope and J.M. Barrie, composer Edward Elgar and artists such as John Everett Millais and Dante Gabriel Rossetti and actors Henry Irving and Sir Laurence Olivier. AA Milne, creator of *Winnie the Pooh*, and a member of the club until his death in 1956, included the Garrick as one of the beneficiaries in his will. In 1998 the Disney Corporation paid the club about $40 million for the right to continue using Milne's characters in its films and cartoons; as a result the Garrick is one of the richest clubs in London. Despite recent criticism, the club continues to refuse female members. Continue down Bedford Street where Goupil & Cie, the French art dealers, were formerly located at number 25. The artist Vincent van Gogh (1853-1890) worked at their offices in 1875 before falling out with the owner and being sent back to Paris.

On the left you pass Henrietta Street where Jane Austen (1775-1817) lived at **28** **number 10** when staying with her brother between 1814 and 1815. The author of *Pride and Prejudice* and *Emma* described the building she was staying in as 'all dirt and confusion, but in a very interesting way'.

Until 2019 ㉙ **number 38** Bedford Street was the headquarters of *The Lady* magazine, the oldest weekly publication aimed at women in Britain, founded in 1885. In recent decades the magazine's staple diet of adverts for domestic help gave it a dowdy image, however all that changed in 2009 when Rachel Johnson – sister of Boris Johnson – became the editor. Her attempts to modernise the magazine were controversial and became the subject of a Channel 4 programme *The Lady and the Revamp* (2010). The building was sold in 1019 and the magazine has now moved to the country.

At the junction with Maiden Lane and Chandos Place look up at the building on the right to see a ㉚ **blue plaque** commemorating where **Charles Dickens** worked in a blacking factory as a young boy between 1824 and 1825. His father was languishing in a debtor's prison in Southwark for part of this time, and Charles worked in awful conditions to try to help his family.

Head up Maiden Lane and on the right-hand side you can see ㉛ **plaques** commemorating where painter **JMW Turner** was born (1775), and the French writer and philosopher **Voltaire** lived (1727-28). Voltaire moved to London after falling out with a vengeful family in France who then had him imprisoned in the Bastille. He persuaded the French authorities to let him live in exile in England and the three years he spent in London influenced the development of his own political philosophy.

At number 35 is **㉜ Rules**, the oldest restaurant in London. It was founded as an oyster bar by Thomas Rule in 1798 and is one of the best places in London to visit if you are searching for a taste of classic old-fashioned British cooking in a high Victorian setting. It is particularly well known for its game: the restaurant owns its own estate in the Pennines where much of its meat is sourced.

Rules was popular with Charles Dickens, Arthur Conan Doyle, HG Wells and Edward VII. The latter often entertained his married mistress Lilly Langtry here, the couple arriving and departing through a special door leading to a discreet private dining room that became the most celebrated 'table for two' in London. Langtry once complained that her royal lover 'always smells so very strongly of cigars'. Dickens had a table reserved for him in an alcove towards the back of the first floor.

Turn left at Southampton Street to return to the piazza and the end of the walk. ●

VISIT...

The Royal Opera House
Covent Garden, WC2E 9DD
www.roh.org.uk/

Bow Street Police Museum
28 Bow Street, WC2E 7AW
www.bowstreetpolicemuseum.org.uk

London Transport Museum
Covent Garden Piazza, WC2E 7BB
www.ltmuseum.co.uk

Freemasons' Hall
60 Great Queen Street,
WC2B 5AZ
www.ugle.org.uk

The Phoenix Garden
21 Stacey Street, WC2H 8DG
www.thephoenixgarden.org

EAT, DRINK...

Angel Public House
61-62 St Giles High St, WC2H 8LE

Lamb and Flag
33 Rose Street, WC2E 9EB
www.lambandflagcoventgarden.co.uk

Rules
34-35 Maiden Lane, WC2E 7LB
www.rules.co.uk

Paddington Street Gardens, see p.41

2 Marylebone Walk

Marylebone

Baker Street

1. Marble Arch
2. 'Tyburn Tree'
3. Tyburn Convent
4. Church of the Annunciation
5. Portman Square
6. Home House
7. Manchester Square
8. Wallace Collection
9. EMI
10. Hinde Street Methodist Church
11. Marylebone Lane
12. St James, Spanish Place
13. Farmers' Market
14. Paddington Street Gardens
15. Garbutt Place
16. Plaque (Octavia Hill)
17. Grotto Passage
18. Grotto Ragged & Industrial School
19. Memorial Garden of Rest
20. St Marylebone church
21. One Devonshire Terrace
22. Royal hunting lodge
23. Devonshire Place Mews
24. Number two
25. Number six
26. Number 50
27. Number 57
28. Wimpole Mews
29. Harley Street
30. Portland Place
31. Chinese Embassy
32. Royal Institute of British Architects
33. BBC Broadcasting House
34. All Souls Church
35. Langham Hotel
36. Medical Society of London
37. Empty plinth
38. Quintin Hogg
39. Wigmore Hall
40. St Christopher's Place

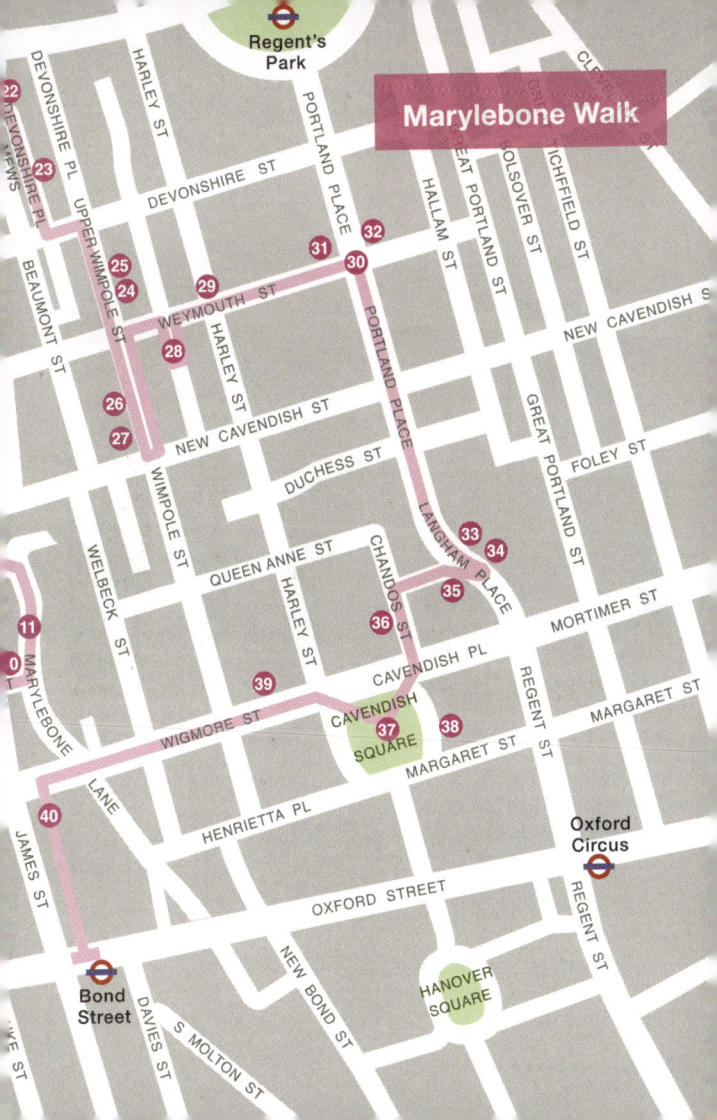

Marylebone Walk

Regent's Park

22
23

DEVONSHIRE PL
DEVONSHIRE MEWS

UPPER WIMPOLE ST
BEAUMONT ST

HARLEY ST

DEVONSHIRE ST

PORTLAND PLACE

GREAT PORTLAND ST
HALLAM ST
BOLSOVER ST
TICHFIELD ST

31 32
30

25 29
24

WEYMOUTH ST

28

HARLEY ST

NEW CAVENDISH S

NEW CAVENDISH ST

26
27

WIMPOLE ST

PORTLAND PLACE

GREAT PORTLAND ST

FOLEY ST

DUCHESS ST

LANGHAM PLACE

33 34

WELBECK ST

QUEEN ANNE ST

HARLEY ST

CHANDOS ST

35

36

MORTIMER ST

REGENT ST

11

CAVENDISH PL

0

39

WIGMORE ST

CAVENDISH
SQUARE

37 38

MARGARET ST

MARGARET ST

MARYLEBONE LANE

40

HENRIETTA PL

Oxford
Circus

JAMES ST

OXFORD STREET

REGENT ST

Bond
Street

DAVIES ST
S MOLTON ST
NEW BOND ST

HANOVER
SQUARE

Marylebone Walk
Start: Marble Arch underground station
Finish: Bond Street underground station
Distance: 2.5 miles

Marylebone is a district in the West End of London that lies between Oxford Street to the south and Marylebone Road and Regent's Park to the north. Before exploring the area it is worth stopping for a moment outside the tube station to look at ❶ **Marble Arch** opposite. It stands on the site of the medieval village of Tyburn, better known as London's main site for public executions for over 500 years.

The village was named after the Tyburn stream (or 'Ty Bourne', meaning two brooks) which was once open to the air but is now hidden deep underground. The stream still runs from

South Hampstead through central London, following the line of Marylebone Lane (seen later) before passing through St James's Park and emptying into the Thames near Vauxhall Bridge. The name Marylebone is a corruption of 'St Mary-by-the-bourne', the old name for the parish church that stood near the Tyburn stream between 1400 and 1740, and the remains of which can be seen later on in the walk.

2

The ❷ 'Tyburn Tree' or gallows stood near Marble Arch, the approximate site marked with a memorial stone in the middle of the traffic island where Edgware Road meets Bayswater Road. From 1196 to 1783 London's criminals, political victims and religious martyrs were executed here, having first travelled by cart from prisons such as Newgate (now the site of Old Bailey) along Tyburn Street (now Oxford Street). The prisoners would stop for a final drink at the Mason's Arms (still found today just north of Marble Arch at the corner of Berkeley Street and Seymour Place). Execution days were also public holidays, and crowds of up to 200,000 would gather at Tyburn to watch the condemned being strung up and then hanged as the carts they stood in were driven away. Relatives would rush forward to pull down on prisoners in order to hasten their death, whilst others tried to touch the fresh corpses in the belief they contained magical healing properties.

In 1571 permanent and more efficient gallows were set up, a measure that in 1649 allowed a record 24 prisoners to be hanged simultaneously. Over the centuries an estimated 50,000 prisoners were hanged at Tyburn, among them Oliver Cromwell (already dead but whose body was disinterred in 1661 by a vengeful Charles II); Roderigo Lopez, doctor to Elizabeth I and presumed inspiration for Shakespeare's 'Shylock'; 'Gentleman' Jack Sheppard, a notorious thief and jail-breaker who escaped from prison four times in 1724 before his fifth and final arrest; and Robert Hubert, a Frenchman who falsely confessed to starting the Great Fire of London in 1666.

The village of Tyburn and its gallows have long disappeared, but they are remembered by the ❸ **Tyburn Convent**, which is situated not far from Marble Arch at 8 Hyde Park Place, just along Bayswater Road. Since 1903 it has been home to a French order of Benedictine nuns and is dedicated to the souls of the 105 Catholic martyrs who died on the Tyburn gallows. The crypt chapel can be visited and contains a replica of the Tyburn Tree itself. A sister is available for guided tours of the shrine daily. Groups should make a prior appointment (see the website at www.tyburnconvent.org.uk).

Marble Arch dates from 1828 and was designed by John Nash (1752-1835), one of the great architects of Regency London. It was modelled on the Arch of Constantine in Rome, although today it looks rather small and insignificant beside the endless traffic rushing by. It was originally situated on the Mall as an entrance to Buckingham Palace, however legend has it that it was too narrow for the royal coach to pass through and as a result it was moved to this site in 1851. Inside are three small rooms that were once used by the police. In 1855, 250,000 people gathered in Hyde Park as part of a political demonstration, and many were surprised when a troop of policemen emerged from within Marble Arch in order to try to control the crowd. The arch is made out of white marble sourced from the same quarry at Carrara that supplied Michelangelo.

From Marble Arch walk up Great Cumberland Place and turn right along Bryanston Street, passing the vast ❹ **Church of the Annunciation** (designed by Walter Tapper in 1911) at the far corner. Head left up Old Quebec Street and turn right at Seymour Street.

Ahead is ❺ **Portman Square**, laid out between 1764 and 1784, and the centrepiece of the Portman Estate. The estate occupies land originally given by Henry VIII to Lord Chief Justice Portman in 1533, although it remained largely rural until Portman's descendants began to develop the area during the 18th century. One of London's great private estates, it comprises around 110 acres of the western part of Marylebone including Manchester Square, Gloucester Place and parts of Baker Street. It is currently under the control of billionaire Christopher (b.1958), the 10th Viscount Portman.

The square is built around a large residents-only garden, and the north-west corner contains a notable house at number 20. It was designed by the eminent architect Robert Adam in the mid-1770s and is known as ❻ **Home House** because it was built for Elizabeth, Countess of Home. It is one of the finest grand houses from that era to survive in London and until 1989 housed the Courtauld Institute of Art. Anthony Blunt (1907-1983), the art historian and Soviet spy, was director of the Institute and lived in a flat here. This was where he was first interrogated by MI5 in 1964. In recent years the house has become a private members club.

Leave the Square on the north-east side and walk up Fitzhardinge Street to reach the smaller, but prettier, ❼ **Manchester Square**. Laid out between 1776 and 1788, it was

Wallace Collection

named after the then Duke of Manchester who also commissioned Hertford House (originally known as Manchester House) on the north side. Today this building contains the magnificent **8** **Wallace Collection**, which boasts a wide variety of art works collected in the 18th and 19th centuries by the first four Marquesses of Hertford, and Sir Richard Wallace, the son of the 4th Marquess.

Sir Richard was born plain Richard Jackson, the illegitimate son of the 4th Marquess of Hertford. The latter never acknowledged his paternity, but softened the blow by leaving his son (who later took his mother's maiden name, Wallace) the family art collection and 60,000 acres of land in Ireland. This was despite a desperate attempt by the Marquess's legitimate family to contest the will. Sir Richard later bought the lease of Hertford House from the 5th Marquess of Hertford and after his death in 1890 his widow left the collection to the nation.

The collection displays around 5,500 treasures in its 25 galleries, including paintings by Titian, Rembrandt, Canaletto, Gainsborough, Velázquez as well as Frans Hals' most famous work, *The Laughing Cavalier*. It also contains fine examples of porcelain, furniture, sculpture, and armour. The collection is open daily from 10am-5pm and it has an excellent restaurant if you want to spend some time here before continuing on the walk.

The offices of recording company **9** **EMI** once stood on the north-west corner of the square at number 20, and the Beatles were regular visitors, both to the offices and local pubs. It was at EMI's offices in 1963 that the Beatles posed for a famous photograph that showed them looking down

from the atrium. This was used on the cover of their first album *Please Please Me*, and in 1969 the Beatles — now going for the hippy look — posed again at the same location (for the never-released *Get Back* album), the transformation they had undergone very evident. The pictures later featured on the *Red* and *Blue* compilation album covers. The original offices were demolished, however the stairs the Beatles posed on were moved to EMI's offices in Hammersmith.

Leave the square to the east along Hinde Street and pass on your left the mighty ❿ **Hinde Street Methodist Church**. One of many surprisingly large churches in Marylebone, it was first founded here in 1810. The current building was designed by James Weir in a classical style and dates from 1887. Head left up ⓫ **Marylebone Lane**, below which flows the Tyburn stream.

You soon reach **Marylebone High Street**, the heart of the old village. The street is lined with cafés and upmarket shops, and whilst those who describe it as resembling a village perhaps need to get out of London more often, it certainly does seem more like an English market town than a thoroughfare barely five minutes away from busy Oxford Street.

Just before you reach the High Street you pass the entrance to George Street. Walk up this street to see the Roman Catholic church of ⓬ **St James, Spanish Place** on the right. Designed by the ecclesiastical architect Edward Goldie, the building dates from 1890 and its magnificent cathedral-like Gothic interior is well worth a visit, particularly for those seeking an escape from the bustle of Marylebone.

The name 'Spanish Place' recalls when Hertford House was occupied by the Spanish Embassy in the 18th century, and its chapel — protected by diplomatic privileges

– was discreetly used by London's Catholics in an age when it was still difficult for them to worship openly. The Spanish connection to the original chapel continued up until 1827 when many of its original records were taken back to Spain.

Continue up the High Street and head left at Moxon Street. A small but excellent **13 Farmers' Market** takes place just around the corner on Aybrook Street every Sunday. Walk to the end of Moxon Street to reach **14 Paddington Street Gardens**, the sort of hidden gem only locals tend to know about. It occupies the site of St George's Burial Ground where 80,000 people were interred between 1731 and 1857. There is an excellent children's playground on the south side, while to the north are pleasant gardens and the remains of old burial tombs. In the 18th century the northern side of the gardens was also home to the Marylebone workhouse.

Head back along Moxon Street to follow the map up **15 Garbutt Place**, looking out on the right-hand side for a **16 plaque to Octavia Hill** (1838-1912). Marylebone was not always as prosperous a place as it appears today and, like most areas of London during the 19th century, contained a number of slums. Hill was a well-connected philanthropist and social reformer who raised funds for the provision of low-cost housing and recreational space for the poor. Her interest in the latter led her to co-found the National Trust in 1894. Number two Garbutt Place (then, ironically, named Paradise Place) is where she began her work in 1864, buying

41

houses from funds borrowed at a rate of five per cent interest from the famous Victorian art critic John Ruskin.

Continue north and head right down **17 Grotto Passage**. On the left look out for a building that still retains the original carved name of the **18 Grotto Ragged and Industrial School**, founded in 1846. Ragged schools were attended by the very poorest pupils, and located throughout the slums of London in the 19th century. Most were founded by philanthropists such as Lord Shaftesbury (chairman of the Ragged School Union), and it is estimated that 300,000 children passed through them between the early 1840s and 1881.

Continue ahead down a narrow passage onto Paddington Street and turn right to rejoin the High Street and continue northwards. Shortly on the left you reach the **19 Memorial Garden of Rest** which stands on the site of the old parish church of St Mary, which was originally founded here in 1400. Before then the parish church had been St John the Evangelist, built in around 1200 and located near the south end of Marylebone Lane (approximately where it meets Oxford Street today). St Mary's became known as St Mary-by-the-bourne as it sat on the banks of the Tyburn stream, and thus is responsible for the name of Marylebone itself.

St Mary's was rebuilt in 1741, but even then it was too small to continue as the parish church for an area whose population had grown from around 5,000 in 1740 to 64,000 in 1801. A larger replacement parish church was built just to the north and St Mary's became a subsidiary chapel-of-ease. Damaged during the Blitz of WWII, St Mary's was demolished in 1949.

Forty-five year old Sir Francis Bacon (1561-1626), philosopher and statesman, married his fourteen year old bride in St Mary's in 1606. Charles Wesley (1707-1788), brother of John Wesley, and an early leader of the Methodist movement, was buried here in 1788 and his grand monument can still be seen. Charles lived

in Marylebone where he wrote the lyrics of many of the 5,500 hymns credited to him. The Methodists at this time were still part of the Church of England and the dying Charles told the rector of St Mary's: 'Sir, whatever the world may say of me, I have lived, and I die, a member of the Church of England. I pray you to bury me in your churchyard'. When he died his body was carried here by eight clergymen of the Church of England.

Lord Nelson, hero of Trafalgar, worshipped in St Mary's and his daughter Horatia was baptised here in 1803. At this point she was already two years old, the illegitimate child of Nelson and his married mistress Emma Hamilton. To avoid a scandal a story was concocted that Horatia's father was Vice-Admiral Charles Thompson, with her real parents named as her godparents.

Nelson adored Horatia, and even as the Battle of Trafalgar approached, found time to think of her, writing just a few days before his death in 1805: 'The Combined Fleets of the Enemy are now reported to be coming out of Cadiz; and therefore I answer your letter, my dearest Horatia, to mark to you that you are ever uppermost in my thoughts'.

The poet Lord Byron was also baptised here in 1788, and the interior of the church was portrayed by the artist William Hogarth (1697-1764) in the marriage scene from his famous series of eight pictures entitled *The Rake's Progress* (1735).

Continue up the High Street and soon on the left you will reach the entrance to the grounds of ⓴ **St Marylebone church**. Designed by Thomas Hardwick, it was consecrated in 1817 and from that point replaced St Mary's (just visited), becoming Marylebone's fourth parish church.

Hardwick's church was built over a vaulted crypt that was already serving as a burial ground, and it continued this function until the 1850s when it was bricked up. In the 1980s the old coffins were removed and reburied in Surrey, and the vault redeveloped. It now houses a chapel and a Healing and Counselling Centre. The church of 1817 was extensively rebuilt in 1884 in a neo-classical style, with a memorial stone laid by Prime Minister Gladstone's wife.

The poets Robert Browning (1812-1889) and Elizabeth Barrett (1806-1861) were married secretly in the church on 12 September 1846, their relationship one of the great love stories in English literary history. Elizabeth was a bedridden invalid who lived with her family in Wimpole Street (seen later on in the walk). Browning read some of her published verses, and even though they had never met he wrote to her praising her work and declaring his love.

However, Elizabeth's father was determined to block any relationship developing, and was so protective a parent he tried to prevent any of his children from marrying. The poets did, however, manage to meet, and soon decided to marry in secret. After the ceremony Elizabeth returned home to her unsuspecting father, behaving as if nothing had happened until she suddenly eloped with her new husband to Italy.

In Italy her health recovered remarkably and they enjoyed a further fifteen years of happy marriage before Elizabeth died in Robert's arms. Her most famous work is *Sonnets from the Portuguese*, and number 43 contains some of the best-known lines in the English language:

> *How do I love thee? Let me count the ways.*
> *I love thee to the depth and breadth and height*
> *My soul can reach, when feeling out of sight*
> *For the ends of Being and ideal Grace.*

Their relationship was immortalised in the popular 1930 play (later a film) *The Barretts of Wimpole Street*, and the church contains a Browning Chapel, which you can ask to see. On the 12th September each year poetry fans mark the anniversary of the marriage by coming to the church.

Charles Dickens (1812-1870) lived at ㉑ **One Devonshire Terrace** between 1839 and 1851, the site now occupied by Ferguson House (15 Marylebone Road) just beside the church. During this important period in his life, five of his children were born (some of whom were baptised in the church) and he wrote *A Christmas Carol*, *The Old Curiosity Shop*, *Martin Chuzzlewit* and *Dombey and Son*. A relief depicting Dickens surrounded by his characters can be seen around the corner on Marylebone Road.

21

Walk back down Marylebone High Street and about 20 meters down on the left look out for the plaque marking the site of the old medieval manor house of Marylebone that was sold in 1544 to Henry VIII. He turned it into a ㉒ **royal hunting lodge**, and his children (and future monarchs) Edward, Mary and Elizabeth all hunted in the King's fields around here. The manor house later passed into private hands, became a school, and was eventually demolished in 1791.

The hunting grounds to the north would later be

incorporated into Regent's Park, and other fields in this vicinity were transformed into the **Marylebone Pleasure Gardens**, a popular London attraction between 1650 and 1778. The attractions on offer included bear-baiting, dog-fighting, boxing matches and bowling greens. Despite the bloodshed and violence that must have occurred here, diarist Samuel Pepys visited in 1668 and thought it a 'pretty place'. The gardens struggled to keep out the more unruly elements, and they feature as a haunt of highwaymen in John Gay's *The Beggar's Opera* (1728).

Follow the map take a left along ㉓ **Devonshire Place Mews** to reach **Dunstable Mews.** These are typical of the mews found throughout Marylebone and which originally served as stables and servants' quarters for the grand houses built in the area during the 17th and 18th centuries. Number 26 Devonshire Place Mews was where Elizabeth Barrett and Robert Browning lived in 1850, four years after secretly marrying at Marylebone's parish church.

Follow the map and turn right into Upper Wimpole Street. ㉔ **Number two** was where the writer Arthur Conan Doyle (1859-1930) briefly practised as an ophthalmologist in 1891, his lack of success affording him plenty of time to write his Sherlock Holmes stories, including *A Scandal in Bohemia* and *The Red-Headed League*. ㉕ **Number six** was once the home of Sir Frederick Treves (1853-1923), a surgeon at the Royal London Hospital in Whitechapel who befriended Joseph Merrick, better known as the 'Elephant Man'.

28 Wimpole Mews

Continue south into Wimpole Street. Elizabeth Barrett lived with her domineering father at ㉖ **number 50** from 1838 until she eloped with Robert Browning.   Paul McCartney lived at ㉗ **number 57** between 1964 and 1966, a lodger at the family home of his then-girlfriend, the actress Jane Asher. He used to escape the press by climbing out over the flat roof to number 56 where the Ashers' neighbour would let him leave by another exit. The Beatles wrote *Yesterday* and *I Want To Hold Your Hand* while staying here.

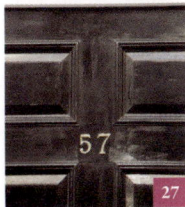

Retrace your steps to Weymouth Street and continue east. On the right is ㉘ **Wimpole Mews** where society osteopath Stephen Ward (1912-1963) lived at number 17 in the early 1960s. It was here that the Profumo Affair, the defining political scandal of the 1960s, began to unfold after an incident on 14 December 1962. Johnny Edgecombe, an embittered former minder of Ward's protégée and showgirl Christine Keeler, came to the house to confront Keeler. Edgecombe fired shots against the outer wall and the resulting media interest uncovered Ward's connection to Keeler and Rice-Davies, and to Keeler's affairs with both War Secretary John Profumo and Russian naval attaché Yevgeny Ivanov.

Initially Profumo denied the affair to the Commons, but later had to admit he had lied and was forced to resign. The Conservative government was badly damaged, helping secure Harold Wilson's Labour victory in 1964. Ward was charged with living off immoral earnings but committed suicide on the last day of his trial in 1963.

Continuing east you cross over ㉙ **Harley Street**, the home of London's medical profession since the early 19th century. It was built in 1729 and is named after Edward Harley, the second Earl of Oxford. In 1860 there were only around 20 doctors practising in Harley Street but this figure rose dramatically during the 20th century and today there are thought to be some 2,000 doctors and dentists based here, many working in one of the eight private hospitals found nearby.

Today Harley Street is part of the de Walden Estate which owns around 92 acres of east Marylebone. In the early 18th century the land was owned by the Harleys, Earls of Oxford. It then passed to the Dukes of Portland, and when the 5th Duke died unmarried in 1879 the estate was passed to his sister and the Howard de Walden family. The estate office is based at 23 Queen Street nearby, and is jointly controlled by the four daughters of the 9th Baron Howard de Walden who died in 1999.

Ahead is ㉚ **Portland Place**, a wide 18th-century street that is amongst the grandest in London. It was laid out by Robert and James Adam in 1778 and named after the Duke of Portland. The width is said to have been necessary because of a promise made to then-resident Lord Foley that his house (situated where the Langham Hotel is now based) would not have its views of the countryside to the north blocked by the development.

On the left is the ㉛ **Chinese Embassy** (number 49) and on the other side of the road lies the elegant 1930s Grade II listed art deco building that houses ㉜ **The Royal Institute of British Architects**

32

(RIBA) (number 66). RIBA has an excellent restaurant-café and bookshop, and is worth a detour if you would like to look inside this august institution.

Turn right at Portland Place and you will shortly arrive at ③③ **BBC Broadcasting House** – another notable art deco building – which opened in 1932. The exterior features statues and reliefs by Eric Gill (1882-1940), and caused controversy at the time of construction due to the substantial size Gill intended to give to the private parts of his statue of Ariel. A deeply religious but complex man, Gill was a prominent sculptor and typeface designer closely associated with the Arts and Crafts Movement. His Gill Sans typeface is still used today, but his reputation has been damaged by the revelations in his diaries that he had sexual relations with his children, his sister and even the family dog.

There is a statute of George Orwell on the east side (Hallam Street). Orwell is believed to have based Room 101 in his novel 1984 on the real room 101 inside Broadcasting House. He worked for the BBC during WWII.

34

34

35

37

Ahead is the distinctive spire of the Anglican Evangelical church of **34** **All Souls Church Langham Place,** designed by John Nash (1752-1835) and consecrated in 1824. His bust stands within the church porch looking out over Langham Place. Nash remained the favourite architect of the Prince Regent, later George IV, and was responsible for laying out much of Regency London. He is particularly remembered for his work on Regent Street, Buckingham Palace, Marble Arch and Trafalgar Square.

Cross over to pass the **35** **Langham Hotel**. When this was built in the 1860s it was the grandest establishment of its kind in London, and quickly became a favourite with notable figures such as Arthur Conan Doyle (who featured it in several Sherlock Holmes stories), Mark Twain, Napoleon III, Oscar Wilde, Noel Coward and Emperor Haile Selassie.

Follow the map down Portland Place into Chandos Street. On the right is the distinctive façade of the **36** **Medical Society of London,** founded in 1773 by the Quaker physician and philanthropist Dr John Coakley Lettsome. It moved here from the City in 1871 and is today the oldest medical society in the United Kingdom.

Continue south to reach the pleasant but rather soulless **Cavendish Square**. This was laid out from 1717 and designed by John Prince for Edward Harley, 2nd Earl of Oxford, and named after the Earl's wife Henrietta Cavendish Holles. Work on the square was delayed for some time due to the financial crisis caused by the South Sea Bubble. Notable people who have lived here include Admiral Nelson, painter George Romney and poet Lord Byron, who was born in 1788 near to where John Lewis deparment store is now situated. The square, unusually, contains an **37** **empty plinth**. In 1770 a statue of the Duke of Cumberland, infamous as the Butcher of Culloden (1746), was erected here but evidently was never popular and was removed in 1868.

53

On the east side of the square is a plaque on the former home of the remarkable Victorian philanthropist ③⑧ **Quintin Hogg,** who did so much to make education a right rather than a privilege and founded Regent Street Polytechnic.

Continue along Wigmore Street looking out on the right for ③⑨ **Wigmore Hall** at number 36. The Hall's fantastic acoustics have earned it the reputation as one of Europe's best small venues for classical music, and it is particularly well known for the concerts held here each Sunday (visit www. wigmore-hall.org.uk for concert details). It was opened in 1901 by the German piano maker Bechstein whose offices were next door, and for many years it was called the Bechstein Hall. However, its German ownership meant it was seized by the authorities during WWI and later re-opened as the more English sounding Wigmore Hall in 1917.

Continue west passing Marylebone Lane on your left. The lane continues south following the path of the now hidden Tyburn stream. Keep straight on however, and shortly on the left you will see some arches marking the entrance of ④⓪ **St Christopher's Place.** Walk through the arches to enter one of London's most attractive central shopping streets – a narrow lane heading south towards Oxford Street and lined with cafés and boutiques that follows the route of the old Tyburn steam. This was actually a slum in the 18th century known as Barrett's Court. In the 1870s social reformers – including Octavia Hill (mentioned earlier) – revitalised the area by building decent low cost housing for the inhabitants. However, a century later many of the buildings were empty and run-down despite the growth of Oxford Street just to the south. There were plans to demolish the buildings but they were saved by a developer named Robin Spiro who turned the lane into the up-market shopping boulevard seen today.

Carry on to Oxford Street, with Bond Street tube station opposite marking the end of the walk. ●

St Christopher's Place

SHOP...

Farmers' Market
Aybrook Street, W1U 4DF
www.lfm.org.uk
Sunday 10am-2pm

Marylebone High Street, W1U
www.marylebonevillage.com

St Christopher's Place, W1U
www.stchristophersplace.com

VISIT...

Wallace Collection
Manchester Square, W1U 3BN
www.wallacecollection.org

RIBA
66 Portland Place, W1B 1AD
Bookshop, café
www.architecture.com

EAT, DRINK...

Bonne Bouche
2-3 Thayer Street, W1U 3JD

La Fromagerie
2-6 Moxon Street, W1U 4EW
www.lafromagerie.co.uk

Pickering Place, see p.75

3 St James's Walk

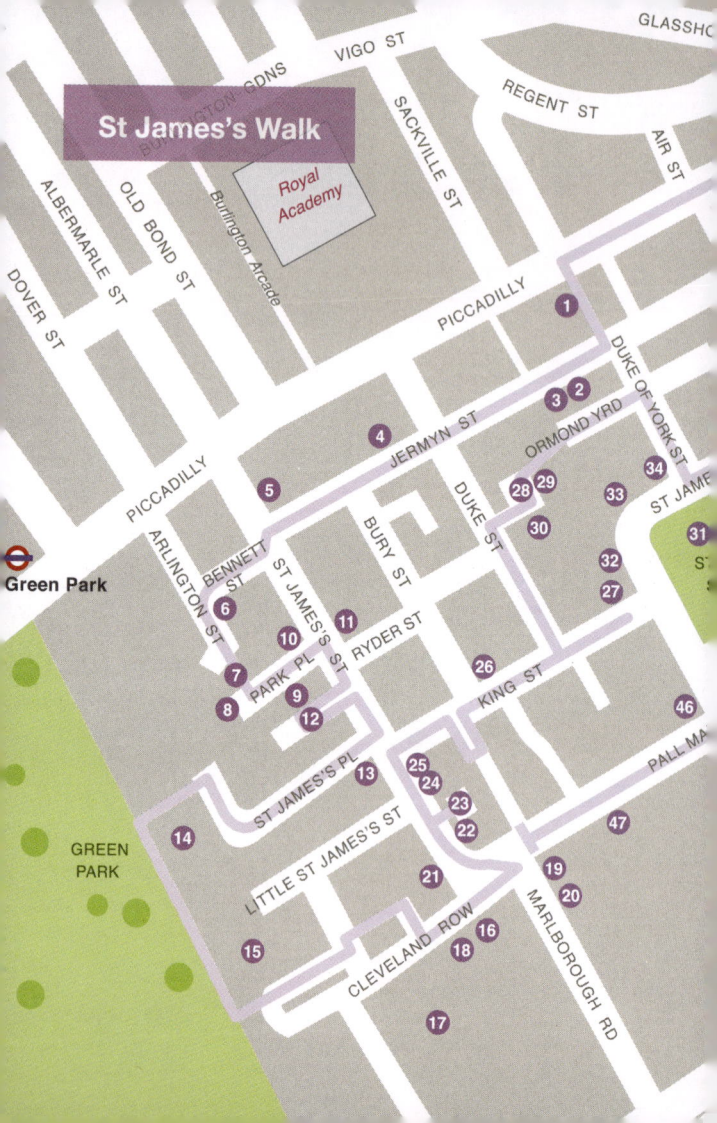

St James's Walk

Royal Academy

Burlington Arcade

VIGO ST

GLASSHO

BURLINGTON GDNS

SACKVILLE ST

REGENT ST

AIR ST

ALBEMARLE ST

OLD BOND ST

DOVER ST

PICCADILLY

DUKE OF YORK ST

1

3 **2**

ORMOND YRD

34

ST JAME

4 JERMYN ST

33

5

DUKE ST

28 **29**

30

31

PICCADILLY

BENNETT ST

ST JAMES'S ST

BURY ST

32

27

🚇 **Green Park**

ARLINGTON ST

6

11

PARK PL

RYDER ST

10

26

46

7

9

KING ST

8

12

ST JAMES'S PL

13

25

24

PALL MA

14

23

22

47

GREEN
PARK

LITTLE ST JAMES'S ST

21

19

20

15

CLEVELAND ROW

18 **16**

MARLBOROUGH RD

17

1 St James's Piccadilly
2 Floris
3 Sir Isaac Newton
4 Beau Brummell
5 White's
6 Blue Posts public house.
7 Tiny passageway
8 Royal Over-Seas League
9 Pratt's
10 Brooks's
11 Boodle's
12 Blue Ball Yard
13 Carlton Club
14 Spencer House
15 Bridgewater House

16 St James's Palace
17 Clarence House
18 The Chapel Royal
19 The Queen's Chapel
20 Queen Alexandra
21 Mark Mason's Hall
22 Berry Bros & Rudd wine merchants
23 Pickering Place
24 James Lock & Co
25 John Lobb, Bootmaker
26 Christie's
27 Blue plaque
28 White Cube gallery
29 Scotch of St James

30 Indica bookshop
31 St James's Square
32 The East India and Sports Club
33 London Library
34 Chatham House
35 Naval and Military Club
36 PC Yvonne Fletcher
37 William III
38 Norfolk House

39 Athenaeum Club
40 Duke of York
41 Carlton House Terrace
42 Giro the dog
43 The Travellers Club
44 Reform Club
45 RAC
46 Army and Navy Club
47 United Oxford & Cambridge Club

National Gallery
TRAFALGAR
COCKSPUR ST
SQU

PALL MALL
WATERLOO PL
CHARLES
CARLTON GDNS
CARLTON HOUSE TERRACE
Institute of Contemporary Art
HORSE
Horse Guards Parade
ST JAMES'S PARK

1 St James's Piccadilly

St James's Walk

Start/Finish: Piccadilly Circus underground station
Distance: 1.5 miles

The walk begins at Piccadilly Circus, from where you head west along Piccadilly, shortly to see on your left Sir Christopher Wren's church of ❶ **St James's Piccadilly.**

Wren built many churches during his career, but nearly all were constructed on the foundations of City churches destroyed by the Great Fire and he therefore often had to compromise his designs. St James's was an exception being commissioned by the Earl of St Albans on a fresh plot of land – and this may explain why Wren regarded it as his best parish church design.

The church was consecrated in 1684 and is Wren's only surviving West End church; despite damage suffered during the Blitz it boast one of Wren's most pleasing and elegant interiors. St James's also contains a rare example of an external pulpit, while inside the galleried nave there is a beautifully carved white marble font, depicting Adam and Eve on either side of the Tree of Knowledge. The latter is the work of Grinling Gibbons (1648-1721), Wren's finest craftsman, who also produced the fine limewood carvings on the altar and reredos. The artist and poet William Blake was baptised in the church in 1757, as was the prominent abolitionist Quobna Ottobah Cugoano in 1773. A new artwork by Che Lovelace has now been installed at the church's entrance to mark the 250th anniversary of Cugoano's baptism.

Walk through the church (or through the coffee shop by the side) to come out into Jermyn Street, home to many upmarket men's outfitters, whose famous shirts are popular with the well-heeled members of the exclusive clubs of St James's. The street is also home to a number of long-standing shops such as ❷ **Floris** at number 89 which has been selling toiletries here since 1730. It was founded by Juan Famenias Floris, an immigrant from Menorca. James Bond wore Floris no.89, and real-life customers included Beau Brummell, Florence Nightingale and *Frankenstein* author Mary Shelley.

Next door you can see a plaque on the wall (opposite the entrance to Prince's Arcade) that remembers the great scientist ❸ **Sir Isaac Newton** (1643-1727), who lived at numbers 87 and 88 between 1696 and 1709. Further along there is also a statue of ❹ **Beau Brummell** (1778-1840), the first great dandy, and close friend of the Prince Regent. Brummell's keen sense of fashion, insisting on perfect tailoring and an immaculately tied cravat, made him an influential figure in London and the clubs of St James's were his main haunt.

Continue on until you reach St James's Street. This contains one of the highest concentration of members' clubs in St James's – an area known as 'Clubland'. Few of the clubs display their names outside, emphasising their exclusivity, and behind the permanently drawn shutters they remain hidden to the public. The number of members inside the clubs of St James's on

any given day is probably never in excess of a few hundred; however, more than any other group found in Britain this elite best exemplifies the term 'the Establishment'. Visiting a club is nearly impossible without having connections to a member but on this walk we will visit at least the outside of some of the most prestigious ones.

The first – **5 White's** – is found at number 37 (just to the right of the junction of Jermyn Street and St James's Street) and is the oldest and arguably the most exclusive club in the world. The early clubs developed out of the 18th-century coffee and chocolate houses that became fashionable venues for gambling and gossip amongst the upper classes. White's began as White's Chocolate House in 1693, owned by Italian Francis White (originally Francesco Bianco). Later it was run by White's assistant John Arthur, and quickly became notorious for its members' flamboyant drinking and betting habits,

such as the famous episode when Lord Arlington wagered £3,000 on which of two raindrops would first reach the bottom of a window pane. More recently, it has become the club of choice for those who run the country's intelligence services, including MI6. The club building dates largely from around 1780, and look out for the celebrated bow window where Beau Brummel and his fashionable friends used to station themselves.

White's set the model for the other clubs, offering fine dining, gaming and billiard tables, a library, a smoking room and bars, as well as grand accommodation for those members travelling into London from their country estates. Membership is intentionally expensive, although the key to entry is who you know – applicants risking the potential indignity of being 'blackballed' by existing members. Brummell used to gamble here, but this stopped after he fell out with the Prince Regent after being rude to the future King in public – famously asking an acquaintance, 'Alvanley, who's your fat friend?'. Without royal protection Brummell's creditors came after him – the last wager recorded by him in White's betting book in 1815 is marked 'not paid'. British Prime Minister David Cameron, whose father was once chairman of the club, resigned as a member due to its controversial policy of not admitting women as members. He is still thought to visit the club socially however.

Cross over onto Bennet Street then turn left at the **6** **Blue Posts public house**. There has been a tavern here since the 17th century and it is named after the blue posts used to advertise the services of a local sedan chair company. The poet Lord Byron lived next door in 1813.

Continue left along Arlington Street where at the end is a **7** **tiny passageway** (easy to miss) leading to steps that take you down to Park Place. On the right is the London clubhouse of the **8** **Royal Over-Seas League**. This was founded by Sir Evelyn Wrench in 1910 to foster international understanding and friendship and has over 20,000 members worldwide. The clubhouse boasts 80 bedrooms and a large garden that overlooks St James's Park.

Head along Park Place towards St James's Street. **9** **Pratt's** is on the right hand side at number 14. A modestly-sized club compared to some others, it is principally a private dining venue that can only accommodate 14 members at a time. It was founded after the Duke of Beaufort went to see his steward William Nathaniel Pratt one night in 1841 and enjoyed himself so much that he and his friends kept coming back. After Pratt died in 1860 his widow and son continued to run the club. Unlike most of the other clubs, it is only open in the evenings and oddly all the servants at the club are known as George.

Opposite Pratt's (on the corner) is **10** **Brooks's**, which in typically secretive clubland style does not bear a street number. It was founded in Pall Mall in 1764, and moved here in 1778 under the management of William Brooks. It also became notorious for the heavy gambling habits of its members, with the politician Charles James Fox having to resort to borrowing from the waiters. The club became associated with the Whig liberal aristocracy, and is in the very upper tier of the great clubs in the area, along with White's and Boodle's. One of the odder wagers recorded in the Brooks's betting book is 'Ld. Cholmondeley has given two guineas to Ld. Derby, to receive 500gs whenever his lordship f**** a women

in a balloon one thousand yards from the earth'. Past members have included William Wilberforce, Sir Joshua Reynolds, and Edward Gibbon.

Opposite Brooks's on the other side of St James's Street at number 28 is ⑪ **Boodle's**. Founded in 1762 by Lord Shelburne, it was named after the head waiter – Edward Boodle – and is particularly popular amongst the country set when visiting London. The club has been based here since 1783, and notable members have included the politicians Charles James Fox, Pitt the Elder and the Younger, and William Wilberforce; the philosopher David Hume, the economist Adam Smith and the Duke of Wellington. Traditionally the most senior officers of MI6 belong to White's, while more junior officers belong to Boodle's. Ian Fleming, Bond creator and a member of the intelligence services, joined Boodle's from White's because he thought members of the latter 'gas too much'. He based the 'Blades' club found in the Bond novels on Boodle's. Unsurprisingly Boodle's members have a reputation for bravery – four having received the Victoria Cross.

Continue down St James's Street where on the right (after number 63) is the hidden ⑫ **Blue Ball Yard.** This is worth a brief detour as it contains some small cottages from the 1740s that once housed coachmen, and together with a vast network of old underground cellars is now part of the Stafford Hotel.

Retrace your steps and continue along St James's Street until on the right-hand side just after the junction with St James's Place, you will find the ⑬ **Carlton Club** at number 69. This is the great Tory club, founded in 1832 by Tory peers and MPs as a place to organise their resistance to the Whigs after their rivals had just won a stunning general election in 1831 running on a reform mandate. The modern Conservative Party owes much of its development to the Carlton, although it stopped being the central party office in the 1860s.

At the infamous 'Carlton Club meeting' on 19 October 1922 backbench Conservative MPs decided to overthrow their leader Austen Chamberlain and withdraw from the David Lloyd George–led coalition. The club moved to its current premises after its previous home in Pall Mall was bombed during WWII but it suffered another bombing in 1990 when the IRA attacked it. In 2008 members finally voted to allow women to have full membership rights – 127 years after the club was founded. The only exception prior to this was for Margaret Thatcher, who was granted an honorary membership giving her the same rights as male members.

12 Blue Ball Yard

14 Spencer House

Walk down St James's Place (beside the Carlton) passing the entrance to **14 Spencer House** on the left, and bear right. Just opposite the Stafford Hotel is a small alleyway that you walk down to reach Green Park, then head left to see the Spencer House again with its fine garden. This was once the London home of the Spencer family, of which Diana, Princess of Wales was the most famous recent member.

Commissioned by the 1st Earl Spencer in 1756, the house is an early example of Neoclassical architecture, with palatial interiors designed by James 'Athenian' Stuart with later re-modelling by Henry Holland. The Spencers lived here until 1895 and although they returned sporadically after that, it was normally let out to tenants. In recent years the building – one of the few great 18th-century private houses remaining in central London – has been splendidly restored by a consortium led by Lord Rothschild. It can be visited on Sundays by guided tour (www.spencerhouse.co.uk).

Just after Spencer House is another aristocratic pile, the even grander **⑮ Bridgewater House,** which was designed in the Italian Renaissance style by Sir Charles Barry (the architect of the Houses of Parliament) and completed in 1854. Immediately after the end of the House head left through a narrow entrance in the gates and continue up Cleveland Row until you see the Tudor gatehouse of **⑯ St James's Palace** on the right-hand side.

Henry VIII built the Palace in the 1530s on the site of a leper hospital and it was his principle London residence during his marriage to Anne Boleyn. The palace became one of the main residences of the English monarchy for the next 300 years, and the most senior of them all after the Palace of Whitehall was destroyed by fire in 1698. It was only in 1837 that the newly crowned Queen Victoria decided to move the main home of the monarchy to Buckingham Palace, but St James's remains the official royal residence – the reason why foreign ambassadors are still formally accredited to the Court of St. James.

Parts of the building survive from Henry's period, including the Chapel Royal, the gatehouse, some turrets and two Tudor rooms in the State apartments. Beside St James's Palace is **17 Clarence House,** completed in 1827 and designed by John Nash for the third son of George III, Prince William Henry, Duke of Clarence. Based on the south-western corner of St James Palace, it is identifiable by the heavy police presence outside. It was in recent years the home of the Queen Mother, and the main residence of Charles and Camilla before he became King Charles III. Even after coronation the couple remained here while Buckingham Palace underwent renovation. Few people realise it is possible to visit Clarence House on a guided tour between August and September (www.rct.uk).

The Chapel Royal is an historic organisation comprising singers and priests who traditionally accompanied the court as it travelled around the country. However, over time it became permanently based within two chapels at this palace – the Chapel Royal and the Queen's Chapel.

18 The Chapel Royal – whose window can be seen to the right of the gatehouse – was constructed under the patronage of Henry VIII and decorated by Hans Holbein in honour of the King's short-lived fourth marriage to Anne of Cleves. The arms of Anne and the mottos of Anne Boleyn and Catherine of Aragon are featured in the ceiling. Mary I's heart is buried beneath the choir-stalls and Elizabeth I said her prayers in the chapel for an English victory against the Spanish Armada in 1588. Queen Victoria was married in the chapel, and in 1997 the coffin of Diana, Princess of Wales, lay here before her funeral in Westminster Abbey. The chapel is also considered to be the centre of English church music and past organists have included Henry Purcell and George Frideric Handel, the latter appointed by George II in 1723 as 'Composer of Musick of His Majesty's Chappel Royal'.

From the gatehouse walk along Cleveland Row and turn right down Marlborough Road. ⑲ **The Queen's Chapel,** is on the left and was built during the reign of James I for Henrietta Maria, the Catholic bride of his son, later Charles I, and designed by Inigo Jones. Although the public cannot visit the chapels as tourists, they can attend services. These are held in the Chapel Royal every Sunday from the first Sunday in October until Easter Day, and in the Queen's Chapel from Easter Sunday to the last Sunday in July.

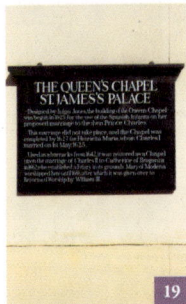

Immediately after the Queen's Chapel on Marlborough Road is a poignant monument to ⑳ **Queen Alexandra (1844-1925),** the long-suffering wife of Edward VII. The sculptor was Sir Alfred Gilbert (1854-1934), creator of the more famous 'Eros' on Piccadilly Circus. He had to be persuaded to return to England to accept the commission after a long self-imposed exile in Europe. However the monument helped secure his knighthood and revitalised his reputation.

From the memorial retrace your steps to Pall Mall. Its name derived from a French mallet-and-ball game named 'Paille Maille', which had become a craze in early 17th-century London. Head up St James's Street, looking over to number 86 where ㉑ **Mark Mason's Hall** is located. This is the grand lodge of the Mark Master Masons, headed by Grand Master Prince Michael of Kent. It is also the administrative centre of many other exotically named Masonic Orders including the Ancient & Honourable Fraternity of Royal

Ark Mariner, the Great Priory & Great Priory of Malta, the Order of the Secret Monitor and the Royal Order of the Masonic Knights of the Scarlet Cord. While you cannot visit the hall as a member of the public, you can walk around the back and down a small alleyway to see the Masonic emblems on the windows of the main room.

On the right at number 3 St James's Street is one of London's most fascinating shops, **㉒ Berry Bros & Rudd wine merchants.** It is the country's oldest wine merchant and has occupied this shop and the massive cellars underneath for over 300 years. It was founded as the 'Coffee Mill' in 1698 by the Widow Bourne, and was originally a grocer's shop before later developing its wine speciality. The size of the interior gives little hint of the vast cellars underneath that until fairly recently held thousands of bottles and stretched out under Pickering Place next door. Napoleon III once held secret meetings in the cellars during his stay in London in the mid 19th century.

The enormous set of scales that reside on the ground floor date from the shop's days as a grocery. Many of the personal details of the 30,000 people who paid to be weighed here over the decades can still be read in the grand ledger books (you can ask to see them). Notable visitors included the Duke of Wellington, Lord Byron (famously obsessed by his weight), Beau Brummell, William Pitt, Laurence Olivier and 'Fighting' George Fitzgerald.

Fitzgerald was a madcap eccentric born in 1748 who was educated at Eton and was hanged in 1786. One day he came to Berry Bros to be weighed and an acquaintance stopped to remark *'I smell the blood of an Irishman'*. Fitzgerald jumped off the scales and drew his sword, cutting off the man's nose and shouting *'I'll be damned if you'll ever smell another'*. If that seems unreasonable behaviour, it compares favourably to the time Fitzgerald became so angry with his father that he imprisoned him in a cave with a wild bear. The shop has details of the many wine-tasting events and courses on offer, many of which are hosted in the cellars.

23 Pickering Place

Beside number 3 is ㉓ **Pickering Place,** the smallest square in London, and once home to the Republic of Texas Legation in the years before Texas joined the United States of America. Pickering Place was notorious in the 18th century for its gambling dens and duels, and Beau Brummell is said to have fought a duel here. The houses date from the 1730s and were built by William Pickering, son-in-law of the founder of the original grocer's shop next door.

Continue north past hatters ㉔ **James Lock & Co.** – founded around 1676 – which commissioned Thomas and William Bowler to create the famous bowler hat in 1850. The shop actually calls it the 'Coke' hat after their customer William Coke, who originally asked them to create a robust design that would help protect the heads of his gamekeepers from low-hanging trees. The staff are very friendly and will show you the strange machine used to measure the size of a customer's head, the result being a card displaying the key dimensions. On the shop wall are the framed cards for, among others, Lord Lucan, Charlie Chaplin, General de Gaulle and Evelyn Waugh. Others who have worn hats from Lock's include Oscar Wilde, the Duke of Wellington and Lord Nelson (who was wearing a hat from Lock's when killed on board *The Victory* in 1805).

Just beside Lock's is ㉕ **John Lobb, Bootmaker**. Based here since the 1850s, Lobb's contains around 12,000 foot lasts – individual wooden models made for each customer's feet. Past customers include

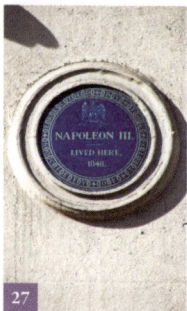

Enrico Caruso, Frank Sinatra, Dean Martin, Aristotle Onassis, George Bernard Shaw, Cole Porter and Rex Harrison. Visitors can see on display the foot outlines of some of the shop's distinguished clientele. Lobb's can take 6 months to make a pair of shoes and a typical price is around £2,200.

Continue on and head right onto King Street. On the north side you pass 26 **Christie's** auctioneers – founded in 1766 by James Christie and based here since 1823. Few tourists to the main art galleries in London know that Christie's can be visited on weekdays, and often has museum-quality pieces on display. Call for more visiting information on 020 7839 9060. If you need refreshment at this point, opposite Christie's is the atmospheric Golden Lion public house, built near the site of the long-demolished St James's Theatre where Oscar Wilde used to premiere his plays in the late 19th century. Napoleon III (1808-73) lived in exile from France at number 1c in 1848 – the 27 **blue plaque** remembering him is the oldest in London and bears the French Imperial eagle.

Follow the map back and head right up Duke Street St James's, looking out on the right-hand side for the narrow entrance into Mason's Yard. Enter the Yard, now dominated by the stunning 28 **White Cube gallery** which opened in 2006 and was the first new stand-alone building to be constructed in the district for several decades. Founded by Jay Jopling in 1993, the original White Cube gallery was based near here, and became famous for hosting exhibitions for the Young British Artists (YBAs). The other White Cube gallery is in Bermondsey (see p.374).

Walk to the north-east corner of the Yard. In the 1960s this was for a while the epicentre of Swinging London, an oasis of hedonism and radicalism amongst the stuffy clubs of St James. First look out for a night club called **29** **Scotch of St James**. In the 1960s this exclusive venue attracted regulars such as the Beatles, the Rolling Stones, the Who and Eric Clapton. The Stones' manager Andrew Loog-Oldham later remembered how 'Lennon and McCartney, Jagger and Richards and I and our ladies would sit back in a dark corner and smoke and gloat'. It was also where in September 1966 Jimi Hendrix first played in public after arriving in London. The venue closed for many years but reopened baring the same illustrious name in 2011.

Number 6 nearby once hosted the **30** **Indica bookshop** and gallery, founded in 1965 by Peter Asher (of Peter and Gordon fame, and brother of actress Jane Asher), Barry Miles (a prominent player in London's underground movement) and John Dunbar (then married to singer Marianne Faithfull). Paul McCartney, then in a relationship with Jane Asher, was also involved in the enterprise, designing the wrapping paper, helping put up the shelves, and putting his hand in his pocket when the bills mounted up. The seminal 60's London underground journal – The International Times – was also founded by the bookshop. One of the most famous events in rock history took place at the Indica when on 7th November 1966 John Lennon attended an art exhibition by Yoko Ono and met his future wife for the first time. Indica was named after Cannabis indica.

In the corner by the former Scotch of St James walk through a very narrow passageway that leads you into Ormond Yard. Continue along, turning right on Duke of York Street and heading downhill to reach ㉛ **St James's Square**. The Square, which is dominated by Georgian and neo-Georgian architecture, has a large private garden at its centre and has traditionally been one of the most fashionable addresses in London. At one time in the early 18th century seven dukes and seven earls lived here.

On the right-hand side (west) at number 16-17 is ㉜ **The East India and Sports Club**, which was founded in the mid-19th century. Its original members were 'the servants of the East India Company and Commissioned Officers of Her Majesty's Army and Navy'. The club later amalgamated with the Devonshire, the Sports and the Public Schools Clubs and also the Eccentric Club. The club regards this mix as representing 'the very best diversity of English tradition' although sadly the club notes that in 'accordance with its constitution, membership of the East India is available only to gentlemen'.

It was here that the Prince Regent (later George IV), while attending a dinner party on 21 June 1815, received news of victory at the Battle of Waterloo. The bloodstained messenger laid down captured French flags and eagle at the Regent's feet and announced 'Victory, sir! Victory!'.

Just past the East India Club at number 14 on the north-west of the Square stands the ❸❸ **London Library**, a relatively unknown institution to most Londoners, but which has been based here since 1845. It is the library of choice for the capital's literary establishment, and was founded largely due to the energies of the great Victorian essayist, critic and historian, Thomas Carlyle (1795-1881). This beautiful building is currently the world's largest independent lending library and past members have included WM Thackeray, William Gladstone, Charles Dickens, George Eliot, Aldous Huxley, Henry James, HG Wells, John Betjeman, Rudyard Kipling, TS Eliot and Isaiah Berlin.

In recent years Sir Tom Stoppard, Sir Tim Rice and Helena Bonham Carter have each served as president of the library. The library is not generally open to non-members, but if you want to submit a membership application you can contact the library for a tour beforehand. There are also regular introductory tours held on the last Saturday of every month at 11am, no booking required (call 020 7766 4712 for more information).

Walk around St James's Square clockwise passing at number 10 ❸❹ **Chatham House**, home of the Royal Institute of International Affairs. This non-profit-making organisation was set up to promote the understanding of major international issues and current affairs, and gave birth to the 'Chatham House Rule'. This rule allows those attending seminars to talk afterwards about what was discussed, but without specifying who attended or revealing who said what, the purpose being to encourage honest and frank conversation. The house itself is Grade I listed, and since being

built in the 18th century has been home to three Prime Ministers – Edward Stanley, William Gladstone and William Pitt.

On the north-east corner at number 4 is the 35 **Naval and Military Club**. Traditionally the club has provided a London home for Officers of the Royal Navy, the Royal Marines, the Army and the Royal Air Force, although in recent years the membership has been expanded to include civilians of both sexes. The club moved here in 1996, and the original house was built here in 1679. From 1912 to 1942 this was the home of Viscount Astor and his wife Nancy Astor, the first female Member of Parliament. The club came to be known as the 'In and Out' on account of the prominent signs on its previous premises, and the current entrance also bears the same markings.

Just opposite the club is a memorial to 36 **PC Yvonne Fletcher** (1959-1984). The Libyan Embassy once occupied number 5, and in 1984 Fletcher was policing an anti-Gaddafi demonstration when someone inside the embassy shot her dead. The subsequent siege of the embassy lasted 11 days – the longest in London's history – embassy staff eventually returned to Libya and her murderer has never been convicted. Look for the 18th century limestone mounting block on the kerb outside number 7. It has listed status and was used for mounting and dismounting from a horse.

Walk to the south-east corner of the square looking out for the bronze statue of ③⑦ **William III (1650-1702)** at its centre, which portrays the king as a Roman general riding his horse Sorrel and which has stood here since 1808. Look out for the molehill under the horse's hooves: William fell from his horse and broke his collar bone after stumbling over a molehill, which indirectly led to his death as he fatally contracted pneumonia while recovering from his injuries. The incident led to his Jacobite enemies customarily toasting the mole – or 'the little gentleman in the black velvet waistcoat'.

Continue along the south-east side of the square, passing ③⑧ **Norfolk House** at number 31. General Eisenhower used this as a base from which he directed the Allied war effort during WWII. He had a frosty relationship with Britain's General Montgomery and arrived here one day in January 1944 to find 'Monty' had deliberately taken Eisenhower's official parking spot – thought to have been a deliberate act of provocation.

Leave the Square and rejoin Pall Mall to the south. On the eastern side at number 107 is the ③⑨ **Athenaeum Club,** its grand classical frontage overlooking Waterloo Place. Founded by civil servant and author John Wilson Croker in 1824, this magnificent building was designed by Decimus Burton in 1827. The Athenaeum has the strongest intellectual reputation out of all the clubs,

81

and was founded as a meeting place 'for men who enjoy the life of the mind'. The stone block on the pavement outside the club are said to have been placed there in 1830 at the request of the Duke of Wellington, then Prime Minister and a regular visitor to the club, to help him mount his horse.

The majority of members are involved in the fields of science, engineering or medicine, and over 52 of the club's past and present members have won a Nobel Prize. Women have been allowed to join since 2002. The library alone contains 80,000 books and the club was the scene of a famous literary reconciliation in 1863 when Charles Dickens and William Makepeace Thackeray finally made their peace after a bitter 12-year feud. This is an exceptionally difficult club to secure membership of as it operates a secret ballot, followed by the infamous black ball vote. The philosopher, mathematician and Nobel Prize-winner Bertrand Russell had to wait forty years to become a member after his initial rejection.

To the south of the Athenaeum is a memorial column to

40

the **40 Duke of York** (1763-1827), best known for being pilloried in the rhyme *The Grand Old Duke of York*. In real life he was the unpopular second son of George II, who was at one point rumoured to become the first 'King of the United States' before Britain lost control of its American colony in the 1780s. A bungling military commander, he died owing £2 million to his creditors. The column was erected in 1834, and was controversially funded by the deduction of a day's pay from every soldier in the Army. Humorists at the time suggested the column's great height was designed to prevent the Duke being harassed by his many creditors even in the afterlife.

To the south-west of the column is **41 Carlton House Terrace**, designed by John Nash in the early 1830s. Outside number nine and near the base of the Duke of York column is a small tombstone to **42 Giro**, an Alsatian dog that belonged to Dr Leopold von Hoesch, Nazi Germany's ambassador to the Court of St James's between 1932 and 1936. It was originally in the front garden to number nine, now a small space between the Duke of York steps and the garage ramp. The tombstone bears the inscription 'Giro: ein treuer Begleiter!' (Giro: a true companion!). Number nine remained the German embassy until WWII, and was where von Hoesche's successor Ambassador Joachim von Ribbentrop worked between 1936 and 1938 before he became Hitler's Foreign Minister. The building is still thought to retain a marble staircase donated by Mussolini. Other past inhabitants of this grand terrace include three British Prime Ministers – William Gladstone, Lord Palmerston and Earl Grey. There is also a blue plaque remembering Charles De Gaulle's presence here during the war.

Walk down Pall Mall until you come to **43 The Travellers Club** at number 106. It was founded in 1819 and moved to its present purpose-built clubhouse, designed by Sir Charles Barry, the architect of Bridgewater House (described earlier), in 1832.

Its founders wanted a meeting place for gentlemen who had travelled abroad and the original rules excluded from membership anyone 'who has not travelled out of the British Islands to a distance of at least five hundred miles from London in a direct line'. Notable members include politicians such as Canning, Wellington, Palmerston, Balfour and Baldwin. There is also a special category of membership for great explorers and travellers: past and present members include Colonel John Blashford-Snell, Sir Ranulph Fiennes and Sir Edmund Hillary. The club remains a male bastion although ladies are welcome as guests throughout the clubhouse (other than in the Smoking Room and Cocktail Bar).

Continuing west along Pall Mall you pass the **44** **Reform Club** at numbers 104-105. The club was started in 1836 and its Whig founders commissioned Sir Charles Barry to build the imposing building (dating from 1841) in the style of an Italian palazzo. Membership was restricted to those who pledged support for the Great Reform Act of 1832, and the founders felt the need for 'an Association or Club (call it what you will) in London to counter the machinations of the Tory Carlton Club'. As a result the early members were Whig MPs and peers which made this effectively the political headquarters of the Liberal Party. Since the early 1920s the club has served a social rather than political purpose with the criteria for admission being 'character, talent, and achievement'. Members have included JM Barrie, Henri Cartier-Bresson, Winston Churchill, EM Forster, Henry James, Lord Palmerston, and HG Wells. It was also the first London club to admit women in 1981, and contains dining rooms, wine cellars, billiards rooms, accommodation, plus an extensive library of 75,000 volumes. The Reform will forever be associated with Jules Verne's *Around the World in Eighty Days* (1873) as the location where Phileas Fogg accepts the famous £20,000 wager.

Continue down Pall Mall where the **45** **RAC** is located at number 89. This is one of the (relatively) less stuffy clubs in St

James's, founded in 1897 by Frederick Richard Simms and Charles Harrington Moore. The original Automobile Club of Great Britain and Ireland became the 'The Royal Automobile Club' after receiving the patronage of Edward VII who was fanatical about motoring. The current clubhouse was opened in 1911, at a cost of £250,000. In 1905 the club founded the now world famous Tourist Trophy or 'TT' race, and later organised the first British Grand Prix at Brooklands in 1926. To become a member is reassuringly expensive with life membership for someone under 30 costing over £35,000. However, the members enjoy arguably the best facilities in Clubland, including a marble swimming pool, a Turkish bath, squash courts, and over 80 en-suite bedrooms. Members can also use Woodcote Park, an associated clubhouse set on a 350 acre estate on the Epsom Downs.

Continue down Pall Mall and on the right-hand side at number 36-39 is the 46 **Army and Navy Club**, founded in 1837 and based here since 1963. It is known as the 'Rag' because of early member Captain Billy Duff's remark that the food being served was 'a rag and famish affair'.

Further along at number 71 is the 47 **United Oxford and Cambridge Club**. It was formed in 1972 by the amalgamation of the 19th-century United University Club and the Oxford and Cambridge University Club. Surprisingly it was not until 1996 that women were admitted to full membership and now the club has over 3,500 members of both sexes based around the world.

This is also where the walk ends and from here you can return north up to Piccadilly Circus. ●

St James's Park

SHOP...

Floris (see p.62)
89 Jermyn Street, SW1Y 6JH
www.florislondon.com

Berry Bros & Rudd (see p.73)
3 St James's Street, SW1A 1EG
www.bbr.com

Lock & Co Hatters (see p.75)
6 St James's Street, SW1A 1EF
www.lockhatters.co.uk

John Lobb (see p.75)
9 St James's Street, SW1A 1EF
www.johnlobbltd.co.uk

VISIT...

Institute of Contemporary Arts
The Mall, SW1Y 5AH
www.ica.org.uk

Royal Academy of Arts
Burlington House, W1J 0BD
www.royalacademy.org.uk

White Cube Gallery
25-26 Mason's Yard, SW1Y 6BU
www.whitecube.com

EAT, DRINK...

Café Nero
St James's Church, W1J 0DJ

St James's Café
St James's Park, SW1A 2BJ
www.benugo.com

Ship & Shovell public house, Craven Passage, see p.98

4 Strand, Embankment & Fleet Street Walk

1. Trafalgar Square
2. Whitehall Telephone Exchange
3. Former police post
4. Statue of Charles
5. South Africa House
6. Coutts bank
7. Zimbabwe House
8. Charing Cross station
9. Benjamin Franklin House
10. British Optical Association Museum
11. Ship & Shovell
12. Arches
13. Number 43 (plaque)
14. Gordon's
15. Number 12 (plaque)
16. 7 Adam Street
17. New Adelphi
18. Royal Society of Arts (RSA)
19. Remnants of the old Adelphi
20. York Gate
21. Victoria Embankment Gardens
22. Cleopatra's Needle
23. Shell Mex House
24. Robert Raikes
25. Patent Sewer Ventilating Lamp
26. King's Chapel of the Savoy
27. Simpsons-in-the-Strand
28. Savoy Hotel
29. Somerset House
30. St Mary-le-Strand
31. King's College
32. Aldwych underground station

LINCOLN'S INN FIELDS

CAREY

STRAND

ADAM ST

JOHN ADAM ST

ROBERT ST

ADELPHI TERRACE

SAVOY PLACE

YORK BUILDINGS

BUCKINGHAM ST

EMBANKMENT GARDENS

ARUNDEL ST

SURREY ST

Temple

Somerset House

STRAND

SAVOY ST

LANCASTER PL

SAVOY HILL ST

WATERLOO BRIDGE

WILLIAM IV ST

VILLIERS ST

CRAVEN ST

JOHN ADAM STREET WALK

JOHN ST

CARTING LN

SAVOY PL

VICTORIA EMBANKMENT

EMBANKMENT GDNS

Charing Cross

Charing Cross

NORTHUMBERLAND AVE

Embankment

Strand, Embankment & Fleet Street Walk

33 Ornate frontage (Norfolk Hotel)
34 Roman Bath
35 St Clements Watch House
36 Australia House
37 Bush House
38 St Clement Danes
39 The Royal Courts of Justice

53 Distinctive sign
54 Dr Johnson's House
55 Hodge the cat
56 Old Cheshire Cheese
57 Telegraph building
58 Daily Express building
59 The Tipperary (now closed)

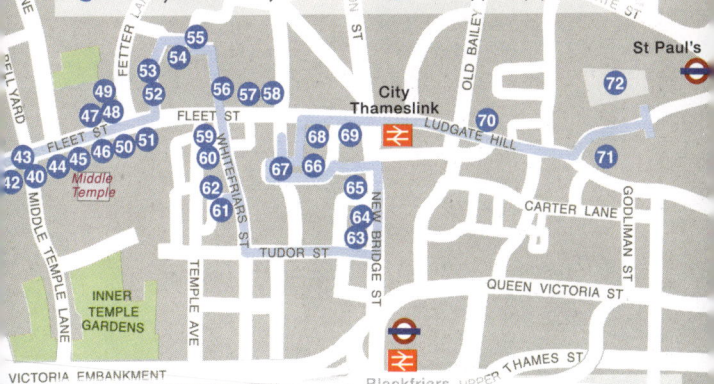

St Paul's

City
Thameslink

Blackfriars

40 Middle Temple Lane
41 Twinings Tea shop
42 Wig and Pen Club
43 Former site of Temple Bar
44 Prince Henry's Room
45 Old fashioned street sign
46 Ye Olde Cock Tavern
47 St Dunstan-in-the-West
48 Red-brick building
49 Hen and Chicken Court
50 C. Hoare and Co.
51 El Vino
52 Red Lion Court

60 Anti-Corn-Law League plaque
61 Ashentree Court
62 Old Priory crypt
63 Former Institute of Journalists
64 Bridewell Palace
65 Bridewell Theatre
66 St Bride's Church
67 Salisbury Court
68 The Old Bell Tavern
69 Punch Tavern
70 St Martin within Ludgate
71 St Paul's Cathedral
72 Temple Bar gate house

Tate
Modern

① *Trafalgar Square*

Strand, Embankment & Fleet Street Walk

Start: Charing Cross underground station
Finish: St Paul's underground station
Distance: 2.5 miles

The walk begins at ❶ **Trafalgar Square** and ends at St Paul's Cathedral. Along the route you will walk in the footsteps of Pepys, Kipling and Franklin who all lived in the Strand and further east explore the remnants of the newspaper industry that for centuries made Fleet Street its home. Before entering the Strand it is worth looking around London's most iconic square, despite it being a tourist trap once described by writer Henry James (1843-1916) as a 'grimy desert'.

The original design for the square was drawn up by the great Regency architect John Nash (1752-1835); however, although he cleared the area of the old buildings that had accumulated on the site of the former royal stables, he died before construction really began. Sir Charles Barry, the architect of the Palace of Westminster, completed the project in 1845. It was originally to have been called 'King William the Fourth's Square'.

The protective lions at the base of Nelson's Column were designed by Edwin Landseer (1802-1873) and installed in 1867. Landseer, better known as a painter of animals, struggled with the commission because of mental health problems, and the delays were a topic of great interest to the newspapers. He used as a model a dead lion from Regent's Park Zoo, which was delivered to his studio by taxi. The lion remained in situ until long after the carcass had begun to rot, with the resulting smell offending Landseer's neighbours.

During WWI a campaign for war bonds saw the square transformed into a mock battlefield, with the fountains filled with mud and the public watching the troops stage twice-daily assaults

on an enemy fortification. Had Hitler won WWII the view today would be very different as the Nazis planned to take Nelson's Column back to Berlin and place it outside the Reichstag as the ultimate symbol of Germany's dominance.

Underneath the square is the ❷ **Whitehall Telephone Exchange**, built in the 1950s at the height of the Cold War, and connected through a network of tunnels to other key command posts in central London. Tucked away in a lamp-post on the south-east corner is a tiny ❸ **former police post**, the smallest in the capital.

Just south of the square is a ❹ **statue of Charles I** made by Hubert Le Sueur in c.1630. The King was executed outside nearby Banqueting House in 1649 and the statue was removed under Cromwell's administration and sold to John Rivett, a brazier. Rivett was supposed to use it for scrap metal but wisely kept it hidden and sold it back to Charles II after the Restoration.

Re-erected in 1665, Charles's statue symbolically looks down to Parliament and Banqueting House. Charles II had some of the men who signed his father's death warrant executed on this spot, and the statue is also where the medieval Charing Cross memorial once stood (see below). Traditionally all distances within London are measured from this location, so it is really the centre of the capital. Behind the statute is a pavement plaque denoting the spot of the original Eleanor Cross (the replica of which stands outside Charing Cross station).

Cross over onto the Strand, passing the South African High Commission in ⑤ **South Africa House** on the north side. Its façade dates from the early 1930s and features unusual sculptures of African animals, including the famous springbok. Until Nelson Mandela's release in 1990, the area outside the building was for many years the scene of demonstrations against the apartheid regime.

To the south is Charing Cross station, which we shall return to shortly. For now continue on the north side of Strand, passing the headquarters of ⑥ **Coutts bank** on the left. Coutts has looked after wealthy clients since it was founded in 1692, and every monarch since George III has held an account here. To be eligible to open an account you need a minimum of £500,000 in liquid assets or an investment portfolio of at least £1 million. The bank has been based here since 1904 and is owned by NatWest Group.

Continue along the Strand and stop outside number 429 ⑦ **Zimbabwe House**, formerly Rhodesia House, originally home to the British Medical Association who sponsored the construction of this building in 1902. The architect was Charles Holden, best known for his work on Senate House and many London underground stations. You can still see the remnants of statues designed by Jacob Epstein that once caused controversy among London's chattering classes. The influential and respected Epstein (1880-1959), was commissioned to produce 18 life-size statues for the exterior of the building. However while the BMA was envisaging decorous statues of famous figures in the history of medicine, Epstein's creations were nude and celebrated the seven ages of man.

When the building was unveiled pandemonium ensued with crowds forming on the street and the alleged eroticism of Epstein's work being vigorously debated in the press – the *Evening Standard* describing the statutes as 'a scandal'. Epstein won the argument, however a few decades later the statues were considered structurally unsound and many were removed. Today only the butchered remains, visible on the third floor, remind us of a long-forgotten London scandal.

Retrace your steps to **8** **Charing Cross station**, named both after the medieval village of Charing and the memorial cross Edward I erected here to mark it as one of the places where the funeral procession of his wife Eleanor of Castile stopped on its way to Westminster Abbey in 1290. The original Eleanor Cross was located where the statue of Charles I now stands, and was destroyed on the orders of Parliament in 1647. The replica outside the station dates from 1863.

The station stands on the site of what was once Hungerford Market. The southern part of the market next to the Thames by Hungerford Stairs was the location of Warren's boot-blacking factory. This was where Charles Dickens (1812-70), aged only 12, was sent by his father John to work for ten hours a day sticking labels onto boot polish jars. His father – the inspiration for the hopeless Micawber in *David Copperfield* (1850) – had ended up in Marshalsea debtors prison and needed money to get himself out. Dickens was so humiliated he never revealed this part of his life even to his own family, and we only know about it because he confided in his close friend and biographer John Forster. The factory itself was immortalised as 'Murdstone and Grinby' in *David Copperfield*. Today the nearest place to the original site is near Embankment tube station.

Leave the station, following the map until you reach Craven Street on your left, which lies between the station and Trafalgar Square. It is a quiet street, containing a number of fine 18th-century town houses. It was at lodgings here that Mr Brownlow interviewed Rose Maylie in Dickens' *Oliver Twist* – an encounter that led to Oliver being recovered. At number 36 is one of London's smallest and most unusual museums – **9** **Benjamin Franklin House** – dedicated to the American statesman, scientist, printer, and inventor Benjamin Franklin (1706-1790). Franklin lodged here at various times between 1757 and 1775, and because of his diplomatic status this is regarded as the USA's first de facto foreign embassy. As the American War of Independence reached its conclusion Franklin returned to America, a political figure second only in stature to George Washington. He helped draft the American Declaration of Independence, and was also a signatory.

While he was a great statesman and scientist, Franklin was also very human. During his time here, and with his wife back in America, he developed a crush on his landlady and perhaps even her daughter. In 1767 an American visitor arrived unexpectedly to find Franklin kissing an unknown young lady in a room on the second floor. Thousands of human bones were recently discovered under the house, most likely illegally obtained corpses discarded by the anatomy school that shared the building while Franklin lived here (see p.131 for more information about the House).

Another unusual museum on this street is the **10** **British Optical Association Museum** at number 42. Founded in 1901, it contains over 11,000 objects including the spectacles of Dr

Crippen and Dr Johnson and a drawer of diseased and deformed eyes. It can only be visited by prior arrangement on weekdays.

Just past the Franklin Museum head left up Craven Passage and pass between the two halves of the ⑪ **Ship & Shovell** public house, the only establishment in London that is split in this way. Walk down into the ⑫ **Arches** that lie behind Charing Cross station where a popular music hall was founded in 1860s by the Gatti brothers, and which is today home to the well-known gay club Heaven and the Charing Cross Theatre.

At the end you reach Villiers Street and turn right. This street name recalls the first and second Dukes of Buckingham, both named George Villiers. The first Duke was the flamboyant favourite, and reputed lover, of James I in the early 17th century. He owned York House which once stood here. The second Duke sold York House to developers in the 1670s and insisted that his family name be remembered in local street names.

The connection with York House is significant as it is the first sign on this walk of the many mansions and palaces that once dominated the land along the Thames between Westminster and the City. This was at its apex in the medieval period when for several hundred years archbishops and aristocrats established ostentatious London residences that were easily accessible from the river, but also near to the centres of political and religious power in the capital. After the Reformation, the influence and economic power of the clergy was greatly diminished and many lost their palaces to the monarchy, or had to sell them to aristocrats and wealthy merchants. Over time the latter also moved out of the area, attracted by the newly developed residential districts of London that became fashionable from the late 17th century.

However during its golden period the Strand and Fleet Street was at the heart of London life. The principal residences we will find echoes of along this walk were (from east to west): York House, Durham House, Salisbury House, the Savoy, Somerset House, Arundel House, Essex House, the Temple, Whitefriars, the Bridewell Palace, and Blackfriars.

As you walk south down Villiers Street, look on the left-hand side for ⑬ **number 43** (there is a plaque) where Rudyard Kipling lived between 1889 and 1891. In his autobiography he wrote 'I could look out of my window through the fanlight of Gatti's music hall entrance, across the street, almost onto its stage. The Charing Cross trains rumbled through my dreams on one side, the boom of the Strand on the other, while, before my windows, Father Thames under the Shot Tower walked up and down with his traffic'. In 1890 Kipling was shocked to witnessed from his window a man commit suicide by stabbing himself.

Beside Kipling House is ⑭ **Gordon's**, London's oldest and most atmospheric wine bar. Founded in 1890, its wood panelled dungeon-like interior is situated within the cellars of the 17th-century building that once stood on the site, and has hardly changed since the days when Kipling drank here.

Just after Gordon's turn left into Watergate Walk, which runs along the side of Victoria Embankment Gardens. On the left are some stairs that take you up to Buckingham Street and on the left-hand corner building at ⑮ **number 12** is a plaque remembering former resident, and London's most famous diarist, Samuel Pepys (1633-1703). He lived here (and also at number 14 – since rebuilt) between 1679 and 1688 after being released from the Tower of London and later moved out to the country – Clapham was then a rural retreat – where he died. Peter the Great – Tsar of Russia – lived at number 15 in 1698 during his incognito stay in London.

At this point if you wish to do the **John Adam Street Walk** make your way up Buckingham Street to reach John Adam Street – if not enter Embankment Gardens with York Gate straight ahead.

JOHN ADAM STREET WALK

This is named after one of the Scottish born Adams brothers (John, Robert and James Adam) who were responsible for designing a number of London's finest buildings in the 18th century. The reason why they are remembered in so many street names in this area can better be understood by turning right onto John Adam Street.

After a short walk pause at the junction with Robert Street on the right. Directly ahead facing down the street towards you is a striking example of the Adam brothers' work at number **16** **7 Adam Street**. This dates from around 1770 and is a rare survivor of the Adelphi development the brothers built at huge cost in this vicinity on the location of what had been the medieval palace of Durham House. The Adelphi buildings ('Adelphi' is Greek for brothers) comprised 24 neoclassical terrace houses furnished to the highest standards of the time, and were built between 1768-72. Sadly the Adelphi slowly went into decline over the following centuries, its terrace and dark vaults overlooking the river becoming the haunt of vagabonds and prostitutes.

The bulk of the 18th-century Adelphi complex was demolished in the 1930s, replaced by the **17** **New Adelphi** – the vast art deco construction you can see at the top of the street that would have probably appealed to Mussolini's architectural tastes. Opposite the New Adelphi you can see another distinctive Adam brothers' building that – amazingly –has served

as the home of The Royal Society for the Encouragement of Arts, Manufactures and Commerce or, for short, the ⑱ Royal Society of Arts (RSA) since 1774.

Some more ⑲ remnants of the old Adelphi can be seen if you turn right down York Buildings and then almost immediately left down Lower Robert Street. This tiny road – perhaps the most obscure in central London, and certainly a rare example of one that is underground – takes you through the vaults that survive from the 18th-century Adelphi complex. You come out beside the Adelphi Terrace – tucked away from the public and a favoured spot of the homeless.

The Adelphi was home to many prominent people over the centuries including George Bernard Shaw, J M Barrie, and Thomas Hardy. As a young man Charles Dickens had lodgings in the Adelphi, a far cry from his time at the boot-blacking factory mentioned earlier. It is surely no coincidence that Dicken's David Copperfield also has lodgings at the Adelphi, and Dickens writes that Copperfield was 'fond of wandering about the Adelphi, because it was a mysterious place with those dark arches...'

As mentioned earlier, the medieval Durham House, built in the 14th century for the Bishops of Durham, used to stand in this vicinity

before the Adelphi was built. This was home at various times to Cardinal Wolsey, Anne Boleyn and Sir Walter Raleigh. It was possibly at Durham House that Raleigh was drenched with water by a servant who thought his master was on fire – in fact Raleigh was enjoying a quiet smoke of tobacco, recently brought back from the New World.

When finished re-trace your steps and walk down Buckingham Street and enter Embankment Gardens with York Gate straight ahead.

20 **York Gate** served as a watergate at the rear of York House, the huge mansion on the Strand that was once owned by the Dukes of Buckingham as mentioned earlier. The first Duke of Buckingham, who acquired the house from the philosopher and writer Francis Bacon, commissioned Nicholas Stone to build the gate in 1626 so the Duke could easily reach boats waiting on the Thames. The rest of York House was demolished in 1670s and, as a result of the creation of Victoria Embankment by Sir Joseph Bazalgette in the 1860s, the gate now stands marooned 150 yards north of the Thames. The name 'Strand' itself is derived from the Old English word for shore or river bank and before the construction of the Embankment, the Strand's proximity to the river would have been much more apparent.

Continue eastwards through **21** **Victoria Embankment Gardens**, built on land reclaimed from the Thames. Through the trees on the south side you can see **22** **Cleopatra's Needle**, originally erected in the Egyptian city of Heliopolis in c. 1450BC, and despite its name far older than the famous Egyptian queen who was born in 69 BC. On the north side (beside the New Adelphi visited earlier) you can see the distinctive art-deco **23** **Shell Mex House**, which was completed in 1931. In the words of architectural historian Nikolaus Pevsner it is 'thoroughly unsubtle, but succeeds in holding its own in London's river front'.

Exit on the north side (by the statue of **24** **Robert Raikes**, founder of Sunday

103

Schools) and walk up Carting Lane. If you walk up a short way on the left-hand side you can see an old lamp post. This is a rare example of a ㉕ **Patent Sewer Ventilating Lamp** and dates from the 1880s. There were once hundreds of these lamp-posts lighting up central London, all supplied by the methane gas being emitted from the sewers below.

Turn right off Carting Lane along Savoy Way and bear left into Savoy Hill, with the ㉖ **King's Chapel of the Savoy** on the right.

This is the only reminder of the great Savoy Palace, which was built by Peter, Count of Savoy – uncle of the queen-consort, Eleanor of Provence – on land here given to him by Henry III in 1246. It was later owned by the hugely wealthy John of Gaunt (1340-99), son of Edward III, whose unpopularity with the mob ensured the Palace was destroyed during the Peasant's Revolt in 1381. It was subsequently rebuilt; however, it was evidently still a target for revolutionaries as recorded by Shakespeare in his play *Henry VI, Part II* when Jack Cade, leader of another popular rebellion against King Henry in 1450, orders his men 'now go some and pull down the Savoy; others to the inns of court; down with them all'.

Henry VII later founded the Hospital of St John of the Savoy

on the site, with the chapel being built as part of the development in around 1505. The hospital remained in use until 1702, after which the buildings were largely abandoned and finally demolished in the 19th century. However, the chapel survived, and despite substantial restoration in the 1860s remains the only pre-Reformation building in this part of London. It is home to the Royal Victorian Order and Order of Chivalry, and is also officially a private chapel of the Queen.

Now very respectable, the chapel once had a reputation for hosting marriages with few questions asked, and was described by Evelyn Waugh in *Brideshead Revisited* as 'the place where divorced couples got married in those days – a poky little place'. The poet and clergyman John Donne (1572-1631) secretly married his employer's niece Anne More here in 1601, after which they eloped. However, her parents were not happy (it is thought she was as young as fourteen). Donne lost his job and was imprisoned in the Fleet Prison (he is said to have written to his wife '*John Donne, Anne Donne, Un-done*'). The chapel is open to the public through the week (www.royalchapelsavoy.org).

Continue up the hill to rejoin the Strand. Turn left onto the Strand, passing on the right ㉗ **Simpsons-in-the-Strand**, one of London's oldest restaurants – originally founded in 1828 as a cigar and chess house. In its heyday, regular diners included Dickens, William Gladstone, Benjamin Disraeli, Vincent Van Gogh, George Bernard Shaw and fiction's greatest detective, Sherlock Holmes.

26

29 Somerset House

Continue along, and on the left you pass the entrance to the ㉘ **Savoy Hotel**, named after the medieval Palace. The short road outside the hotel is the only place in Britain where cars are required to drive on the right-hand side, and the entrance contains a grand statue of Count Peter of Savoy (1203-1268). There are some plaques on the wall outside the entrance which provide further information about the history of the Savoy Palace.

Retrace your steps and continue eastwards on the south side of the Strand, crossing over Lancaster Place which leads onto Waterloo Bridge. Shortly on the right you reach the entrance to the vast ㉙ **Somerset House,** the only substantial survivor of the great mansions that once dominated this route. The original building on the site was the first Renaissance-style palace in England when it was constructed in around 1550 for the Lord Protector Somerset. The construction used stone pilfered under Somerset's orders from a number of other buildings in London, including those closed during Henry VIII's Dissolution of the Monasteries.

The house had a variety of owners over the following centuries, including Elizabeth I who stayed here before becoming Queen. Oliver Cromwell's body lay in state here after his death in 1658 and just over one hundred years later the Tudor mansion was rebuilt between 1776 and 1801 by Sir William Chambers in a grand Palladian design. Today it is home to a number of institutions, including the Courtauld Institute of Art with its fine gallery. The main courtyard also hosts many forms of entertainment from ice-skating in the winter months to open-air pop concerns and film screenings (see p.131 for more information).

Follow the map back onto Strand to the church of **30** **St Mary-le-Strand**, which stands isolated in the middle of the road. The medieval church was destroyed in 1548 to make way for Somerset House, and the parishioners had to go elsewhere until a new church was built in the 1720s as one of the 'Queen Anne Churches'. It was designed by James Gibbs in an extravagant Baroque style, and legend has it that Bonnie Prince Charlie, hero of the Scots, renounced his Roman Catholic faith here during a clandestine visit to London in 1750. Charles Dickens's parents were married here in 1809. Today it is officially the church of the Women's Royal Naval Service. The area around the church is now pedestrianised allowing you to skirt the south side of the church to see the stone tablets describing the burial vaults that lie below.

31 **King's College** stands beside Somerset House, and was founded by George IV and the Duke of Wellington in 1829 – largely as a reaction against the free-thinking non-conformists and radicals who had founded University College London in 1826. The college occupies the site where Richard Thresher's hosiery shop once stood at number 152 Strand. Admiral Nelson – shortly after losing his arm in a naval battle – came to the shop to buy some stockings and received Thresher's sympathies, only to reply 'lucky for you it wasn't my leg'. In 1797 Nelson – minus his arm – also paid a visit to a Navy office situated within Somerset House in order to claim compensation for his war injury. However despite the obvious visible evidence the sceptical bureaucrat dealing with Nelson refused to process the claim on account of the fact the war hero had forgotten to bring along his medical certificate.

Continue eastwards on the south side of the Strand and shortly you will see the distinctive glazed-tile frontage of the disused ㉜ **Aldwych underground station**, formerly part of the Piccadilly Line. Closed in 1994, it originally opened as Strand station in 1907 and was renamed 'Aldwych' in 1917. During WWII it served as an air-raid shelter and the British Museum's Elgin Marbles were stored here. The station still has many of its original features and has often been used as a location for films including *Atonement*, *Patriot Games* and *The Krays*. Past renovations have revealed the original 'Strand' signage.

Follow the map down Surrey Street looking out for another entrance to the disused tube station. The street was named after the Dukes of Norfolk, who also hold the titles Earl of Arundel and Earl of Surrey. Arundel House once stood in this location, originally founded as the medieval town house of the Bishops of Bath and Wells. They lost control of it during the Reformation, and it was sold to the Earl of Arundel in 1549. The Royal Society held their meetings here after their original home was destroyed during the Great Fire of 1666, but the main house was demolished in 1678.

On the right-hand side of Surrey Street look for the ㉝ **ornate frontage** of the former Norfolk Hotel – now part of King's College. This was one of the meeting places used by politician John Profumo and call-girl Christine Keeler during their affair, that helped bring down the Macmillan government.

Just beside the former hotel bear right down a small passage to reach Strand Lane. This contains one of London's most mysterious treasures, the red-brick ❸❹ **Roman Bath**. Whether it really dates from the Roman period or was (more likely) part of the now demolished Arundel House that stood here in Tudor times, is never likely to be known. It was immortalised by Charles Dickens in *David Copperfield*, when he writes of how 'There was an old Roman bath in those days at the bottom of one of the streets out of the Strand – it may be there still – in which I have had many a cold plunge'. You can see the Bath through a viewing window, but to visit you must first contact Westminster Council a week before your visit (see p.131 for more details). Next to the Roman Bath is ❸❺ **St Clements Watch House.** Before the Metropolitan Police was founded, many parishes managed their own security. This was the parish equivalent of a police station dating from the 1720s. The men 'watching' over the parish would also have used this as a temporary gaol.

Return to the Strand. On the other side you will see the crescent-shaped Aldwych, location of the Indian High Commission, the Australian High Commission at ❸❻ **Australia House** and ❸❼ **Bush House**. The Australian High Commission opposite moved here in 1918, making this the oldest continually occupied mission in London. Its interior was used for the scenes featuring Gringott's Bank – staffed by goblins – in the film *Harry Potter and the Philosopher's Stone* (2001).

The basement of Australia House also contains what is thought to be one of London's 'holy wells' – sacred springs whose apparent healing powers were venerated by Londoners right up to the late medieval period. The spring can only be accessed through a manhole cover so is not visible to the public (although see the Clerkenwell Walk if you want to see the physical remains of another of London's wells).

The name *Aldwych* dates back to when the invading Saxons based themselves around here from 600 AD and in later centuries their original town was referred to as 'Ealdwic' (or 'old settlement'), later corrupted to Aldwych.

Continue eastwards and shortly you see the other 'Island Church', 38 **St Clement Danes**. It claims to be the church referred to in the opening line of the nursery rhyme *Oranges and Lemons*, "'Oranges and lemons', say the bells of St. Clement's" although it may equally have been St Clement Eastcheap in the City. In any event the church bells play the tune of Oranges and Lemons four times a day. The church's name is linked to

38

the Danish Vikings that occupied this part of London in the 9th century AD. Although St Clement's escaped the Great Fire it was nevertheless rebuilt in 1681 by Christopher Wren. Today it serves as the Central Church of the Royal Air Force and outside there is a statue to the controversial WWII RAF leader 'Bomber' Harris (1892-1984). William Webb Ellis, inventor of rugby football, was rector here between 1843 and 1855 and on the east side is a statue of Dr Samuel Johnson (1709-1784), who once worshipped here.

Continue east, crossing Essex St with 39 **The Royal Courts of Justice** on your left. This vast Gothic-styled warren of court rooms and corridors was opened in 1882 by Queen Victoria. Today it houses the Court of Appeal and the High Court. The entrance will be familiar to many who have watched television news reports as journalists and photographers often crowd outside during an important case. The public can visit when the courts are in session.

Follow the map to 40 **Middle Temple Lane**, where can be found the entrance to the Middle Temple and to the south-east, Inner Temple, two of the four Inns of Court to which barristers must belong. You can learn more about Middle and Inner Temple on the Inns of Court walk (see Volume One), however it is worth mentioning here that 'Temple' is derived from the medieval Order of the Knights Templar, whose London headquarters occupied much of the land between here and the Thames until the the early 14th century.

Also opposite the courts at number 216 stands **41** **Twinings Tea shop**, one of the oldest shops in London and still owned by the Twinings tea company, which opened its first shop in this street in 1706. The original figures above the shop portray Chinese tea merchants, who were important to Twinings because in the late 18th century China was the main supplier of tea to England. You can buy a wide variety of tea products in the shop – which dates from 1787 – and it contains a small museum that charts the history of the Twining family.

Continue along and at numbers 229-30 you will see the former home of the **42** **Wig and Pen Club**, once a prominent private club for journalists and lawyers that closed in 2003 – a victim of the exodus of journalists away from this area as the newspapers moved out. It occupied two narrow timbered houses. One dates from the early 17th century, and is the only complete house in the street to pre-date the Great Fire.

In the middle of the road is a dragon statue which marks the **43** **former site of Temple Bar**, and the beginning of Fleet Street and the approach to the City itself (a dragon being the City of London's coat of arms). If you cross over to have a look at the reliefs on the base of the statue you can see a depiction of Temple Bar – a stone gate designed by Sir Christopher Wren after the original wooden gate was destroyed in the Great Fire. All the other gates into the City had been demolished by 1800, but Temple Bar survived until 1878. By then its narrowness was causing traffic congestion on the Strand and so it was taken down and moved to a country estate in Hertfordshire. Recently it was returned to London and now stands beside St Paul's Cathedral (see below). Until 1745 the spikes on top of Temple Bar were used for displaying the severed heads and limbs of executed prisoners, with street vendors charging a penny for viewing glasses so onlookers could get a better view.

Continue east to reach the junction with Chancery Lane running to the north. This is where Fleet Street begins and the Strand ends. The street is named after the Fleet river and while later on in the walk we will find out more about the river itself, the origin of the word Fleet has been suggested as being from the Anglo-Saxon flëot meaning "tidal inlet".

Opposite Chancery Lane at 17 Fleet Street is the half-timbered frontage of **44** **Prince Henry's Room.** Part of the structure survives from a tavern called the Prince's Arms – built in 1610 – which contains a first floor Jacobean plaster ceiling displaying the Prince of Wales's coat of arms (with initials 'PH' in the centre). This was probably put there to mark the investiture of James I's eldest son Prince Henry (1594-1612) as the Prince of Wales in 1610. From 1795 to 1816 'Mrs Salmon's Waxworks' were located in the front part

Prince Henry's Room

of the house, while the tavern continued in the rear. Dickens satirises the sweating waxworks here in his novel *David Copperfield*. Samuel Pepys mentions coming here in 1661 when it was the Fountain Inn.

Beside Prince Henry's Room look up to see an **45 old fashioned street sign** with three squirrels. This recalls Goslings Bank, which was founded in 1650 and was based at this location from 1743 – known then by its customers as being underneath the 'Signe of the Three Squirrils'. It later became part of Barclays bank, a branch of which still occupies the site today, and Barclays continue to hold customer records for Goslings Bank going back to 1717.

Continuing along Fleet Street, and stop outside number 22 (also on the south side) – the incredibly narrow late 19th-century **46 Ye Olde Cock Tavern**. Its predecessor of the same name was founded in the mid-16th century and originally stood on the opposite side of Fleet Street. It was popular with the likes of Charles Dickens, Samuel Pepys and Alfred Tennyson. The latter wrote a light-hearted poem entitled *Will Waterproof's*

Lyrical Monologue in the original Tavern in 1842, including the lines 'O plump head-waiter at the Cock, To which I most resort, How goes the time? 'Tis five o'clock, Go fetch a pint of port'. When subsequent customers asked for the 'plump head-waiter', the man concerned was not best pleased given he had not even been aware the Poet Laureate was a customer. Furnishings from the original building were used in the construction of the current public house.

Cross over to visit the church of 🔴47 **St Dunstan-in-the-West**. This medieval church narrowly escaped the Great Fire thanks to the efforts of the then Dean of Westminster and scholars from Westminster School, who tackled the flames with buckets of water. The current building dates from the 1830s and has an interesting octagonal interior, and a beautiful iconostasis (altar screen) brought here from a monastery in Bucharest in 1966. It remains the only church in England to have shrine or chapel to seven different branches of Christendom.

The famous clock hanging over the street dates from 1671 and features Gog and Magog, the traditional guardians of London who strike each hour and quarter-hour. This was the first clock in London to have a minute hand and has been referred to in various books including Oliver Goldsmith's *The Vicar of Wakefield* (1766).

The courtyard contains an original statue of Elizabeth I – the oldest outdoor statue in London – and also figures of the mythical King Lud and his sons, by legend a British king before the Roman era. They all once decorated Lud Gate, the old western gate into the City. John Donne was rector here from 1624 to 1631 and diarist Samuel Pepys worshipped here a number of times, finding time to try to seduce female members of the congregation during services. Lord Baltimore, founder of the State of Maryland in the USA, was buried here in 1632.

Beside the church on the east side you can see a **48** **red-brick building** which still boasts the names of the Evening Telegraph, People's Friend, People's Journal and Dundee Courier. These are still published today by Dundee-based DC Thompson, a Scottish family-run business responsible for creating *The Beano*, and which has been producing newspapers since 1905. They continue to have a small London office here, making this the only traditional publisher to still have a presence on Fleet Street.

Just a few doors down on the same side, walk down the claustrophobic **49** **Hen and Chicken Court** – the fictitious site of Sweeney Todd's barber shop. The story was first set out in detail in the Victorian penny-dreadful *The String of Pearls: A Romance* (serialized 1846-47) by Thomas Peckett Prest. In the story, set in 1785, Todd kills the customers in his barber shop and the bodies are then dropped through a trapdoor.

They are then taken through a tunnel underneath the church to Mrs Lovett's pie shop in Bell Yard where the flesh was cooked in meat pies.

The book has the opening lines 'Before Fleet-street had reached its present importance, and when George the Third was young, and the two figures who used to strike the chimes at old St Dunstan's church were in all their glory – being a great impediment to errand-boys on their progress, and a matter of gaping curiosity to country people – there stood close to the sacred edifice a small barber's shop, which was kept by a man of the name of Sweeney Todd'.

Later, Todd evil deeds are uncovered as the corpses down below begin to rot and 'the pious frequenters of old St Dunstan's church began to perceive a strange and most abominable odour throughout that sacred edifice'. There is no historical evidence that Sweeney Todd ever existed.

Opposite St Dunstan's is 50 **C. Hoare and Co.**, the only one of the great 17th-century private deposit banks to remain family-owned. Others seen on this stretch of Fleet Street, such as Child & Co and Coutts, are now owned by the big banks. Hoare's has been based here since 1690 and customers have included Catherine of Braganza (wife of Charles II), Samuel Pepys, John Dryden, Thomas Gainsborough, Lord Byron, Jane Austen and Lord Palmerston. One of the earliest cheques was written here in July 1676, including the words 'Mr Hoare.. pray pay to the bearer hereof Mr Witt Morgan fifty-four pounds ten shillings and ten pence'. The current building dates from 1829.

Continue westwards passing 51 **El Vino** on the right, a legendary Fleet Street watering hole that was once dominated by newspaper men and barristers. It is famous for its strict dress code, and until a court case in 1982 it refused to allow women to be served at the bar. Rumpole of the Bailey, the colourful barrister

character created by John Mortimer, liked to relax with a cigar and glass of 'Chateau Fleet Street' in Pommeroy's wine bar, thought to have been modelled on El Vinos.

Cross to the north side and (at 170 Fleet Street) walk up **52** **Red Lion Court**, an example of the maze of old-fashioned lanes that lie behind Fleet Street. You will see ahead a **53** **distinctive sign** high up on the wall showing a hand pouring oil into a Greek lamp bearing the motto *Alere Flamman* (feed the flame). This dates from the 1820s and was originally the sign for a printer and publisher named Abraham Valpy (1787-1854) – most notable for publishing a number of important works of classical literature and founding the *Classical Journal* in 1810.

Pass the sign and at the top bear right and follow the sign for **54** **Dr Johnson's House** in Gough Square.

Samuel Johnson (1709-84) rented 17 Gough Square in 1746, and with the help of his six Scottish assistants (or *'harmless drudges'* as he called them) spent the next nine years compiling the first English dictionary. However, it was his friend James Boswell's *Life of Johnson* (1791) that really ensured Johnson would never be forgotten, Boswell superbly capturing the great man's wit and eccentricities in what is perhaps the best biography in the English language. Johnson's wife Hetty died here in 1752. Johnson's House is open throughout the year, see p.131 for contact details.

Bear right past the statue of Johnson's cat **55** **Hodge** ('A very fine cat indeed' he

Red Lion Court

thought) and then left into Wine Office Court to find the **56 Ye Old Cheshire Cheese**. The original tavern was rebuilt after the Great Fire in 1667 and it retains the atmosphere of an old London chop-house with wood-panelled rooms and maze-like corridors. Charles Dickens spent a great deal of time here, sitting at the table to the right of the fireplace by the ground floor bar.

It has also been the haunt of Dr Johnson and James Boswell, Thomas Carlyle, Lord Tennyson, William Thackeray, Mark Twain, Arthur Conan Doyle, and US president Theodore Roosevelt. It even had a famously eccentric pub parrot called Polly who could swear in numerous languages. She died in 1926 and had her obituary placed in 200 newspapers around the world.

Continue south to reach Fleet Street again and cross over. Look back to the north side of Fleet Street to get a good view of the distinctive art deco façades of the **57 old Telegraph** (with the distinctive clock overhanging the street) and **58 Daily Express buildings**, two of the reminders that Fleet Street was until recently dominated by the newspaper industry.

56

The origins of this association began with Wynkyn de Worde (d.1534), who had learnt his trade working under William Caxton (d.1492), the first English printer. After Caxton died, de Worde moved the printing press from Westminster to Fleet Street in around 1500, hoping to attract business from the wealthy clergymen who lived in the grand houses nearby. His business was based at the Sign of the Sun opposite St Bride's. Others soon followed, and in 1702 The Daily Courant, the world's first daily newspaper, was opened here (the site is seen later in the walk on Ludgate Hill).

The importance of the Church on the development of the printing industry is still evident today. The head of a printer's union is known as the Father of the Chapel, type is stored in fonts and black smudges are called monks.

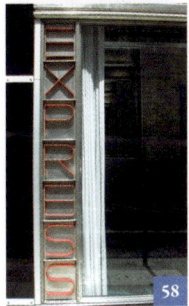

From then until the 1980s all the great British newspapers and news agencies were based in or around Fleet Street, and the pubs, restaurants and wine bars were full of journalists, reporters and printers. However, working practices had become antiquated and in the 1980s Rupert Murdoch made a huge break with the past by moving News International to Wapping. When Reuters left Fleet Street in 2005 the great era was officially dead, and now the area is dominated by other professions. Goldman Sachs bank occupied the old Telegraph and Daily Express buildings from 1991 until they relocated in 2019.

Walk on to stand at the junction with Whitefriars Street. At number 66 once stood **59** **The Tipperary**, said to be London's oldest Irish pub having been bought by a Dublin brewer in around 1700. The pub closed its doors for the last time in 2022.

Just around the corner on Whitefriars Street look out for the **60** **plaque commemorating the London office of the Anti-Corn-Law League.** The repeal of the Corn Laws (that imposed a duty on imported corn), is largely forgotten today, but was as controversial and divisive as the EU Referendum or Iraq War in the mid-19th century. The names of John Bright and Richard Cobden that are on the plaque were household names in their day and the successful repeal of the laws by Prime Minister Robert Peel bitterly divided the Tory party and ended his political career.

Walk down Whitefriars Street, named after the Carmelite or Whitefriars Priory founded in this area in the mid-13th century. Following the Dissolution of the Monasteries the priory was abandoned, and from 1608 to the 1620s part of the crumbling site was occupied by the Whitefriars Theatre. Shakespeare mentions the Priory in *Richard III*, when the Duke of Gloucester orders that Henry's dead body be taken there.

On the left is a modern office development where until recently stood **Hanging Sword Alley**. This was an infamous residential street with a tough reputation in the 18th century. It contained a criminal den known as 'Blood Bowl House', and could be a dangerous place to walk through as one local resident named Thomas Cealey found out to his cost in 1739, when attacked here by two women. A new development has replaced the entire area and none of the narrow alleyways baring ancient names remain.

Continue down Whitefriars Street and then turn right into ⑥ **Ashentree Court**. Look out for some information boards which describe how *The Daily Mail* was printed nearby for many decades until it moved to Kensington in 1988. Bear right and look out for some stairs that take you down to the basement level of an office building. At the bottom you can see through a window the remains of the ⑥ **old Priory crypt**, the only part of Whitefriars still visible. Just ahead is a passageway that contains tiled information boards tracing the history of the newspaper industry in Fleet Street.

Retrace your steps and continue down Whitefriars Street – once named Water Lane when a tributary of the Fleet River flowed through this area giving Fleet Street its name. At the end is Tudor Street, once at the heart of the notoriously lawless area known as 'Alsatia' – named after the Alsace region in Europe that was fought over by France and Germany for centuries, becoming ungovernable as a result. The ecclesiastical privileges associated with the priory meant the area around here was effectively a state within a state, the haunt of vicious gangs and debtors trying to evade prison.

Legislative reforms at the very end of the 17th century began to remove these privileges; however, the term 'Alsatia' became part of the English language. For example in the famous book *The Mill on the Floss (1860)*, the author George Eliot described how the character Maggie 'always appeared in the most amiable light at her aunt Moss's; it was her Alsatia, where she was out of the reach of law'.

Follow the map eastwards along Tudor Street. At numbers 2-4 look out for the former home of ⑥ **The Institute of Journalists**. The building has a foundation memorial stone that dates the building to 1903. Newspapers and journalists were drawn to the area south of Fleet Street after gas works were established south of Tudor Street in late 19th century, thus ensuring a source of power for the huge print machines.

Continue on to reach New Bridge Street and turn left. Outside number 14 you will see a plaque recalling that this was the location of Henry VIII's **64** **Bridewell Palace** and where he lived between 1515 and 1523. The palace was later used to house foreign diplomats and Hans Holbein the Younger's famous work *The Ambassadors* (1553) – was painted here. Edward IV was persuaded to let the palace be used by the City authorities to house homeless children and 'disorderly women'.

Over time the former palace became home to a hospital, a school and a prison – the latter use resulting in the term 'Bridewell' passing into the English language as meaning a place of detention. The site was eventually closed in 1855 and the buildings later demolished, although part of the 19th-century gatehouse has been incorporated into the current entrance. The gatehouse contains a bust of Edward VI – the monarch who donated the Palace to the City of London in 1553.

Head north and then left into Bride Lane, passing the **65** **Bridewell Theatre.** This long established venue offers regular evening performances from March through to December. To find out more about the theatre or the St Bride Foundation of which it is a part, visit their website (www.sbf.org.uk).

Walk up the flight of steps beside the theatre that brings you out into an open courtyard. This gives you a good view of the back of **66** **St Bride's Church**, dedicated to

Bridgid of Ireland (or St Brigid of Kildare), an Irish saint of the 5th century AD. St Bride's was just one of 88 City churches destroyed in the Great Fire of 1666, and was rebuilt by Sir Christopher Wren. The famous steeple stands 226 feet high and is said to have inspired the creation of the original multi-tiered wedding cake by a local baker. Until the 18th century the church was described on maps as St Bridget – subsequently being shortened to perhaps reflect its famous connection with the wedding industry.

It is known as the 'Journalist's Church' as traditionally it has been used by that profession for major services even after the newspapers moved away from Fleet Street. It also contains an interesting crypt that is open to the public and contains remains from the Roman, Saxon and Norman eras. Near the font is a bust of Virginia Dare, the first English girl born in America in 1587, whose parents were married in St Bride's. The church is also known for its choir and the fine music concerts held there on weekday lunchtimes.

66

St Bride's Passage

Carry on through St Bride's Passage into Salisbury Square and continue down ⑥⑦ **Salisbury Court**, which leads to Fleet Street. Look out for the plaque on the left-hand side that records the site where the first edition of The Sunday Times was edited in 1822.

Just after this on the right-hand side is a plaque marking where the diarist Samuel Pepys was born in 1633. Pepys was baptised at St Bride's and when his brother Tom died during the Great Plague of 1665 Pepys tried to have him buried in the church. However, it was too full so Pepys bribed the church sexton sixpence to 'jostle' the other bodies together to make the necessary space.

It was also in Salisbury Court that Pepys was 'cut for the stone' in front of his family in 1658 by Thomas Hollier. The offending gallstone was extracted and was described as being the size of a tennis ball. Such procedures often ended badly, and Hollier's four subsequent operations all resulted in the patient's death. Evidently Pepys recognised his luck – on each anniversary of the operation he held a 'solemn feast for the cutting of the stone'.

You can visit St Bride's church now by walking down the narrow St Bride's Passage off Salisbury Court, or joining Fleet Street and turning right. When finished at the church rejoin Fleet Street and head east. Ahead you will see Ludgate Circus and Ludgate Hill with the dome of St Paul's Cathedral dominating the skyline.

On the right at 95 is ⑥⑧ **The Old Bell Tavern** – a fantastic old Victorian pub, originally founded by Wren as a hostel for his workers who were re-constructing St Bride's after the Great Fire.

Number 99 is another ornate Victorian public house – the ⑥⑨ **Punch Tavern**, named after the magazine Punch (1841-2002) that was founded here. Perhaps the best pub however is the Crown & Sugar Loaf nearby on Bride Lane – a candidate for possessing the finest interior of any pub in London. It was originally part of the Punch Tavern, but was physically split after a disagreement between the co-owners a few years ago.

As you get to the end of Fleet Street pause to look up Farringdon Street (to the north) and New Bridge Street (to the south). You can still discern the shape of the valley that was once dominated by the Fleet River. The river is now hidden but as late as the mid-18th century a pedestrian would have walked over Fleet Bridge (which stood at the junction) in order to reach Ludgate Hill.

The source of the Fleet is on Hampstead Heath, and it remained London's second main river until the 17th century. However by then it was becoming so silted up and full of filth it was almost un-navigable. Attempts by developers after the Great Fire to convert it into a functioning canal failed although nearby street names such as Newcastle Close and Old Seacoal Lane recall the era when coal ships from the north came here.

By the mid-18th century much of the northern section leading up to Holborn was covered over and became the site of Fleet Market. In the following 50 years the last remaining open stretch of the river to the south of here was also covered over and today empties into the Thames under Blackfriars Bridge.

The unhealthy atmosphere once generated by the polluted river explains why the land was the site for a number of prisons that once stood nearby. Cross over and continue up Ludgate Hill on the north side. Just by the corner of Ludgate Hill there is a plaque that remembers the former site of the Daily Courant newspaper mentioned earlier. Continue uphill to pass the church of **70 St Martin within Ludgate**, which once stood next to (hence 'within') the old City gate of Ludgate. The medieval church was destroyed in the Great Fire and rebuilt by Sir Christopher Wren in 1684.

Continue up to **71 St Paul's Cathedral** and bear left to Paternoster Square where you can see the 17th-century **72 Temple Bar gate house** mentioned earlier, which was recently returned to London after 125 years. The walk ends here and you might now take the opportunity to visit the cathedral. St Paul's tube station is just a few minutes' walk to the north-east of the cathedral grounds. ●

VISIT...

Benjamin Franklin House
36 Craven Street, WC2N 5NF
www.benjaminfranklinhouse.org

**The Courtauld Gallery &
Somerset House**
Somerset House, WC2R 0RN
www.courtauld.ac.uk
www.somersethouse.org.uk

Roman Bath
5 Strand Lane, WC2R 1AP

Dr Johnson's House
17 Gough Square, EC4A 3DE
www.drjohnsonshouse.org

St Paul's Cathedral
St Paul's Churchyard, EC4M 8AD
www.stpauls.co.uk

EAT, DRINK...

Gordon's Wine Bar
47 Villiers Street, WC2N 6NE
www.gordonswinebar.com

Ye Olde Cock Tavern
22 Fleet Street, EC4Y 1AA

Old Cheshire Cheese
145 Fleet Street, EC4A 2BU

The Old Bell Tavern
95 Fleet Street, EC4Y 1DU

Punch Tavern
99 Fleet Street, EC4Y 1DE
www.punchtavern.com

St Helen's Bishopsgate, see p.149

5 The City: Eastern Walk

LONDON WALL

LONDON WALL

BLOMFIELD ST

THROGMORTON AVE

MOORGATE

COLEMAN ST

AUSTIN FRIARS

OLD BROAD

LOTHBURY   THROGMORTON ST

PRINCE'S ST

Bank of England

THREADNEEDLE ST

FINCH LN

Bank

CORNHILL

BIRCHIN LN

GEORGE YARD

GRACECHURCH ST

QUEEN VICTORIA ST

LOMBARD ST

KING WILLIAM ST

WALBROOK

ST SWITHIN'S LN

Mansion House

GARLICK HILL

QUEEN ST

CANNON ST

Cannon Street

CANNON ST

Monument

WILLIAM ST

PUDDING LN

BOTOLPH LN

EASTCH

LOWER

1 Old City wall
2 Trinity Square Gardens
3 All Hallows by the Tower
4 Mark Lane Tube Station
5 Muscovy Street
6 Site of the Navy Office
7 St Olave's Hart Street
8 Crutched Friars
9 St Botolph Aldgate
10 Hoop and Grapes
11 Classic police call box
12 Aldgate Pump
13 Mitre Square
14 Priory of the Holy Trinity
15 The Bevis Mark Synagogue
16 Bishops' mitre
17 St Botolph without Bishopsgate
18 18th-century former charity school

19 Turkish bath
20 All Hallows-on-the-Wall
21 Drapers' Hall
22 Dutch church of Austin Friars
23 Adams Court
24 St Helen's Bishopsgate
25 St Andrew Undershaft
26 Lloyd's Building
27 East India House
28 Leadenhall Market
29 St Peter upon Cornhill
30 St Michael Cornhill
31 Smith, Elder & Co.

32 Old water pump
33 Ball Court
34 Simpson's Tavern (closed)
35 Jamaica Wine House
36 First coffee house
37 George and Vulture

The City: Eastern Walk

38 Lombard Street
39 St Mary Woolnoth
40 Mansion House
41 St Stephen Walbrook
42 London Stone
43 St Mary Abchurch
44 King William Street Tube Station
45 The Monument
46 Old Billingsgate Market
47 Custom House
48 Lovat Lane
49 St Mary at Hill
50 St Dunstan in the East

Liverpool Street

18 17
19 16

BROAD ST
WORMWOOD ST
BISHOPSGATE
CAMOMILE ST
OUTWICH ST
HOUNDSDITCH
BEVIS MARKS
BURY ST
GRT ST HELENS
24
UNDERSHAFT
ST MARY AXE
25
15
DUKES PL
MITRE PASSAGE
14 13
MITRE ST
Aldgate
9 11
10
ALDGATE HIGH ST
MANSELL ST

LEADENHALL ST
12
ENHALL ST
27
26
LIME ST
BILLITER ST
FENCHURCH AVE
JEWRY ST
MINORIES

HALL PL

Fenchurch Street

LLOYDD AVE
FENCHURCH ST
8
INCHURCH ST
MINCING LN
MARK LN
SEETHING LN
CRUTCHED FRIARS
COOPER'S ROW
GOODMAN'S YRD

Tower Gateway

ROOD LN
GREAT TOWER ST
7
6
4 5
TRINITY SQ
2
Tower Hill
1

IDOL LN
50
CROSS LN
3
BYWARD ST
TOWER HILL
ES ST
47

TOWER BRIDGE

Tower of London

The City: Eastern Walk
Start/Finish: Tower Hill underground station
Distance: 3.5 miles

The walk begins from Tower Hill tube station. As you exit, the Tower of London – founded by William the Conqueror in the 1070s – dominates the view to the south.

Immediately outside the station you can see one of the best-preserved sections of the ❶ **old City wall**, built by the Romans in the late 2nd century AD as London began to wilt under attacks from tribes such as the Angles and Saxons who lived outside the Empire's borders. The Roman wall ran for over two miles and enclosed around 330 acres.

After the Romans left London in the 5th century AD, the area inside the walls was largely abandoned. It was not until the reign of King Alfred the Great (849-899 AD) that the City was reoccupied and the original Roman wall re-fortified and strengthened. If you look at this section of City wall you can see the Roman tiles making up the bottom portion.

To see another part of the old City wall, and one rarely visited, head down Trinity Square (just north of Tower Hill station). A few yards down on the right is the Leonardo Royal Hotel : walk through the open entrance to find on the other side a substantial section of the wall, the lower half of which dates from the Roman period.

Return to the station and walk into neighbouring ❷ **Trinity Square Gardens.** Head west passing Sir Edwin Lutyens's Mercantile Marine Memorial to sailors who lost their lives in both World Wars. Near the exit on the far side are some plaques in the ground which commemorate prisoners from the Tower who were publicly executed here.

Part of old City wall next to Leonardo Royal Hotel

One such victim was the Duke of Monmouth (1649-85), the illegitimate son of Charles II, who was sentenced to be executed after his failed rebellion against his uncle James II. As he prepared to die the Duke spoke to Jack Ketch – possibly the least proficient executioner in history – saying 'Here are six guineas for you: pray do your business well: do not serve me as you did my Lord Russell. I have heard you struck him three or four times'.

Despite this promise of a bonus if he did his job correctly, Ketch took five strokes of his axe to separate Monmouth's head from his body, even stopping mid-way to see if someone else in the crowd might volunteer to finish the job for him.

After the execution Monmouth's head was allegedly reattached to his body to permit his portrait to be painted – surely one of the strangest compositions ever undertaken. According to one (albeit unlikely) legend James II could not bear his nephew being executed, so switched Monmouth with another man. Monmouth was then spirited away to become a secret prisoner in France under

Louis XIV – possibly becoming the real life 'Man in the Iron Mask' that inspired the novel written by Alexandre Dumas in 1848.

The last execution held here was of Lord Lovat, chief of the Fraser clan, in 1747 on account of his support for Bonnie Prince Charlie's rebellion of 1745. Just before Lovat died a set of scaffolding carrying nearly 1,000 spectators collapsed and twelve people were killed.

Exit the Gardens and cross over Byward Street to reach ❸ **All Hallows by the Tower.** This claims with some justification to be the oldest church in London and was founded by St Ethelburga of Barking Abbey in 675 AD. Inside the church you can see a Saxon arch from the original church that was uncovered after bomb damage during WWII.

Notable figures associated with All Hallows include Samuel Pepys, who in 1666 watched the Great Fire of London from the church tower; John Quincy Adams, sixth President of the United States who was married here in 1797; William Penn, founder of Pennsylvania, baptised here in 1644; and Nobel prize winner Albert Schweitzer, who recorded organ recitals inside All Hallows for Columbia records in 1935. Legend has it that the heart of Richard I was buried in a chapel that once adjoined the church.

The bodies of those executed on Tower Hill were often brought to rest at the church, including those of St Thomas More, Bishop John Fisher and Archbishop William Laud. The Saxon undercroft contains a fascinating collection of treasures including part of a

2nd-century AD Roman pavement, an altar stone originally from the Templar Crusader's castle of Athlit, Saxon burial remains, Shackleton's barrel-shaped crow's nest used on his last Antarctic expedition, and copies of the parish records that show the entries relating to Penn and Quincy Adams. The nave of the church also contains a font by Grinling Gibbons (1648-1721), the great Dutch craftsmen whose carving skills were so valued by Christopher Wren when he rebuilt the City's churches after the Great Fire.

When finished cross the road. The subway entrance opposite the church, and the building now occupied by All Bar One, were once part of the ❹ **Mark Lane tube station** that opened in 1884. It was closed in 1967 and replaced by the current Tower Hill underground station.

Walk up Seething Lane, passing ❺ **Muscovy Street** on the right. The latter is named after the Muscovy Company, the first company in the world, which was once based nearby and enjoyed a trading monopoly with Russia between 1555 and 1698. The vicinity has another Russian connection as Tsar Peter the Great (1672-1725) used to drink in a tavern near this street when he stayed in London in 1698, and the tavern (now demolished) was later renamed the *Czar of Muscovy* in his honour.

As you walk up Seething Lane you pass on the right a small park that contains a bust of the famous diarist Samuel Pepys (1633-1703). This marks the ❻ **site of the Navy Office** where Pepys worked

and lived, moving into a ten-bedroom house with his wife Elizabeth in 1660. He wrote most of his diary while living here, only stopping in 1669 for fear he was going blind. In September 1666, during the Great Fire of London, he recorded in his diary how all his household goods were taken away by cart for safety, although he chose to dig a pit and in it place his true treasures, 'my Parmazan cheese, as well as my wine'.

Continue up the Lane looking out on the left for the ominous 17th-century skull and crossbones carvings that sit on top of the entrance to the former graveyard of **7** **St Olave's Hart Street**. This church, one of the smallest in the City, is also unusual for largely pre-dating the Great Fire. It is dedicated to King Olav II of Norway (995-1030 AD), that country's patron saint who fought alongside the Anglo-Saxons against the Danes in the Battle of London Bridge in 1014, an event that possibly inspired the children's rhyme *London Bridge is falling down*. St Olave's was described by Pepys as 'our own church', and both he and his wife were buried here. You can see their memorials inside.

The atmospheric graveyard inspired Charles Dickens to describe the church as 'St Ghastly Grim' in his book *The Uncommercial Traveller* (1861). A mysterious 'Mother Goose', possibly the inspiration for the famous pantomime character, is recorded as being buried here in 1586. Another person interred here was Mary Ramsey, the woman who by tradition is thought to have brought the Great Plague to London in 1664.

Follow the map up **8** **Crutched Friars**, passing a cavity in a wall containing the figures of two friars. The Crutched Friars was a religious order that founded a monastery here in 1249 after having arrived from Italy, and they were so named because they carried a wooden staff surmounted by a cross.

Crutched Friars leads to Jewry Street, this area originally known as 'Poor Jewry' when it was at the heart of London's medieval Jewish ghetto. At the top you can see **9** **St Botolph Aldgate**, one of three

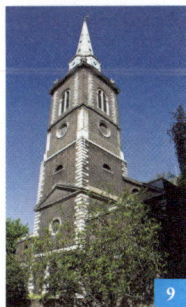

surviving churches that originally stood near a gate in the City wall and which were dedicated as a result to the Saxon patron saint of travellers. A church has stood here for 1,000 years and the current building dates largely from 1744.

During the Great Plague of 1665, 5,000 corpses were buried in the churchyard. In the 19th century St Botolph's became known as the 'Prostitutes' Church' as it stood in the middle of a red light area where in 1888 a number of Jack the Ripper's victims plied their trade. During this period the authorities offered prostitutes an amnesty from arrest if they restricted their activities to the triangular island on which the church is located.

The City gate of Aldgate (or 'old gate') was the oldest of the six original vast Roman gateways into the City. It was rebuilt many times over following centuries and the poet Geoffrey Chaucer (1343-c.1400) lived in rooms within the medieval gateway between 1374 and 1385. Aldgate was finally demolished c.1760.

Head right along Aldgate High Street to find at number 47 the wood-framed ⑩ **Hoop and Grapes**, possibly the oldest public house in the City, with foundations dating back to the 13th century. The date of the current building is debated but it probably existed before the Great Fire. The cellar is rumoured to have once been connected by tunnel to the Tower of London.

Retrace your steps, visiting St Botolph's and looking out for the ⑪ **classic police telephone call box**, dating from c.1935 and

Grade II listed. Continue west to the junction of Leadenhall Street and Fenchurch Street.

At this junction stands **12** **Aldgate Pump**, a rare reminder of how Londoners fetched their water before houses were connected to a mains supply. The pump you see today dates from around 1870, and was once connected to a nearby well that had served the local population since the 13th century. However, after a damning report on the standard of water coming from the well (not helped by the fact the supply was filtered through the local graveyard) the pump was reconnected in 1876 to the New River Company's water supply that originated from outside the City.

Follow the map into **13** **Mitre Square**. It was here that 46 year-old prostitute Catherine Eddowes was murdered by Jack the Ripper in the early hours of 30th September 1888, just hours after Elizabeth Stride, the Ripper's third victim, had been murdered in nearby Whitechapel. Shortly before she died Eddowes was seen with a man with a dark moustache and wearing a deer stalker, red neck scarf and tweed-jacket

12

—the only likely sighting of the Ripper ever recorded. Eddowes's was found with her throat cut and her body horribly mutilated.

The square stands on the site of the ⑭ **Priory of the Holy Trinity**, an Augustinian monastery founded in 1108 by Queen Matilda, the wife of Henry I. It survived until 1532 when it was dissolved during the reign of Henry VIII.

At the end of the square on the left, walk through the narrow Mitre Passage passing under a building, into Creechurch Place and then right along Creechurch Lane into Bevis Marks. Creechurch Lane was the site of a synagogue founded by a small number of Spanish and Portuguese Jews in the mid-17th century. The congregation were the first to openly worship in London since the Jews were expelled from England in 1290, and it was Oliver Cromwell who relaxed – or at least turned a blind eye to – the anti-Semitic laws still on the statute book.

This original synagogue has long since gone (there is a plaque remembering it halfway up Creechurch Lane), but its successor dating from 1701 can be seen on the left-hand side as you walk up Bevis Marks. ⑮ **The Bevis Mark synagogue** is the oldest synagogue in the country, and the only one in Europe that has hosted continuous services for over 300 years.

The building bears a great resemblance to Christian churches of the same era, unsurprisingly given Quaker Joseph Avis and other local men were charged with its design and construction. Two times Prime

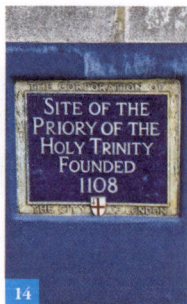

Minister and author Benjamin Disraeli (1804-1881) was born into the congregation; however, his father Isaac fell out with the Jewish authorities in 1813 and had his son baptised into the Christian faith. This allowed Disraeli to pursue his great political career in an era when Jews were still excluded from high office.

Continue up Bevis Marks, its name a corruption of 'Buries Marks'. This original name reflected how in the medieval period the street marked the perimeter of where burials could take place upon lands owned by the Abbots of Bury St Edmunds.

Continue along Camomile Street, named after the medicinal plant once grown here. At the junction with Bishopsgate look out for the emblem of the **16 Bishops' mitre** on the office wall opposite. This marks the site of Bishop's Gate, one of the original City gates built by the Romans and later rebuilt by Eorconweald, a 7th-century Bishop of London. Bishop's Gate was finally demolished in 1760.

Walk north up Bishopsgate, once a residential street, which even up until the late 19th century contained a number of grand late-medieval mansions. These have now all been built over, however two examples survive elsewhere in London: the frontage of the house that belonged to Sir Paul Pindar (1565-1650) can be found in the Victoria & Albert Museum; and Crosby Hall, part of the 15th-century Crosby Place, was moved to Cheyne Walk in Chelsea in 1910 (see the Chelsea walk). Crosby Place was mentioned by Shakespeare in *Richard III* and was once owned by Sir Thomas More.

On the left you can see the spire of **17 St Botolph without Bishopsgate**, the second City church on this walk dedicated to the Saxon patron saint of

travellers. Head left through the church's garden and former burial ground. The poet John Keats (1795-1821) and Elizabethan actor Edward Alleyn (1566-1626) were both baptised in St Botolph's.

Just north of the church stands the site of the hospital of St Mary Bethlehem, founded as part of a priory in 1247. It is better known by its nickname of 'Bedlam', defined in the dictionary as meaning a 'madhouse' or 'scene of uproar'. This was on account of the hospital's attempt to aid London's mentally ill, although the patients were treated more like prisoners, shackled to the walls and fed on scraps. They later became a popular tourist attraction, with the hospital staff provoking the patients before visits to ensure the visitors could be cruelly entertained.

Shakespeare refers in *King Lear* to 'Bedlam beggars, who, with roaring voices/Strike in their numb'd and mortified bare arms/ Pins, wooden pricks, nailes...' – a description that gives some idea of the chaos that must have reigned within the hospital.

In 1675 Bedlam moved to Moorfields, and then to Lambeth in 1815. After the hospital moved out of London its Lambeth building became (and still remains) home to the Imperial War Museum.

Pass the netball courts on the south side of St Botolph's,

flanked by an ⑱ **18th-century former charity school** on the north side. You then pass a curious tiled building, that has served many purposes, but was originally a ⑲ **Turkish bath** built in 1895. The unusual design is said to have been based on a shrine at the church of the Holy Sepulchre in Jerusalem.

Follow the map onto London Wall and bear right, passing the church of ⑳ **All Hallows-on-the-Wall**. This was first recorded in 1130 and, as can still be seen, was attached to the old City wall.

19 *Turkish bath*

The medieval church, that was known for its resident hermits, survived the Great Fire of London but was rebuilt by George Dance the Younger in 1765-67.

Follow the map down Throgmorton Avenue, named after Sir Nicholas Throckmorton (c.1515/1516–1571), statesman and ambassador to France during the reign of Elizabeth I. Towards the bottom of the Avenue is ㉑ **Drapers' Hall**, home of the Drapers' Livery Company. Livery Companies were originally founded in the medieval period as trade associations or guilds with the purpose of protecting their members' economic interests and regulating their respective trades and professions.

The Drapers were originally merchants who specialised in woollen cloth, and received their Royal Charter in 1364. Today the Drapers' Company is officially ranked third out of the 109 Livery Companies that still exist, the ranking being based on prestige and history. The organisation is now principally concerned with charitable activities, and has been based here since buying the land from Henry VIII in 1543.

Just before Drapers' Hall hall turn left into Austin Friars with the modern ㉒ **Dutch church of Austin Friars** on the right. Austin Friars is named after the Augustinian monastery founded here in 1253 and dissolved during the reign of Henry VIII. In 1550 the nave of the former monastery church was given to Dutch refugees at a time when there was, as yet, no Protestant church in the war-torn Netherlands.

The church was rebuilt a number of times and finally destroyed during the Blitz. The current structure dates from the 1950s and the church retains its Dutch congregation, making it the oldest Dutch-language Protestant church in the world. Vincent Van Gogh sketched the church in 1876 while living in London, and the drawing is today held in the Van Gogh museum in Amsterdam.

Exit Austin Friars on the south side to meet Old Broad Street and cross directly over heading through the narrow entrance of ㉓ **Adams Court**. Walk through this little-known and hidden part of the City, eventually passing through some gates to reach Threadneedle Street. Bear left up Bishopsgate and turn right into Great St Helen's.

Dominating the scene is the towering 'Gherkin' building that re-defined London's skyline when completed in 2003. In its shadow is the church of ㉔ **St Helen's Bishopsgate**. It is dedicated to St Helena (c.250-c.330 AD), the mother of Constantine, the first Christian Emperor of Rome. By tradition the church was founded by Helena in the 4th century AD and once contained a piece of the 'true cross' of Christ that she had discovered in the Holy Land.

A medieval nunnery once stood beside the parish church, but after the dissolution of the nunnery in 1538 the two buildings were joined together, hence the unusual 'double nave' shape. Inside is the finest collection of monuments and tombs within any City parish church, including the spectacular tombs of City grandees Sir Thomas Gresham (d. 1579), Sir William Pickering (d. 1575), and Sir John Crosby (d.1476 – of Crosby Hall mentioned above). St Helen's also contains a rare example of a squint (or 'hagioscope'), which allowed the medieval nuns to view the church altar from the nunnery. The church is normally open each morning from Monday to Friday.

25 *St Andrew Undershaft*

William Shakespeare lived in the parish of St Helen's, probably after he had moved from nearby Shoreditch where he first lived after arriving in London. In 1597 a 'William Shackspere' appears in a parish list of tax defaulters suggesting either he was struggling with his finances or he had already moved south of the river to Southwark where he is thought to have lived whilst working at playhouses such as the Globe.

Follow the map along Undershaft and bear right at St Mary Axe passing ㉕ **St Andrew Undershaft** on your left. Named after a famous medieval maypole that stood outside the church, the pole or 'shaft', stood much higher than the church tower and was used during May Day celebrations. At other times it may have been stored under the eaves of local houses. The maypole was permanently taken down in 1517 after a bloodthirsty May Day anti-immigrant riot was started by City apprentices, an event recorded in a scene from the Elizabethan play *Sir Thomas More* by Anthony Munday, to which Shakespeare is believed to have contributed several pages.

St Andrew Undershaft largely dates from around 1520 and so is another rare example of a City church that survived the Great Fire. It contains the tomb of John Stow (c.1525-1605) whose *Survey of London* (1598) is a unique and detailed account of Elizabethan London.

Leave the church and cross over Leadenhall Street heading for the innovative ㉖ **Lloyd's Building** designed by Richard Rogers and opened in 1986.

26

Cross over Leadenhall Street and walk down Lime Street with the Lloyd's Building on your right. ㉗ **East India House** once stood at the junction of the two streets, and served as the headquarters of the East India Company. The company was founded under a Royal Charter by Elizabeth I in 1600 and by the early 19th century controlled much of India, Burma, Singapore and Hong Kong, together comprising around a fifth of the world's population.

The Company played an important part in the foundation of the British colonies of Hong Kong and Singapore, and was also responsible for the importation of opium into China, a trade that caused terrible drug problems among the Chinese population. The company also paved the way for the British Empire in India but its pre-eminence swiftly declined after the Indian Mutiny of 1857 and its London headquarters were demolished four years later with Lloyd's taking over the site. By 1874 the East India Company's role and territories had been formally taken over by the British Crown, thus ending what was arguably the most influential commercial enterprise in world history.

Shortly you will see on the right the entrance to 28 **Leadenhall Market**, originally founded in 1445 as a market for wool, leather, meat and fish. The market's walls helped stop the spread of the Great Fire, but it was later demolished by the Victorians to make way for the current structure that was opened in 1881. It is worth taking time to explore the warren of little streets around the market including Bull's Head Passage on the south side. This contains a shop at number 42 that was used to portray 'The Leaky Cauldron', the entrance into 'Diagon Alley' in the film version of *Harry Potter and the Philosopher's Stone* (2001).

Exit the market on the west side and cross over Gracechurch Street to walk up the narrow St Peter's Alley. This leads to the church of 29 **St Peter upon Cornhill**, founded on the highest hill in the City and site of the great Roman Basilica and Forum, which survived until the end of the 3rd century AD.

St Peter's is traditionally believed to have been founded by King Lucius in 179 AD, although there is no evidence to support this. However, the fact that other churches in medieval London appear to have ranked St Peter's first in terms of prestige and age suggests there is some substance to this claim of Roman origins. The current church was rebuilt by Wren after the Great Fire.

Dickens often mentions Cornhill in his books. In *A Christmas Carol* Scrooge's office is based here, near an 'ancient tower of a church, whose gruff old bell was always peeping slily down at Scrooge out of a gothic window in the wall'. In Our *Mutual Friend* Lizzie Hexham and Bradley Headstone come to the church, Dickens describing 'a churchyard; a paved square court, with a raised bank of earth about breast high, in the middle, enclosed by iron rails. Here, conveniently and healthfully elevated above the level of the living, were the dead, and the tombstones; some of the latter droopingly inclined from the perpendicular, as if they were ashamed of the lies they told'.

Follow the path round to the exit onto Cornhill and head left. Shortly you pass ㉚ **St Michael Cornhill**, a church with Saxon foundations and notable for its Gothic tower that was built partly by Nicholas Hawksmoor between 1718 and 1722. The interior was re-ordered by Sir George Gilbert Scott in 1857 and 1860, and is regarded as one of the more drastic Victorian attempts to impose their style on an existing City church.

Continue down Cornhill as far as number 32 on the left-hand side. This used to be the office of publishers ㉛ **Smith, Elder & Co**., who in 1848 were paid a surprise visit by their clients Anne, Emily and Charlotte Brontë. Until this visit the publishers had been corresponding with the sisters under their pseudonyms; Acton, Currer and Ellis Bell – and unsurprisingly thought they were dealing with male writers. The sisters had taken this approach as they thought it would help them be taken more seriously, but as a result they had to show copies of their correspondence with the publishers before their identities were accepted.

The Brontës also met the Victorian literary giant William Makepeace Thackeray at these offices, a difficult encounter by all accounts with Thackeray quoting lines from *Jane Eyre* that its author Charlotte failed to recognise. The wooden panels on the doorway to number 32 portray a number of scenes depicting Cornhill's past, including this famous meeting.

Look out for the **32** **old water pump** on the other side of the road, marking the spot of a medieval well and prison. It was erected in 1799 and funded by the Bank of England and other City companies. Retrace your steps and walk up the tiny **33** **Ball Court** (on the same side as St Michael's and St Peter's). This takes you to the former site of **34** **Simpson's Tavern,** founded in 1757. It was one of the most atmospheric restaurants in London, famous for its hearty menu in the style of the traditional 'chop house'.

33

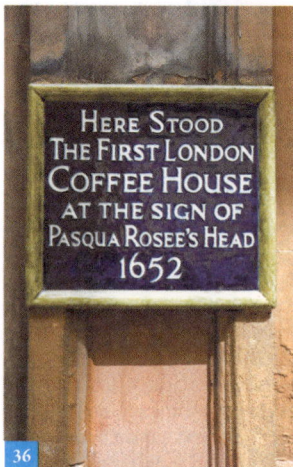

The friendly but eccentric staff and generous portions had been popular with city workers for over 250 years, but in December 2022 the landlords took possession of the property despite the efforts of the restaurant management to keep the business running.

Exit on the other side of the former Simpson's, leading into the City's narrowest and most confusing warren of back-alleys, which seem to have hardly changed since the days of Pepys or Dickens. Look out on the left for a sign to the **35 Jamaica Wine House** along St Michael's Alley, originally the Jamaica Coffee House when founded in the 1670s. It is named after its original clientele who were mainly merchants connected to trade in the West Indies. Messages for merchants would be left here, and news and gossip about the West Indies exchanged over a pipe and coffee, a way of dong business that continued at the Jamaica until the mid-19th century.

Beside the Jamaica Wine House is a plaque on the wall commemorating the site of London's **36 first coffee house**, which was opened in 1652 by an Armenian named Pasqua Rosée. He had arrived in London as the servant to a merchant named Daniel Edwards, and so impressed Edwards' friends with the coffee he made that the merchant encouraged him to open the shop. Its popularity saw similar coffee houses spread throughout London like wildfire: by 1739 over 550 could be counted. Many became associated with particular trades or political beliefs with some, like Lloyd's Coffee House (which was frequented by early insurance agents) giving rise to global commercial ventures that still exist today.

Walk away from Cornhill down St Michael's Alley, passing the **37 George and Vulture** chop house on the right. This is another traditional City eatery, founded in the 17th century and rebuilt after a fire in 1748. It is referred to by Dickens as where Mr Pickwick stays during the trial of *Bardell vs. Pickwick* in *The Pickwick Papers*. The City Pickwick Club, founded because of Dickens's book, had its inaugural dinner here in 1909. Dickens once hosted a dinner here in 1834 for 34 of his friends and the restaurant still has the original bill. During the 18th century the George and Vulture became known as one of the haunts of the 'Hellfire Club' – a notorious group of aristocrats rumoured to indulge in Satanism and other immoral practices.

Continue ahead until you reach George Yard and then enter **38** **Lombard Street** and bear right. This was the original banking centre in London, and where Barclay's and Lloyd's banks used to have their head offices. It is named after the Lombard merchants from Italy who first came here in the 12th century and who filled a gap left by the Jewish money lenders who had been expelled from the City. The Lombardians used to work on benches – or *banco* in Italian – giving rise to the word 'bank'. The trade signs that hang from buildings on the street are a medieval tradition that now only survives in this part of the City.

Charles Dickens's first great love, Maria Beadnell (1811–1886), used to live at number 2 while her father managed the bank next door. The 18-year-old Dickens met Maria in 1830 and pursued her for four years; however, he was then still a poor young reporter with few prospects. After a long courtship, Maria ended the relationship and Dickens would later record how as a young, heart-broken man, he would come to Lombard Street during the night and stand outside staring at her window.

Years later Maria contacted Dickens – by now a world-famous and married author – and he agreed to meet her. Perhaps both were hoping to rekindle the flames of their romance, but Dickens was saddened to find Maria was no longer the young woman he had loved and he recorded with some relish how her beauty and wit had faded and his feelings for her had died

Outside the supermarket (10-15 Lombard Street) a plaque marks the location of Lloyds coffee house between 1691-1785. It was here that insurers would do business that eventually led to the foundation of Lloyds insurance.

At the end of Lombard Street you pass by Nicholas Hawksmoor's elegant **39** **St Mary Woolnoth**, his only City church. Hawksmoor (1661-1736) – regarded as Wren's most talented pupil – built the church between 1716 and 1727. It is the only City church with an underground station (Bank) occupying its crypt. John Newton (1725-1807), a former slave-ship captain, was rector here and is perhaps best known for co-writing the hymn *Amazing Grace*.

The poet TS Eliot used to work for Lloyd's Bank in Lombard Street and immortalised the church in his poem *The Waste Land* (1922), describing how the morning commuters walked over London Bridge, 'And each man fixed his eyes before his feet/ Flowed up the hill and down King William Street/To where Saint Mary Woolnoth kept the hours/With a dead sound on the final stroke of nine'.

From the church cross over King William Street, with the Bank of England to your right. Head left down Mansion House Place which runs alongside **40** **Mansion House**, the official residence of the Lord Mayor of London designed by George Dance the Elder in the mid-18th century. As the Lord Mayor is the chief magistrate in the City, Mansion House is also in theory a law court and contains eleven cells, one of which briefly held suffragette campaigner Emmeline Pankhurst in the early 20th century.

Mansion House Place becomes St Stephen's Row in an area known as Walbrook, named after the now-hidden river that once bisected the City and which is thought to have its source near Holywell Lane, not far to the north of here around Shoreditch High Street. The river was largely covered over during the late medieval period, and today – now rather more prosaically known as the London Bridge Sewer – empties into the Thames from an outflow about 100 feet to the west of Cannon Street Station.

Wren's church **41** **St Stephen Walbrook** lies immediately on the left, and is often described as his finest London parish church. The original church was founded in Saxon times and the 15th-century building was destroyed in the Great Fire. Wren rebuilt the

church in the 1670s with a beautiful dome, then very innovative in English church construction, and seen as a trial run for St Paul's. At the heart of the church is Henry Moore's marble altar installed in 1987.

Look out for a telephone kept inside a glass case. This was the original telephone used in 1953 by rector Dr Chad Varah (1911-2007) to provide a crisis hotline for the suicidal. This gave rise to the Samaritans organisation founded by Varah, which now has branches worldwide.

41 *St Stephen Walbrook*

Follow the map to Cannon Street and head eastwards. Shortly on the left, opposite Cannon Street station, look out for a small stone projection on ground level behind which is the ㊷ **London Stone**. The stone's origins are obscure, however it is commonly suggested that it was used by the Romans as a central measuring point for all official distances in their province of Britannia. Others believe it may have been the stone that held King Arthur's sword Excalibur. In any event it later became seen as the symbolic heart of the City where official proclamations were made and oaths sworn.

It is referred to in the works of William Blake, Charles Dickens and Shakespeare. The latter in his play *Henry VI* describes Jack Cade, leader of a popular rebellion in 1450, observing the tradition of striking his sword against the stone as a symbol of his sovereignty. The stone used to be set into the wall of St Swithin's church that once stood here but which was destroyed in the Blitz and not rebuilt.

Carry on along Cannon Street, taking a left at Abchurch Lane to visit the atmospheric ㊸ **St Mary Abchurch** – another Wren church built after the original was destroyed in the Great Fire. It is a rival for the title of Wren's greatest London parish church, and like St Stephen Walbrook contains a fine dome. It also features a reredos carved by Grinling Gibbons. Only this, and the font in All Hallows by the Tower, can be proven to be authentic works by Gibbons.

SITE OF
KING WILLIAM STREET
UNDERGROUND STATION
FIRST CITY TERMINUS
1890—1900

Follow the map along Cannon Street into King William Street to reach Monument Street. At the start of Monument Street look out for a blue plaque on the right that marks the site of the abandoned **44 King William Street tube station**. This was the first deep tunnel underground station in London when it opened in 1890 and was the northern terminus of the City & South London Railway. However, it was never economically successful and soon closed in 1900. It remained shut, despite plans in 1910 to use its tunnels for growing mushrooms. It finally found a purpose during WWII when it was used as an air raid shelter. Much of the subterranean remains of the station were absorbed into remodelling of nearby Bank station.

45 The Monument is one of London's best-known landmarks, and was completed in 1677. Standing 61 metres high, it was designed by Christopher Wren and Robert Hooke, and commemorates the Great Fire of London that started 61 metres away in Thomas Farriner's baker shop in Pudding Lane just after midnight on 2 September 1666.

45

Over the next three days the fire destroyed over 13,200 houses and 87 out of 109 City churches, leaving over 70,000 people homeless. 436 acres were razed to the ground, about four-fifths of the City. Only 51 churches and 9,000 houses were rebuilt, and perhaps the only good statistic to come of the fire is that only around ten people are thought to have died in it.

Farriner was questioned as part of the official investigation into the fire but not charged and returned to work as a baker. The anger of Londoners was instead directed at a Catholic Frenchman named Robert Hubert who confessed to starting the fire even though the authorities found out he was not even in London at the time it broke out. Nevertheless he became a scapegoat and was executed at Tyburn. The original inscription on the base of the Monument included the anti-Catholic statement '...but Popish frenzy, which wrought such horrors, is not yet quenched'. The offensive phrase was not removed until 1831. 11 years later the cages around the top of the Monument were added to end its unenviable reputation as a popular jumping spot for suicides.

Robert Hooke (1635-1703), one of the greatest scientists of his era, had intended the Monument to be used for scientific experiments, and in particular to act as a zenith telescope. From a cellar laboratory located below the Monument he intended to make measurements of a selected fixed star and discover evidence of the Earth's annual motion about the sun by looking through the hollow column at the night sky. The top of the column had a hinged trapdoor which could be opened at night; however, it proved useless as the building turned out to be too unstable for Hooke to take accurate readings.

From the Monument walk down the hill, passing Pudding Lane on your left, to reach Lower Thames Street. On the right-hand side is 46 **old Billingsgate Market** which served as the main fish market in London for 900 years until the market relocated to the Isle of Dogs in 1982. The infamous Kray twins used to work at the market in their early years, as did writer George Orwell. Beside it is 47 **Custom House**, by David Laing and completed 1817. The site had been used for the collection of customs duties since 1275, but is now due for development.

Do not cross Lower Thames Street but instead head left up the steep and narrow 48 **Lovat Lane** until you reach Wren's church of 49 **St Mary at Hill**. First mentioned in 1177, it was rebuilt by Wren after the Great Fire; its charming interior has recently been refurbished after having been gutted by a fire in 1988. Beside the church is a narrow

50 *St Dunstan in the East garden*

alleyway that leads to St Mary at Hill Street, and from here you can see the other side of the church with its fine clock overhanging the pavement. If the alleyway is shut, you may need to continue up to Eastcheap, turn right then right again down St Mary at Hill Street.

Cross over again down St Dunstan's Lane to visit the remains of **50** **St Dunstan in the East**. Originally founded in Saxon times, the later medieval church largely survived the Great Fire, and needed only partial rebuilding in a Gothic design by Christopher Wren. However, Wren's elegant church was bombed during the Blitz and a pleasant garden was later laid out within the ruins.

Walk up St Dunstan's Hill to reach Great Tower Street with the distinctive steeple of All Hallows visible on the right. From here retrace your steps to Tower Hill and the end of the walk. ●

SHOP

Leadenhall Market (see p.152)
1a Leadenhall Market, EC3V 1LT
www.leadenhallmarket.co.uk

VISIT...

All Hallows by the Tower
Byward St, EC3R 5BJ (see p.139)
www.ahbtt.org.uk

Monument (see p.163)
Monument Street, EC4R 8AH
www.themonument.info

Tower of London
Tower Hill, EC3N 4AB
www.hrp.org.uk

EAT, DRINK...

Hoop and Grapes
47 Aldgate High St, EC4A 4BL

Jamaica Wine House
St Michael's Alley, EC3V 9DS
www.jamaicawinehouse.co.uk

George and Vulture
3 Castle Court, EC3V 9DL

Walrus & Carpenter
45 Monument St, EC3R 8BU
www.nicholsonspubs.co.uk

6 Clerkenwell Walk

Charterhouse Square, see p.173

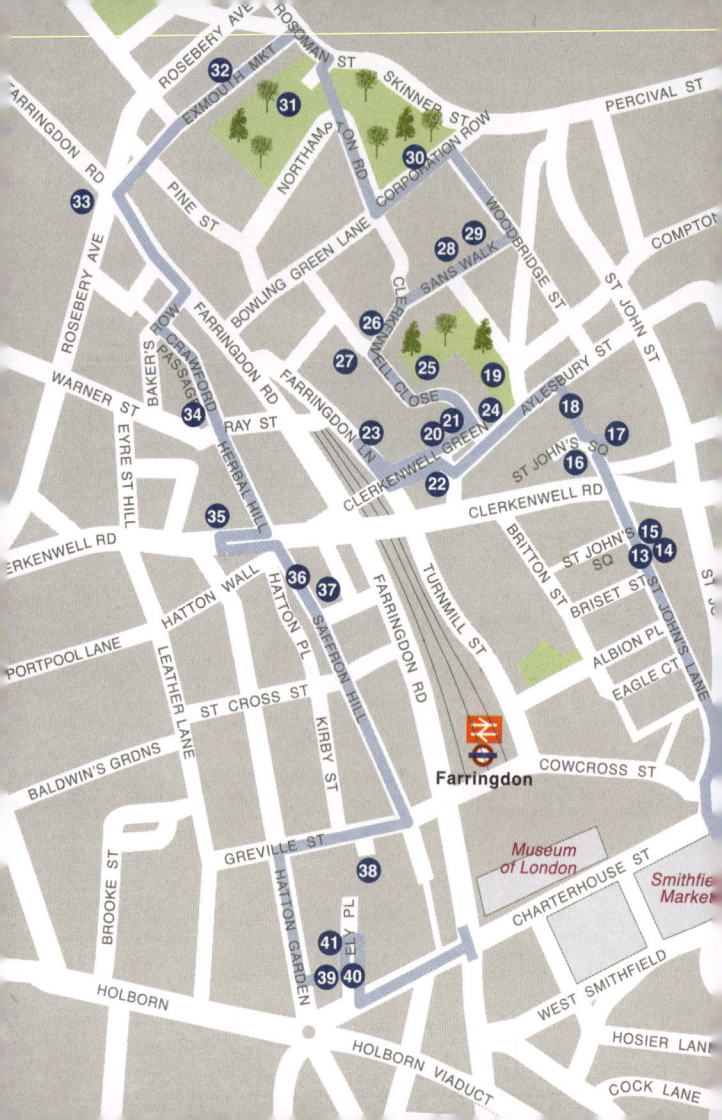

Map

ROSEBERY AVE

ROSOMAN ST

SKINNER ST

PERCIVAL ST

FARRINGDON RD

EXMOUTH MKT

32

31

NORTHAMPTON RD

CORPORATION ROW

30

PINE ST

BOWLING GREEN LANE

WOODBRIDGE ST

COMPTO

28 29

SANS WALK

ST JOHN ST

33

ROSEBERY AVE

FARRINGDON RD

CLERKENWELL

26

27

CLERKENWELL CLOSE

25

19

AYLESBURY ST

WARNER ST

BAKER'S ROW

CRAWFORD PASSAGE

34

RAY ST

23

20 21

24

18

17

EYRE ST HILL

HERBAL HILL

CLERKENWELL GREEN

22

ST JOHN'S SQ

16

CLERKENWELL RD

CLERKENWELL RD

35

PORTPOOL LANE

HATTON WALL

36

37

HATTON PL

SAFFRON HILL

FARRINGDON RD

TURNMILL ST

BRITTON ST

ST JOHN'S SQ

15

13 14

BRISET ST

ALBION PL

ST JOHN'S LANE

EAGLE CT

LEATHER LANE

ST CROSS ST

KIRBY ST

COWCROSS ST

BALDWIN'S GRDNS

🚇 Farringdon

Museum of London

CHARTERHOUSE ST

Smithfie Marker

BROOKE ST

GREVILLE ST

HATTON GARDEN

ELY PL

38

41

39 40

WEST SMITHFIELD

HOLBORN

HOLBORN VIADUCT

HOSIER LANE

COCK LANE

1. Carthusian Street
2. Florin Court
3. Charterhouse
4. Fox and Anchor
5. Smithfield Meat Market
6. West Smithfield
7. William Wallace
8. St Bartholomew-the-Great
9. 41-42 Cloth Fair
10. Number 41
11. St Bartholomew's Hospital
12. St Bartholomew-the-Less
13. St John's Gate
14. St John's Ambulance Association
15. Order of St John Museum
16. St John's Square
17. Priory Church of St John
18. Jerusalem Passage
19. Clerkenwell Green
20. Marx Memorial Library
21. Scotti's Snack Bar
22. Middlesex Sessions House
23. 'clerk's well'
24. Crown Tavern
25. St James
26. The Horseshoe
27. Peabody Trust
28. Hugh Myddleton School
29. Clerkenwell House of Detention
30. Corporation Row
31. Spa Fields
32. Exmouth Market
33. Mount Pleasant Mail Centre
34. The Coach Pub
35. St Peter's Italian Church
36. Saffron Hill
37. Ziggurat Building
38. Bleeding Heart Yard
39. Ye Olde Mitre Tavern
40. Ely Place
41. St Etheldra's

OLD ST

CLERKENWELL RD

OLD ST

CHISWELL ST

GOSWELL RD

CHARTERHOUSE ST

Charterhouse Gardens

Barbican

BEECH ST

SILK ST

Barbican Centre

LONG LANE

CLOTH FAIR

LITTLE BRITAIN

Clerkenwell Walk

LONDON WALL

SUTTON'S HOSPITAL IN CHARTERHOUSE

STOP

PRIVATE

3 *Charterhouse*

Clerkenwell Walk

Start: Barbican underground station
Finish: Farringdon station
Distance: 2.5 miles

From Barbican underground station follow the map down ❶ **Carthusian Street**, passing the cosy Sutton Arms pub that dates from 1891. Press on to reach Charterhouse Square, flanked on the right by the elegant art deco apartments of ❷ **Florin Court** (dating from 1936 and Poirot's home in the ITV series of the same name). Cross over to the other side of the square to reach the largely medieval gatehouse of ❸ **Charterhouse**, a former Carthusian monastery that was founded here in 1371 by Walter de Manny on the site of a Black Death plague pit. The Carthusian Order originated with Saint Bruno of Cologne and its name (and the English equivalent Charterhouse) was derived from the Chartreuse Mountains where the saint built a hermitage in the 11th century.

The Clerkenwell monastery was the largest of nine Carthusian houses in England, but was closed in 1538 during Henry VIII's Dissolution of the Monasteries. Prior John Houghton was hanged, drawn and quartered at Tyburn as punishment for his resistance to Henry VIII, and one of his severed arms was pinned to the front of the gatehouse. Ten other monks died in captivity or by execution, and are among those known as the Carthusian Martyrs. Sir Thomas More, himself a prisoner of Henry VIII, is said to have seen the brave monks being led out to execution from his cell in the Tower of London, and remarked to his daughter:

'Look, do you see Meg, that these Blessed Fathers are now going to their deaths as cheerfully as bridegrooms to their marriage'.

Following the Dissolution, Charterhouse was home to the nobility, including the Duke of Norfolk in 1571 before his execution for involvement in the Ridolfi Plot against Elizabeth I. Elizabeth stayed here before her coronation, while her successor James I held a court at Charterhouse in 1603. Recent Crossrail building works in the Square revealed the site of a 14th century plague pit.

Charterhouse exists today because it was bought in 1611 by Thomas Sutton, the wealthiest commoner of his time. Sutton died the same year and endowed a charity on the site, named the King James's Hospital in Charterhouse. It contained almshouses for 80 poor men who later became known as the 'Brothers', and also a school for 40 foundation scholars. The latter developed into the well-known public school Charterhouse which stayed here until 1872 when it moved out to Godalming in Surrey. Former pupils of the Clerkenwell-based school include the preacher John Wesley, the Earl of Liverpool who was Prime Minister in the early 19th century, writer William Makepeace Thackeray (who called the school 'Slaughterhouse' in his fiction), and Robert Baden-Powell.

While the school has gone, Charterhouse continues as a charitable home to pensioners under the title of Sutton's Hospital. Despite considerable damage done during the Blitz, much of the medieval monastic building still remains within the chapel, the Norfolk Cloister and around Washhouse Court. The main archway at the gatehouse dates from 1405 and the magnificent Great Hall dates from the mid-1540s when Lord North made his home here.

The chapel also contains the tombs of Thomas Sutton, dating from 1614, and Sir Walter de Manny.

Charterhouse is a large complex of buildings — over twice the area of Charterhouse Square itself. It is now home to a museum that tells the 650 year history of this remarkable building (see p.195).

Follow the map around the edge of the square until you reach the gates onto Charterhouse Street and look out for the **4** **Fox and Anchor** on the right. Decorated with Doulton tiles, it dates from the 1890s and is a good example of the Art Nouveau style used in many London public houses.

Continue ahead and you see the site of **5** **Smithfield Meat Market** on the left. Livestock and butchered meat have been traded here for over 800 years, although the livestock market was shut down in the 1850s. In the late 19th century the current market buildings were constructed to house the butchers and wholesalers working in the early hours supplying fresh meat to London's growing population. In 2023 it was announced the market would leave Smithfield and move to Dagenham, changing the character of this area and ending a tradition going back over 800 years.

Walk through the market to face **6** **West Smithfield**, 'Smithfield' being a corruption of the medieval 'smooth field'. Today the open area is very civilised, surrounded by shops, restaurants and bars. However, in the past it was one of the most vibrant and often cruel places in London,

where medieval jousting tournaments were held and public executions carried out.

In Dickens's *Oliver Twist* (1838), Oliver walked across West Smithfield with his tormentor Bill Sikes while the market was taking place one morning and found 'the ground was covered nearly ankle deep with filth and mire; a thick steam perpetually rising from the reeking bodies of the cattle'.

Follow in Oliver's footsteps through the Victorian market building to see on the far side two plaques on the wall of St Bartholomew's Hospital. One recalls how ❼ **William Wallace**, Scotland's 'Braveheart', was hanged, drawn and quartered here in 1305, while the other remembers the many **Protestant martyrs** who were burnt or boiled alive at the site in the 1550s, during the reign of Queen Mary. It is said Mary watched the burnings whilst dining on chicken and red wine inside the half-timbered gatehouse of St Bartholomew's church nearby.

Next to Wallace's plaque, and behind the 13th-century gatehouse with its later half-timbered additions, is the church of ❽ **St Bartholomew-the-Great,** the finest Norman period church in London. It was originally part of a far larger church contained within a Priory dedicated to St Bartholomew founded on this site in 1123

by Rahere, once a jester to Henry I. Rahere had vowed to open a monastery here after his apparently miraculous recovery from an illness contracted during a pilgrimage to Rome. After the Dissolution of the 1530s a truncated parish church was allowed to continue. The atmospheric Norman choir, near to the tomb of Rahere, may be familiar to visitors as it has been used for scenes in many films including *Four Weddings and a Funeral, Shakespeare in Love* and *Robin Hood Prince of Thieves.*

8　*St Bartholomew-the-Great*

Exit through the side entrance of the church onto ⑨ **Cloth Fair** looking out for a plaque in Cloth Court that commemorates former resident and Poet Laureate Sir John Betjeman (1906-1984). He lived here between 1955 and 1977, finally moving out because of his frustration with the growing traffic congestion.

Just ahead at ⑩ **number 41-42 Cloth Fair**, is a rare survivor of the Great Fire. It has even been the focus of a fascinating book – *The Oldest House in London* by Fiona Rule.

Retrace your steps to visit ⑪ **St Bartholomew's Hospital** – commonly known as 'Barts' – which is the oldest institution of its kind in London and was originally part of the priory. After the latter was dissolved the hospital was re-founded on a secular basis in 1546 with Henry VIII's approval. Above the entrance is the only statue of the Tudor tyrant in London.

The hospital is a parish in its own right with the ⑫ **St Bartholomew-the-Less**, located just inside the main entrance. It also contains an interesting museum (see p.195 for details) covering the history of the priory and the hospital. A visit to the museum also gives access to the Grand Staircase which is flanked with paintings by William Hogarth (1697–1764). Hogarth, born in nearby Bartholomew Close and baptised in St Bartholomew-the-Great, offered his services to the hospital when he heard they might commission a foreign painter instead.

Sherlock Holmes fans may be interested to know that the hospital is where the great detective first meets Dr Watson in Arthur Conan Doyle's book *A Study in Scarlet (1887)*.

Walk back through the market buildings and then turn right into St John Street, heading left down St John's Lane where at the end you pass under **🅱 St John's Gate.**

Dating from 1504, this is the main surviving part of the medieval Priory of the Knights of St John of Jerusalem, better known as the Knights Hospitaller, an order founded in Jerusalem in 1099. The priory was founded in 1140, and its Great Hall was where in 1185 Henry II and his barons met to discuss a Crusade to the Holy Land. The church was consecrated by Heraclius, Patriarch of Jerusalem, who also consecrated the church used by the Knights Templar in London in the same year (see the *Inns of Court walk* Volume One for more information on Temple Church).

In 1187 the Muslim leader Saladin attacked the Crusaders and Heraclius was due to march at the head of the Crusader army carrying the 'True Cross' of Jesus, the most sacred relic in Christendom. However Heraclius was too ill to take

13 *St John's Gate*

part and thus avoided the massacre of the Crusaders at the Battle of Hattin where the relic was lost. Heraclius later took part in the futile attempts to stop Jerusalem falling to Saladin, and died soon after as the Crusader Empire fell apart.

The Clerkenwell Priory recovered from being burnt by Wat Tyler's followers during the Peasants' Revolt in 1381, although it suffered the ignominy of its Prior being beheaded on Clerkenwell Green nearby. However, it could not escape Henry VIII who shut the priory in 1540 during the Dissolution.

Henry VIII used the former church to house his hunting tents. Its six acres were also home to the Master of the Revels, the official who organised (and censured) plays and feasts for the Tudor monarchs. Thirty of Shakespeare's plays, often performed at Court, were licensed here and it is thought many rehearsals would have taken place within the old priory buildings and under the watchful eye of the Master and his officials.

Most of the priory was later demolished to provide building materials for new housing. However, the priory church, used as a private chapel after the Dissolution, became Clerkenwell's second parish church – St John's – in 1723 (see below). The gatehouse also survived and served as the office for the ground-breaking *Gentleman's Magazine* founded in 1731, which included Dr Johnson amongst its contributors. In the mid-19th century the gatehouse was turned into a popular public house known as the Old Jerusalem Tavern.

The closure of the priory mark the end of the Hospitallers as an institution. Although they were forced out of the Holy Land, they set up new headquarters in Cyprus, then Rhodes, before moving to Malta in around 1530. Here the Knights paid a single falcon as an annual tribute to the King of Sicily, an act that inspired the title of Dashiel Hammett's novel *The Maltese Falcon*, which was made into a famous film in 1941 directed by John Huston and starring Humphrey Bogart as detective Sam Spade.

The Hospitallers were expelled from Malta by Napoleon in 1798 and splintered into a number of different organisations. The most authentic is the Sovereign Military Hospitaller Order of Saint John of Jerusalem, of Rhodes and of Malta. This Roman Catholic organisation – today based in Rome – can trace its roots all the way back to the original Hospitallers, and has membership of many international bodies as well as observer status at the United Nations.

Beside St John's Gate is the home of the British version of the Hospitallers, with its origins in a non-Catholic revivalist movement from the 1830s. In 1874 the British Order of St John bought the freehold of St John's Gate and three years later founded the ⑭ **St John's Ambulance Association**, famous today for its provision of medical assistance to the public. The British Order of St John also went back to its 11th-century heritage by founding the St John Ophthalmic Hospital in Jerusalem in 1882.

The ⑮ **museum** just beside the gatehouse is worth visiting for information on the history of the Hospitallers and St John's Ambulance and is open Wednesday to Saturday 9.30am to 5pm, (www.museumstjohn.org.uk).

Continue north across Clerkenwell Road and into ⑯ **St John's Square**. On the right is the ⑰ **Priory Church of St John,** where the the 16th-century Priory church and 12th-century crypt can be admired. The spectacular church is not open to the public except by guided tour which can be organised through the museum (call 020 7324 4005 or book via the museum website).

If you look down on the ground in St John's Square you can see studs that mark the shape of the church's long-demolished nave, another victim of Wat Tyler's rebels. Head up the narrow ⑱ **Jerusalem Passage** – its name evocative of the Hospitaller legacy – and turn left to reach ⑲ **Clerkenwell Green.**

This is the heart of Clerkenwell, and whilst it is picturesque any hint of greenery disappeared 300 years ago. In the late 17th-century Clerkenwell became one of London's first suburbs, attracting wealthy inhabitants leaving the City. It became a fashionable place, gaining a reputation for its spas, tea gardens and theatres.

Many French Huguenots fleeing the anti-Protestant persecutions in France during the late 17th century also settled here and set up artisan workshops. The tradition of craft workshops and small-scale enterprises continues to this day in Clerkenwell.

As London expanded westwards many of the wealthier classes moved on to places such as Mayfair, and Clerkenwell became home to breweries, distilleries and printers. As London's population grew (ballooning from 1 million in 1801 to 5.5 million in 1891), Clerkenwell became increasingly less prosperous and known for its over-crowded slums and politically radical inhabitants.

Clerkenwell Green was at the centre of this radicalism, and many marches started from here, particularly those organised by the Chartists in the mid-19th century. The world's first May Day march began from the Green in 1890, a date now celebrated around the world as International Workers' Day.

The most famous radical associated with Clerkenwell Green is Vladimir Lenin (1870-1924), leader of the Russian Revolution of 1917. In 1902 he was living in London and editing the Russian-

language radical publication *Iskra* (or 'The Spark'). In the same year he moved production into premises at number 37a and 38 Clerkenwell Green, which was then home to the British Social Democratic Federation. Today the building is occupied by the Marx Memorial Library.

It is said that between stints editing the paper Lenin used to drink with Joseph Stalin (1878-1953) – another revolutionary who spent time in London – in the Crown Tavern (formerly the Crown and Anchor), which is still open on the green.

The **20** **Marx Memorial Library** is housed in an 18th-century building that was originally used by a Welsh charity school. The library opened in 1933 and holds around 150,000 volumes related to Marxism and socialism. It can be visited by appointment, and the staff are happy to let you visit the tiny office, no larger than a garden shed, where Lenin used to edit *Iskra*. A copy of *Iskra* is laid out as if waiting for the great revolutionary to return and read the final proof. In 1920 the son of Harry Quelch – the socialist activist and journalist who helped Lenin publish *Iskra* here – travelled to Russia and met the new Soviet leader. The first thing Lenin enquired of the young man was 'how is everyone at Clerkenwell Green?'.

If you would like at break at this point then just beside the library is **21** **Scotti's Snack Bar**, a fine example of the type of old-fashioned Italian café that was common in London during the 1950s but which is increasingly rare today.

Otherwise walk over to the south-west side of the road to view the grand 18th-century building that once served as the ㉒ **Middlesex Sessions House** between 1780 and 1920 and was said to have been the busiest court in England. The basement dungeon was where prisoners would await trial, many to be taken to Newgate prison nearby or transported to the colonies. The former court house was later used as a Masonic lodge and conference centre but has more recently been converted into luxury apartments complete with a rooftop pool.

The Green also has a fictitious criminal connection, as it was here that the Artful Dodger robbed Mr Brownlow in Dickens's *Oliver Twist*, the thief running away to let the hapless young Oliver be arrested in his place (see more below).

To see the reason behind Clerkenwell's name follow the map for a small detour onto Farringdon Lane to the west. In medieval times London's parish clerks performed their annual mystery plays with a biblical theme beside a well. This ㉓ **'clerk's well'** was rediscovered

in the early 20th century and can be seen behind glass at number 14 Well Court.

Head north from the green by the **24 Crown Tavern** – a good place for a stop now as in Lenin's day – into Clerkenwell Close.

On the right is the beautiful church of **25 St James.** The current building largely dates from around 1780 and stands on the site of an earlier church that was part of St Mary's Nunnery, another of the great religious houses that were once so integral to Clerkenwell's early history. St Mary's was founded in 1140 on 14 acres of land and closed during the Dissolution in 1539. Most of the remaining buildings were demolished by the 1780s. Clerkenwell Green itself was originally part of the fields that lay between the Nunnery and the Hospitallers' Priory visited earlier.

Just inside the church can be seen a 19th-century 'modesty board' running along the staircase to prevent men looking up ladies' skirts. Beside it are the wooden parish benefactor boards listing names going back to the 16th-century.

Continue along Clerkenwell Close, which follows the outline of the old Nunnery buildings, and look out for **26 The Horseshoe** – an excellent example of an early 19th-century public house. To the left of the pub is a housing estate founded by the **27 Peabody Trust**,

which was established by the American philanthropist George Peabody in 1862 'to ameliorate the condition of the poor and needy of this great metropolis and to promote their comfort and happiness'. Block G was hit by a German bomb in December 1940 killing 12 people.

Head right leading to Sans Walk. On the left is the late 19th-century **28 Hugh Myddleton School** building. This has now been converted into flats and other premises, and stands on the site of the former **㉙ Clerkenwell House of Detention**, opened in 1847 and one of London's busiest prisons until its demolition in 1890. The basement still retains the old prison cells. It has been used as a location for film and television dramas, including Guy Ritchie's *Sherlock Holmes*, *Spooks*, *Harlots* and *Mr Selfridge*. The House of Detention was built on the site of an even earlier prison, the early 17th-century Clerkenwell Bridewell.

Continue down Sans Walk, turning left into Woodbridge Street, before reaching ㉚ **Corporation Row**. In 1867 part of the prison wall and several houses in Corporation Row were blown up when the Fenians, the Irish Nationalist forerunners to the IRA, made an audacious attempt to free some of their colleagues. A memorial to the 12 people killed and 50 injured can be found in St James's church. Michael Barrett, the Fenian ringleader, was the last person to be publicly executed outside Newgate Prison in 1868.

On Corporation Row you can still see the back wall of the old Myddleton School with its original 19th-century entrance signs for 'girls and infants' and also, intriguingly, 'special girls'.

Continue down the Row and follow the map along Northampton Road passing ㉛ **Spa Fields** on the left – a nondescript park that was once a location for radical political gatherings in the 19th century. The most famous of these were a number of meetings organised in late 1816 by the revolutionary Spenceans, named after the radical democrat Thomas Spence (1750-

1814). Up to 20,000 people attended the meetings but they were disrupted by the authorities, who feared an attempt would be made to overthrow the government. A number of radicals were arrested and some later executed, with the meetings becoming known as the Spa Fields Riots.

Follow the map into the park and through onto Rosoman Street and continue to **32 Exmouth Market**, once home to a popular resort named London Spa founded here in around 1730. As you walk along the street, look for the Exmouth Arms Pub and the Italianate-style Church of Our Most Holy Redeemer which dates from 1887 and has a superb interior. A market has been here since the 1890s but this has in recent years dwindled to just a few street food stalls. The area used to be fairly run-down but now boasts upmarket restaurants, including the world renowned Moro.

At the end of Exmouth Market you reach Farringdon Road. To the right is the Royal Mail's **33 Mount Pleasant Mail Centre**, which stands on the site of Coldbath Fields Prison. The prison was built in 1794 and demolished in 1889. It ran a harsh regime, including the use of a treadmill and a strict policy of enforced silence for prisoners. John Williams – the man charged with the infamous Ratcliffe Murders of 1811 – committed suicide in the prison before his trial. He was later buried at a crossroads by the Ratcliffe Highway with a stake through his heart. The Post Office Railway – an underground driver-less mail train that ran to and from Paddington and Whitechapel between 1927 and 2003 – had one of its eight stations at Mount Pleasant. To find out more, visit the Postal Museum just a few minutes from here (see p.195).

Head downhill along Farringdon Road following the path of the River Fleet, which flows underneath. The Fleet begins in Hampstead and empties into the Thames by Blackfriars Bridge. Part of the river was converted into the New Canal in 1680 and just to the south off Farringdon Street is Old Seacoal Lane, whose name recalls the coal barges that once berthed there. The canal did not prosper and was filled in during the 1730s. The remaining parts of the open Fleet were also covered over in the following decades, the process being completed by the construction of Farringdon Road in the 1860s.

On the right-hand side of Farringdon Road, take a right into Bakers Row then left down Crawford Passage. Near the junction with Ray Street is the ㉞ **The Coach** pub. If you bend down at the grating in the road immediately outside the pub you can hear the Fleet burbling along underneath.

At the junction of Ray Street and Herbal Hill look for the old parish boundary marker for St Andrew, Holborn dating from 1804. Continue up Herbal Hill onto Clerkenwell Road. Just to the right at number 136 is ㉟ **St Peter's Italian Church,** or *Chiesa Italiana di San Pietro*, situated in the heart of what was once known as 'Little Italy'. During the early 19th century many Italians arrived in London looking for a better life. By 1850 around 2,000 lived in this area, and St Peter's was founded in 1863 to serve this local Italian Catholic community. In recent years the Italian presence in the area has largely disappeared, however St Peter's remains a focal point for the Italian community in London and the procession of St. Mary of Carmel has been held here each July since 1883. If you pass by while a wedding is taking place you will see a flamboyant piece of Italian theatre being played out in what is otherwise a rather drab part of central London.

Boundary marker

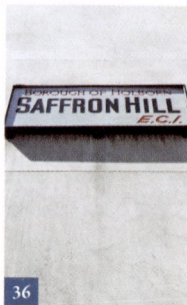

In the late 1920s the Sicilian-dominated Sabini gang emerged from Little Italy. In the next few years it became known as a 'razor gang' that ruthlessly controlled bookmakers at many major racecourses. The power of the Sabinis was effectively ended after they lost a vicious fight against the rival gang the Elephant Boys at Lewes racetrack in 1936.

Follow the map into ㊱ **Saffron Hill,** whose name derives from the saffron fields that flourished here in medieval times when the spice was in great demand, particularly with plague victims who believed its medicinal qualities could alleviate their suffering.

By the 19th century Saffron Hill had degenerated into one of the worst slums in London. Thomas Beames in his book *The Rookeries of London* (1852) regarded it as a 'notorious plague spot' and the second-worst rookery in London after the parish of St Giles. Field Lane, which formed the lower part of Saffron Hill before being demolished during the construction of Farringdon Road in the 1860s, was the inspiration for Dickens when he described Fagin's Den in *Oliver Twist*. In the book Oliver's first impression of the area is that it is 'very narrow and muddy, and the air was impregnated with filthy odours... disclosed little knots of houses where drunken men

and women were positively wallowing in filth'. Dickens knew Saffron Hill and Field Lane well because he visited and wrote articles about the workhouse and ragged school once found here, so his fiction was based on the brutal reality of Clerkenwell's slums.

Field Lane was also the site of an 18th century gay brothel (Mother Clap's Molly House) whose proprietor Margaret Madam Clap was charged in 1725 with having encouraged 'persons to commit sodomy'. Clap was the victim of a wave of persecutions encouraged by the Society for the Reformation of Manners, who spent much of their time trying to expose homosexual meeting spots. The brothel also inspired Mark Ravenhill's play *Mother Clap's Molly House* (2001).

Continue along Saffron Hill looking out for the distinctive stepped ③⑦ **Ziggurat Building** on the left. This was originally an industrial building, converted into flats in 1997, and today individual apartments can sell for several million pounds.

At the end turn right into Greville Street. On the left is ③⑧ **Bleeding Heart Yard**, home to the Plornish family in Dickens's *Little Dorrit*. The unusual name of the yard is derived from an old London legend concerning Lady Elizabeth Hatton, a prominent figure in early 17th-century London society. During a Winter Ball in 1626 she is said to have danced with her spurned lover the Spanish Ambassador (or alternatively she danced with the Devil) and was found dead in the yard the next morning, her heart still pumping blood onto the cobblestones. In reality Lady Elizabeth was not murdered, and died of natural causes in 1646.

Continue along Greville Street until you reach Hatton Garden, named after Sir Christopher Hatton (1540-1591) who served as Lord Chancellor to Elizabeth I. Said to have been her lover, he built a large house and garden here in 1576 on land that the Queen forced the Bishops of Ely to lease to him at a cheap price. The house and garden have long since disappeared and Hatton Garden is now best known for its jewellery shops and diamond trade. In 2015, 88-90 Hatton Garden was the victim of a £14 million burglary which became famous when most of the gang were found to be in their 60's and 70's. 54 Hatton Garden once housed Hatton Garden Police Court. The fictional magistrate Mr Fang, who deals with Oliver Twist after his arrest near Clerkenwell Green, was based upon an irritable magistrate called Mr Laing who worked at the court. Dickens visited the court to see Laing in action while writing *Oliver Twist*.

Walk down Hatton Garden and on the left, between numbers 8 and 9, is ❸❾ **Ye Olde Mitre Tavern,** almost certainly London's most hidden public house. Its origins date from around 1546 when it was built for the use of servants who worked in Ely House – home to the Bishops of Ely when they were in London. The current building dates from the late 18th century. A stone bishop's mitre from the old gatehouse is built into a wall, and the trunk of a cherry tree in the front bar marked the boundary of the Bishops' property and the land leased to Sir Christopher Hatton.

Ye Olde Mitre Tavern

Continue past the tavern down a tiny alleyway to emerge into **40 Ely Place** where Ely House once stood. The Bishops of Ely who lived here controlled large swathes of sheep-rearing countryside throughout England and the profits produced ensured Ely House was one of the grandest residencies in Medieval London.

The Bishops would stay here whilst attending Parliament and entertained in a grand scale. In 1531 Henry VIII and his wife Catherine of Aragon were the guests of honour at a grand feast that lasted for five days and saw the consumption of 100 sheep, 168 swans, 91 pigs and 51 cows.

The Bishops stayed in Ely House from the 13th century until the 18th century, after which time, with the sole exception of the Chapel (see below), the buildings were demolished. The 60 acres of buildings, vineyards and orchards around the house were technically part of the Bishops' diocese in Ely, Cambridgeshire and so outside the jurisdiction of London's authorities. This meant that the tavern just visited continued to obtain its alcohol licence from Cambridgeshire until the early 20th century and even today Ely Place remains a private road administered under a special Act of Parliament.

Walk up Ely Place to see the Catholic chapel of **41 St Etheldra's** on the left. This dates from 1290 and is the only surviving part of Ely House. Originally Catholic until the Reformation, it was the first such place of worship to revert back to Catholicism in 1873.

In Shakespeare's *Richard II*, the character of John O'Gaunt gave the following famous speech from Ely House:

'This royal throne of kings, this scepter'd isle,
This Earth of majesty, this seat of Mars,
This other Eden, demi-Paradise,
This fortress built by Nature for herself
Against infection and the hand of war,
This blessed plot, this Earth, this realm, this England'

Head east along Charterhouse Street until you reach Farringdon Road, the walk ends at Farringdon station. ●

VISIT...

Museum of the Order of St John
St John's Lane, EC1M 4DA
www.museumstjohn.org.uk

St Bartholomew's Museum
St Bart's Hospital, EC1A 7EB
www.bartsandthelondon.nhs.uk/
museums

The Charterhouse
Charterhouse Sq, EC1M 6AN
www.thecharterhouse.org

The Postal Museum
15-20 Phoenix Place, WC1X 0DA
www.postalmuseum.org

EAT, DRINK...

The Coach
26-28 Ray Street, EC1R 0EG
www.thecoachclerkenwell.co.uk

Crown Tavern
43 Clerkenwell Green, EC1R 0EG
www.thecrowntavernec1.co.uk

Fox and Anchor
115 Charterhouse St, EC1M 6AA
www.foxandanchor.com

The Horseshoe
24 Clerkenwell Close, EC1R 6AA

Scotti's Snack Bar
38 Clerkenwell Green, EC1R 0DU

Ye Olde Mitre Tavern
1 Ely Place, EC1N 6SJ
www.yeoldemitreholborn.co.uk

7

Hoxton &
Shoreditch Walk

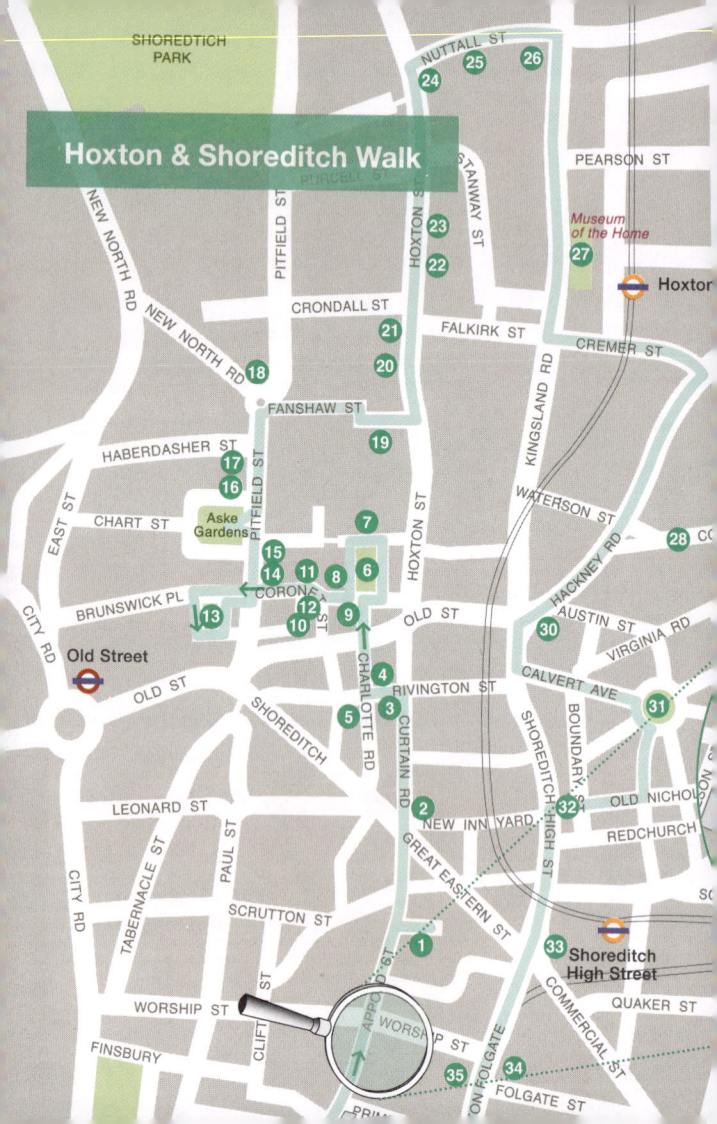

HAGGERSTON PARK

QUEENSBRIDGE

HACKNEY RD

COLUMBIA RD

Hackney City Farm

RD

29

CLIFTON

APPOLD

WORSHIP ST

34

35

NORTON FOLGATE

FOLGATE S

PRIMROSE ST

PINDAR ST

ST

SUN ST PASSAGE

Exchange Square

BISHOPSGATE

Liverpool Street

Spital Mar

BRUSHFIELD S

BRUSHFIELD S

BETHNAL GREEN RD

WEAVERS FIELDS

Bethnal Green

Broadgate Circus

Gardens

BUXTON ST

Hoxton & Shoreditch Walk

Start/Finish: Liverpool Street station
Distance 3.5 miles

From Liverpool Street station follow the map through Broadgate Circle and walk up the steps and take a right onto Appold Street. This leads into Curtain Road which was once at the heart of London's furniture-making industry from the 19th century until the mid-20th century but is today a fashionable area with many cafés and bars. You are now in Shoreditch, first recorded as 'Soerdich' in 1148. It is thought to have been named after an open sewer that once flowed through the area down to the Thames and which was possibly part of the 'lost' river Walbrook (more about later).

For many centuries the Augustinian Priory of St. John the Baptist in Haliwell (or Holywell) dominated around eight acres of land in this part of Shoreditch, its sacred water still remembered in the name of today's Holywell Lane nearby. The priory was founded in the 12th century and lasted until 1539 when it was closed during Henry VIII's Dissolution of the Monasteries. The shape of the priory lands can still be seen, however, if you draw a line on the map connecting Shoreditch High Street, Holywell Lane, Batemans Row and Curtain Road. The latter is named after the old curtain wall of the priory.

It was in the decaying gardens of the old priory that the first permanent playhouses in London since Roman times were established in the 1570s, making this the birthplace of English theatre. The first evidence of Shoreditch's unique theatrical legacy can be found by taking a right down Hewett Street. At the very end on the right-hand side is a plaque commemorating the former site of the ❶ **Curtain Theatre**. The Curtain was built in 1577 as a rival to the neighbouring playhouse known as *The Theatre*, founded the year before by actor-manager James Burbage (1531-97). It was in these two theatres that William Shakespeare established his reputation as both an actor and playwright after arriving in London in his mid-20s.

James Burbage was one of the leading Elizabethan theatrical figures, and his family lived in nearby Holywell Lane. His son Richard (1568-1619) became even more famous as the star of the theatrical troupe The Lord Chamberlain's Men (later the King's Men). Richard was the first to play many of the great parts written by his friend and fellow actor William Shakespeare, including the roles of *Hamlet, Othello, Richard III* and *King Lear*. Recently remains of The Curtain were discovered during the construction of the neighbouring tower block, greatly adding to historians' knowledge of the venue.

The Burbage family made The Theatre into the best playhouse north of the river, and later took over the rival Curtain. Shakespeare's early plays were premiered in these two theatres, including *Henry V* in which (mostly likely) the Curtain is described as 'this wooden O'. Other playwrights were also popular, and Ben Jonson's *Every Man in His Humour* was first performed at the Curtain in 1598.

In 1596 The Theatre was shut after Richard Burbage and his brother (having inherited from their father a lease that was near expiry) had a dispute with their landlord. The Lord Chamberlain's Men moved over to the Curtain, but their residency there was short-lived as the Burbages decided to abandon Shoreditch altogether. Fearing the landlord would take possession of The Theatre building itself when the ground-lease expired, the Burbages organised a party of men to dismantle The Theatre in December 1598. The timbers were moved over the river and rebuilt as the world-famous Globe theatre on Bankside. The Curtain in Shoreditch was last mentioned in 1625 and probably demolished not long thereafter.

In Shakespeare's time Shoreditch was outside the jurisdiction of the puritanical City authorities, and as a result was a popular location for gambling dens, brothels, animal-baiting houses and theatres – a wild streak that lives on today in some of the down-at-heel pubs that still survive the gentrification on the north side

of Shoreditch High Street. On his arrival in London Shakespeare lived in Shoreditch and probably worshipped at the parish church of St Leonard's (seen later in the walk). In 1596 he moved south to the parish of St Helen's in Bishopsgate where he was recorded as failing to pay his taxes.

The area around the junction of Curtain Road and Holywell Lane is thought to be the source of the Walbrook river that flows underground through the City (hence Walbrook Street to the south of this walk) and exits into the Thames just under Cannon Street station. The name 'Holywell' originated with a sacred healing spring once located near here, which was probably venerated in pagan times, and later becoming a holy site for Christians. In medieval times around 20 such springs were venerated by Londoners although few remain visible today. Later, as the city expanded, the spring was no longer considered 'special' and the historian John Snow noted in his Survey of London (1598) that "Holywell is much decayed and spoiled, with filthiness purposely laid there for the heightening of the ground for garden plots."

Continue up Curtain Road and cross over Great Eastern Street. Immediately on the right-hand side (where a branch of Foxtons

now stands) is a plaque commemorating the site of ❷ **The Theatre**. There were travelling theatre troupes performing in public spaces, taverns and inns for many years, but it is here in 1577 that the first purpose built theatre stood. It's foundations were recently uncovered during building works.

Continue along Curtain Road and take a left into Rivington Street. The ❸ **Barley Mow** on the corner and the ❹ **Bricklayers Arms** just ahead are two of the pubs most associated with the transformation of Hoxton

4 *Bricklayers Arms*

and Shoreditch in recent decades from dingy backwaters into London's bohemian heartland. The genesis of this change took place in the late 1980s and early 90s when artists began to move here, attracted by the cheap studio space that was available in old warehouses and office blocks.

However this migration would have probably gone largely unnoticed had the media not picked up on the 'Young British Artists' (YBAs) such as Damien Hirst and Tracey Emin whose radical new brand of contemporary art hit the headlines in the early 90s. Both artists now have global profiles with Hirst becoming perhaps the richest artist ever. This creative explosion earmarked Hoxton, seemingly overnight, as possibly the trendiest place in London, and for over a decade it has continued to attract media types and artists who live, work and socialise here.

On the left-hand side at number 32 Rivington Street is an ❺ **old electric sub-station** dating from 1907 that used to power street trams and was built by the old London County Council. Retrace your steps until you reach The Bricklayers Arms and take a left along Charlotte Street to reach Old Street, then cross over and walk up Rufus Street into ❻ **Hoxton Square**.

Hoxton, formerly part of Shoreditch, is the area north of Old Street. It was largely rural even up until the 18th century and was once famed for its market gardens and nurseries. The square was laid out on the then open 'Hogsden Fields' in 1683.

It was on these fields that the playwright Ben Jonson (c.1572-1637), a contemporary and rival of Shakespeare, killed the actor Gabriel Spencer during a duel in 1598 over some long-forgotten dispute. Jonson escaped execution for the murder by requesting the 'benefit of clergy', an ancient right that allowed those who could read out a Latin passage from the Bible to be treated as if they were a clergyman and thus receive a more lenient sentence. The right was seen as increasingly absurd even in Jonson's time particularly as the tested passage was normally Psalm 51, which could be memorised by non-Latin scholars. Although Jonson passed the test, he was imprisoned for a short period and as he could not prove he was a clergyman he had to suffer the indignity of being branded on his thumb in order to prevent him using the defence again. The less fortunate Spencer was buried in St Leonard's church, which is seen later on in the walk.

Very little remains of the square's original buildings, although the recently restored house at number 32 dates from the late 17th century or very early 18th century. The north side contains the Roman Catholic church of ❼ **St Monica's Priory**, built in 1865-6 by EW Pugin (1834-75) for the Augustinian Fathers and described as 'a cheap building that nevertheless has

considerable distinction' by English Heritage, who gave it a Grade II listing. Pugin's father was the more famous Augustus Pugin, the architect and designer who contributed much to the Gothic design and furnishing of Sir Charles Barry's Houses of Parliament.

8 **Number one** on the Square has a blue plaque remembering past resident Dr James Parkinson (1755-1824). His work *An Essay on the Shaking Palsy* (1817) was the first to describe the condition today known after him as 'Parkinson's Disease'. A more recent unofficial blue plaque remembers the legendary DJ Andrew Weatherall (1963-2020) who worked here when it was home to Bass Clef jazz club, and then from 1993 the Blue Note club that helped transform night life in the area.

Hoxton Square is the epicentre of the Hoxton 'scene', which was best exemplified by the **9** **White Cube gallery** that occupied number 48 until it up sticks and left in 2012. There are numerous trendy bars and eateries on the square and on fine days the small central park is full of London's most fashionable characters complete with intricate tattoos and lustrous beards. The square has been transformed since the early 1990's but still remains an island of prosperity amid the still run down Hoxon estates to the north of here.

Leave the Square at it's southwest corner and follow the map along Coronet Street to enter ⑩ **Hoxton Market**. The market was founded in 1687, but over time lost out in popularity to others nearby in Bethnal Green and Dalston. However, a Saturday street market also known as Hoxton Market takes place along Hoxton Street (see later on the walk).

On the north side of Hoxton Market is ⑪ **The National Centre for Circus Arts**, an academy for circus performers. It is based in an 1896 building that once housed The Shoreditch Borough Refuse Destructor and Generating Station. This power plant took in local waste and generated power for nearby facilities such as the public baths in Pitfield Street and street lights. The façade contains the Latin motto '*E Pulvere Lux Et Vis*', meaning from dust, light and power.

On the east side of Hoxton Market is a former ⑫ **Christian Mission**, which was founded in 1886 and retains its original signage describing how the mission moved to this site in 1915. It provided local children with free dinners and boots.

Such philanthropic missions were common in 19th-century Hoxton. The laying out of the early squares in the late 18th century suggested developers were hopeful that the area would become prosperous. Instead it became overcrowded and largely poor, swamped by the large numbers

of people arriving in London during the Industrial Revolution. The population of Hoxton and Shoreditch grew from around 10,000 in 1750 to 130,000 in 1861 and the district suffered some of the very worst crime and mortality figures in London. The philanthropist Charles Booth (1840-1916) in his 1902 work *Life and Labour of the People of London* described the area as 'working-class. Poverty is everywhere, with a considerable admixture of the very poor and vicious ... '.

Follow the map back onto Coronet Street, across Pitfield Street and into ⓭ **Charles Square**, built at the same time as Hoxton Square. It is grotty now, and very few of the original buildings remain except for number 16 which was built in around 1725 and once served as a magistrates court and registry office. More recently it was the headquarters of the London Labour Party but has now been redeveloped into flats.

Illustrator and adventurer Frederick Catherwood (1799-1854) lived on the Square in the early 19th century. In 1839 he was in the party that discovered the lost Mayan pyramids in the jungles of Central America. John Newton (1725-1807), the ex-slaver turned Anglican cleric and slavery abolitionist, also lived on the Square. He is best known as the author of the hymn *Amazing Grace*.

Head back to Pitfield Street and walk northwards. On the right is the ⓮ **Hop Pole**, an excellent example of an old-fashioned London pub building (now sadly used for other purposes) with its signage dating from around 1900.

Even after The Curtain and The Theatre closed Shoreditch and Hoxton continued to be a popular place for large-scale public entertainment, and during the 19th century could still rival the West End for the size of its theatres and music halls. A variety theatre music hall dating from 1870 once stood at nos 18-20, but was demolished in the 1980s.

Look out for the Victorian building on the right (opposite the tennis courts) which still has lettering on the exterior identifying this as the ⓯ **Passmore Edwards Free Library**. Built in 1897, this is named after John Passmore Edwards, a Victorian philanthropist and politician who funded over 70 hospitals, libraries, schools and art galleries around the country earning him the nickname the 'Cornish Carnegie'. Appropriately, given the area's connections with the birth of the English theatre, the building is today home to the Courtyard Theatre.

A few hundred yards or so to the north look out for the ⓰ **Curzon (formerly Gaumont) Cinema** at 55 Pitfield Street. The original cinema opened in 1914 and was one of the largest in London. It finally closed in 1956 and was then used as a meat storage facility and later lay derelict for decades. In 2008 Jarvis Cocker lived nearby on Haberdasher Street and was against the proposed office development as an 'ugly lump', telling the Hackney Gazette "I don't want office workers to see me parading in my pyjamas." Jarvis has since moved away but would no doubt approve of the new cinema that was opened in 2021. The original building was demolished but the new cinema replicates the stylish Art Deco façade.

⓱ **The George and Vulture pub** just ahead (on the corner with Haberdasher Street) is a characterful pub with fantastic large windows – worth a stop for lunch.

Continue north to cross over Fanshaw Street to reach the 2,000 seater church of **18** **St John the Baptist**, designed by Francis Edwards (a pupil of Sir John Soane) and consecrated in 1826. This elegant classical building represented the first time that Hoxton had its own parish church making it a distinct parish from that of Shoreditch.

To the east of the church is Fanshaw Street. Walk along, passing flats built by the council after WWII, looking out on the right for some late **19** **19th-century former industrial buildings** (numbers 5-9) that have been nicely converted into living space and commercial premises.

Enter Hoxton Street ahead, a vibrant and busy inner-city thoroughfare that is the real heart of the area for Hoxton's locals, and a far cry from the uber-cool aura of Hoxton Square. Immediately in front is New City College, which stands on the site of Hoxton House Asylum. The asylum was founded in 1695 within Hoxton House, a large early 17th-century private residence, and was just one of a number of such institutions in this area. By the early 18th century Hoxton was home to more mental patients than anywhere else in London. The college also stands on the site of an old Jewish burial ground used between 1707 and 1878 by the Hambro Synagogue in Fenchurch Street.

Head left (north) up Hoxton Street. A legacy of the area's theatrical connections can be seen on the left at no.107 where there is a plaque marking the former site of the **20** **Britannia Theatre**, first opened in 1841

St John the Baptist

as 'The Royal Britannia Saloon & Britannia Tavern'. It was later rebuilt in 1858 and could hold over 4,000 people. Charles Dickens once visited and was greatly impressed, comparing it to the Scala in Milan and noting how it was 'lighted by a firmament of sparkling chandeliers'. Sadly it was destroyed during the Blitz of WWII.

The Britannia stood near the site of an even earlier Hoxton place of entertainment, the notorious Elizabethan Pimlico Tavern and Pleasure Gardens. A 1609 poem called *Tis a Mad World at Hogsdon* (i.e Hoxton) described how 'Doctors, Protors, Clerks, Attornies, To Pimlico make sweaty journies'. If you visit Hoxton and Shoreditch on a Friday night you might think little has changed since then.

Continue north up Hoxton Street, looking out on the left-hand side for a plaque on the side of a block of flats (opposite no 96)

relating to the **21 Guy Fawkes Gunpowder Plot.** The flats stand on the site of the house of William Parker, the 4th Lord Monteagle (1575-1622), who received an anonymous letter on October 12th, 1605 warning him not to attend Parliament on November 5th as King James I and others attending 'shall receive a terrible blow, the Parliament, and yet they shall not see who hurts them'.

Lord Monteagle, a Catholic sympathiser, nevertheless informed on the plotters and on 4th November 1605 accompanied the Lord Chamberlain and his men on a search of Parliament's vaults. They discovered Fawkes hiding there and the plot was foiled; Parker was later rewarded with a pension of £700 per annum from the King. Historians including Lady Antonia Fraser have conjectured that Monteagle was the author of the letter, thus enabling him to betray the plot while avoiding any awkward questions about his prior knowledge of the conspiracy.

Continue north up Hoxton Street. Many of the buildings are 19th century, but numbers 124-26 on the right are early 18th century and are set much further back from the street (they would have had fine gardens). Next door is **22 Hoxton Hall** (number 130), founded in 1863 as a 'saloon style' music hall before later serving as a Quaker meeting house. It now serves as an arts centre and community theatre (www.hoxtonhall.co.uk), and you can ring the bell to ask to see inside the fantastic small hall whose period atmosphere often attracts filmmakers. The main entrance was past the hall (on Wilks Place) where the original signage can still be seen.

Further ahead on the right are the distinctive old-fashioned façades of the **㉓ Hayes and English Funerals shop** (number 148) and **Cooke's Eel & Pie shop** (150). The eel & pie shop with its white tiled walls and counter, and sawdust covered floor, is a good place to stop if you want to try some traditional East London fare, although the pie and mash with liquor (or parsley sauce) may be more to your taste than the eels. It is run by East End character Joe Cooke whose family have been in the business since the 1860s.

Continue north and just before Nuttall Street on the right you can see the former premises of the **㉔ St. Leonard's Offices for Relief of the Poor**, otherwise known as the workhouse, which were built in 1863. Turn into Nuttall Street to see on the right the Mary Seacole nursing home, which stands on the main site of the old workhouse, and **㉕ St Leonard's Hospital** further down, which grew out of the workhouse infirmary. The infirmary contained two wards for ill paupers and benefited greatly from a re-organisation undertaken by Dr James Parkinson (mentioned earlier) after he took

charge in 1813. He created separate male and female wards and a fever block for infectious patients. Later changes rather undermined these improvements and a damning report in 1865 made clear the 'general aspect...is one of extreme cheerlessness and desolation'.

At the end is Kingsland Road. On your right is the substantial red-brick Gothic church of ㉖ **St Columba**, which dates from the 1870s. In the late 19th century it served as an important slum mission centre and school. To your left (looking north) you can see the minarets of the Süleymaniye Mosque, one of largest of its type in London, which opened in 1998. Head right (south) down Kingsland Road on the left-hand side until you see the entrance to the ㉗ **Museum of the Home**, one of London's best small museums.

Set in pretty grounds, it is housed within 14 former almshouses built in around 1714 by the Ironmongers' Company and funded from the bequest of Sir Robert Geffrye (1613-1703). For nearly 200 years the almshouses provided shelter for around 50 pensioners, becoming a museum dedicated to interior design in 1914. The traditional museum has had a modern extension added in recent years and a change of name owing to Sir Geffrye's involvement in the slave trade (see p.221).

When finished continue south down Kingsland Road. This stretch of road, and Shoreditch High Street – which continues to the south – were once dotted with music halls during the late Victorian and Edwardian eras. The Shoreditch Empire, also known as the London Music Hall, stood at 95-99 Shoreditch High Street between 1856-1935 and Charlie Chaplin performed there before leaving to find fame and fortune in America.

There are a number of reasonably-priced Vietnamese restaurants along this

29 Columbia Road flower market

stretch of the High Street if you need to stop for a break. Otherwise continue on and turn left into Cremer Street, passing Hoxton Road overground station. You reach Hackney Road and turn right (south), passing the entrance to **28** **Columbia Road**. If you are passing by on a Sunday be sure to visit the vibrant **29** **flower market** held on this road between 8am and 2pm. The market was founded in 1869 by the philanthropist Angela Burdett-Coutts (1814-1906), a scion of the Coutts banking family and a pioneer of many projects to help the poor who lived in the slums of the Victorian East End.

Continue on to the junction of Shoreditch High Street, Hackney Road and Old Street. The original village of Shoreditch grew up around this immediate area which has formed a road junction since Roman times.

Continue along the High Street looking out on the left for **30** **St Leonard's,** London's original 'actors' church'. Many of the Elizabethan actors who rubbed shoulders with Shakespeare in the theatres and pubs of Shoreditch would also have probably stood beside him in the congregation of St Leonard's in an era when non-attendance at church could result in a fine.

An Actor's Memorial tucked away inside lists some of the notable theatrical people buried here including Will Somers, court jester to Henry VIII; James Burbage and his sons Richard and Cuthbert; the Elizabethan comedian Richard Tarlton; the actor Gabriel Spencer (who died fighting a duel with Ben Jonson); and William Sly and Richard Cowley, who were once business partners with Shakespeare. There is another intriguing memorial from 1710 to Elizabeth Benson on the south-east wall, which depicts two skeletons clutching at the tree of life. Shakespeare's great friend and colleague Richard Burbage was buried here in 1619 with the simple epitaph 'Exit Burbage'.

The medieval church was rebuilt in 1736-40 by George Dance the Elder, Surveyor to the Corporation of London, who furnished

his design with a handsome Doric portico and a vertiginous steeple. The building of the new church became controversial after local builders went on strike over poor pay, and were replaced by Irish workers. This led to anti-Irish riots which, at their height, required the local militia to disperse a 4,000 strong crowd.

St Leonard's is immortalised in the children's nursery rhyme *Oranges and Lemons* in the line 'when I grow rich/say the bells of Shoreditch'. The mortuary behind the church was the scene of the inquest into the death of Mary Jane Kelly, the last victim of Jack the Ripper in 1888. No relatives came to her funeral but the verger of the church gave her some dignity in death by paying for a full funeral with a procession that went along Hackney Road to St. Patrick's Roman Catholic cemetery at Leytonstone. Sadly, today the church is often shut, with the grounds a gathering point for local homeless people.

When you leave the church continue towards the City and take the first left down Calvert Avenue to Arnold Circus. This circular park is the centrepiece of the ③ **Boundary Estate**, which opened in 1900 and replaced a notorious slum – or rookery – known as 'Old Nichol'.

In the 19th century Old Nichol was regarded as probably the worst of its kind in London. Henry Mayhew, a prominent Victorian chronicler of London's social conditions, visited the area in 1850 and noted 'An almost total lack of drainage and sewerage was made worse by the ponds formed by the excavation of brick earth. Pigs and cows in back yards, noxious trades like boiling tripe, melting tallow, or preparing cat's meat, and slaughter houses, dustheaps, and 'lakes of putrefying night soil' added to the filth'.

Old Nichol's population of around 6,000 people was dominated by large vicious gangs of villains and thieves that controlled prostitution rings and stole live cattle from those walking past the area on their way to London's meat markets. The mortality rate was twice that even of run-down Bethnal Green nearby, and four times that of London as a whole, with one child in four likely to die before their first birthday. The area was immortalised by Arthur Morrison in his influential book *A Child of the Jago* (1896) which contains an account of the life of a child in a slum closely based on Old Nichol. In the opening page, Morrison writes of 'a narrow passage, set across with posts, [which] gave menacing entrance on one end of Old Jago Street.' This alley Morrison called 'The Posties', still stands today and is all that remains of the 'Jago' – it's real name is ❸❷ **Boundary Passage**. When the then-revolutionary Boundary Estate was opened it boasted 23 new blocks containing over 5,000 residents centred around a bandstand that lies at the heart of Arnold Circus. It has a claim to being the country's first council estate.

Having explored the area, follow the map through Boundary Passage and take a left onto Shoreditch High Street. On your left you pass (just before Commercial Street heads off to the left) the former

site of the ❸❸ **Bishopsgate Goods Yard**, now partly occupied by the recently opened Shoreditch High Street station. The Goods Yard stood on the site of what was originally Shoreditch railway station in 1840, and was renamed Bishopsgate in 1847. It was used for passengers until Liverpool Street station opened just to the south in 1874. Bishopsgate station was soon shut down and in 1881 re-opened as Bishopsgate Goods Depot. Instead of handling London's commuters, it became the main railway station for cargoes being transported to London by rail from the east-coast ports.

The yard was destroyed by fire in 1964 and stood derelict in the following decades, its crumbling arches used to house small businesses. Controversially, much of the remaining 19th-century structure has been demolished in recent years to make way for the extension of the London overground and Shoreditch High Street station. Just south of the station you can see the crumbling remains of part of the old structure.

Follow the map onto ❸❹ **Norton Folgate**, a tiny area of London that was once home to the great Elizabethan playwright Christopher Marlowe and possibly William Shakespeare. Norton Folgate was one of London's old 'Liberties' or manors, which for reasons often

now obscure became districts outside the normal parochial administrative system. As with other Liberties, for centuries Norton Folgate drew its fair share of criminals and other types seeking refuge. Norton Folgate remained an enclave until being absorbed into the Borough of Stepney in 1900. Despite a campaign by the blog *Spitalfields Life* and the historian Dan Cruickshank, much of the area has now been sacrificed to a vast office development, with just a few older buildings still to be found on Folgate Street.

35 **Broadgate Tower** on the right-hand side (number 233 Shoreditch High Street) stands on the site of a converted 19th-century power station – known as the Light Building. The historic building was demolished in 2006 and in 2009 this 161m high tower of steel and glass was opened, designed by Skidmore, Owing & Merrill and costing approximately £240m. It is just one of many new office blocks built in the area in recent years. Broadgate Tower was a location in the Bond film *Skyfall* (representing a skyscraper in Shanghai).

Continue south down Bishopsgate to find Liverpool Street station once more and the end of the walk. ●

SHOP...

Columbia Road Flower Market
Columbia Road, E2 7RG
www.columbiaroad.info
Open: Sun 8am-2pm

VISIT...

The Museum of the Home
(see p.214)
Kingsland Road, E2 8EA
www.museumofthehome.org.uk

Curzon Cinema
55 Pitfield Street, N1 6BU
www.curzon.com

EAT, DRINK...

Bricklayers Arms
147-149 Curtain Road,
EC2A 3PE

The George & Vulture
63 Pitfield Street, N1 6BU
www.georgeandvulture.com

Cooke's Eel & Pie Shop
150 Hoxton Street, N1 6SH

Sông Quê Cafe
134 Kingsland Road, E2 8DY
www.songque.co.uk

8 King's Cross, St Pancras & Camden Walk

St Pancras Church, see p.173

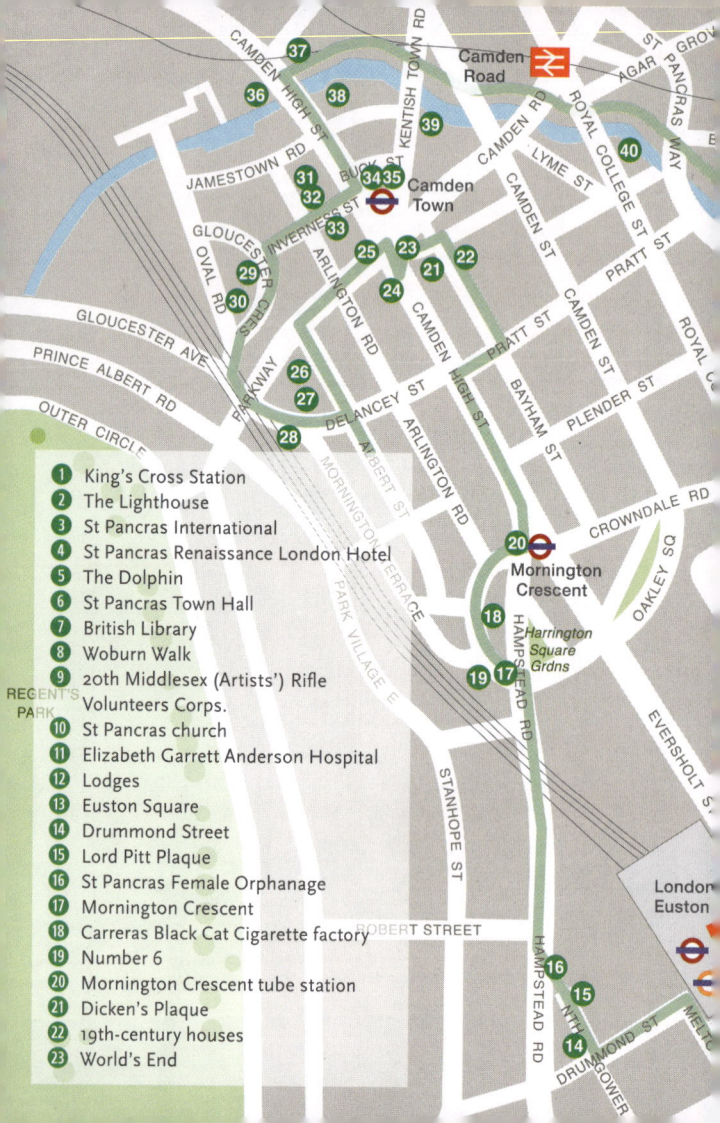

Map labels:

- Camden Road
- CAMDEN HIGH ST
- KENTISH TOWN RD
- CAMDEN RD
- ROYAL COLLEGE ST
- ST PANCRAS WAY
- AGAR GROVE
- JAMESTOWN RD
- BUCK ST
- Camden Town
- LYME ST
- CAMDEN ST
- INVERNESS ST
- GLOUCESTER CRES
- OVAL RD
- ARLINGTON RD
- PRATT ST
- PLENDER ST
- ROYAL COLLEGE ST
- GLOUCESTER AVE
- PRINCE ALBERT RD
- PARKWAY
- DELANCEY ST
- CAMDEN HIGH ST
- ARLINGTON RD
- BAYHAM ST
- CROWNDALE RD
- OAKLEY SQ
- OUTER CIRCLE
- MORNINGTON TERRACE
- PARK VILLAGE E
- ALBERT ST
- Mornington Crescent
- Harrington Square Grdns
- HAMPSTEAD RD
- EVERSHOLT ST
- REGENT'S PARK
- STANHOPE ST
- ROBERT STREET
- London Euston
- HAMPSTEAD RD
- DRUMMOND ST
- GOWER ST
- NTH
- MELT

Legend:

1. King's Cross Station
2. The Lighthouse
3. St Pancras International
4. St Pancras Renaissance London Hotel
5. The Dolphin
6. St Pancras Town Hall
7. British Library
8. Woburn Walk
9. 20th Middlesex (Artists') Rifle Volunteers Corps.
10. St Pancras church
11. Elizabeth Garrett Anderson Hospital
12. Lodges
13. Euston Square
14. Drummond Street
15. Lord Pitt Plaque
16. St Pancras Female Orphanage
17. Mornington Crescent
18. Carreras Black Cat Cigarette factory
19. Number 6
20. Mornington Crescent tube station
21. Dicken's Plaque
22. 19th-century houses
23. World's End

King's Cross, St Pancras & Camden Walk

24 Ghost sign for Boots
25 Ladies' lavatory
26 no.127 Albert Street
27 Dylan Thomas
28 Edinboro Castle
29 Gloucester Crescent
30 Number 70
31 Arlington House
32 The Good Mixer

33 Inverness Street
34 Camden Market
35 Deep-level air raid shelter
36 Camden Lock
37 Hawley Wharf
38 TV-AM
39 Sainsbury's supermarket
40 Two C19th Cottages
41 St Pancras Gardens St
42 Pancras Hospital
43 St Pancras Old Church
44 Hardy's Tree

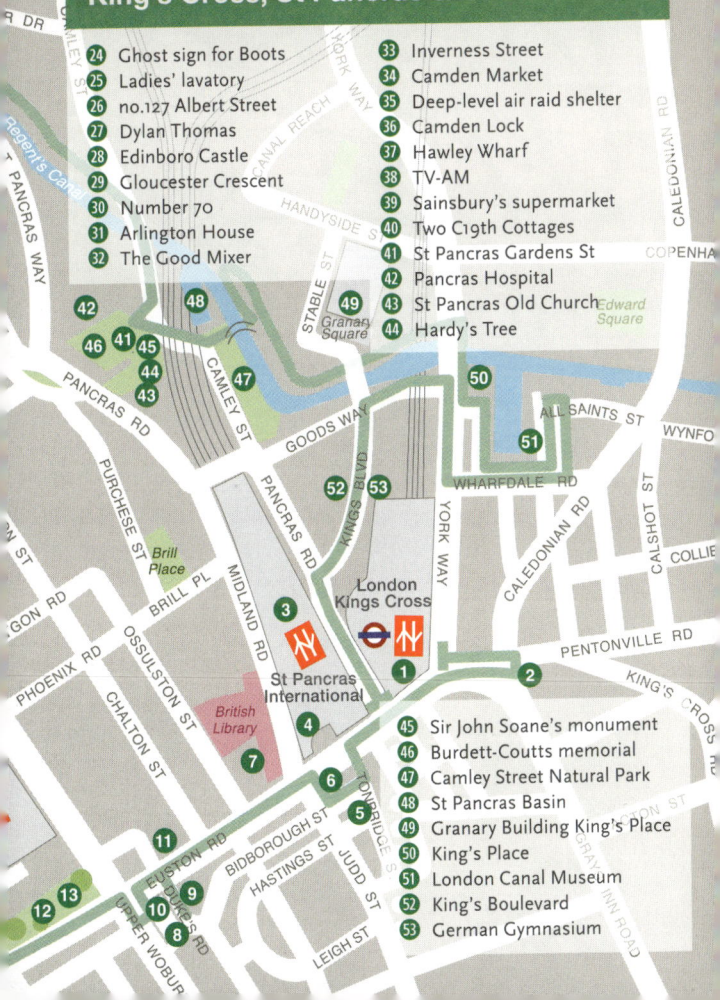

45 Sir John Soane's monument
46 Burdett-Coutts memorial
47 Camley Street Natural Park
48 St Pancras Basin
49 Granary Building King's Place
50 King's Place
51 London Canal Museum
52 King's Boulevard
53 German Gymnasium

London Kings Cross

St Pancras International

British Library

1 King's Cross station

King's Cross, St Pancras and Camden Walk

Start/Finish: King's Cross station
Distance: 5 miles

The walk begins at ❶ **King's Cross Station**, the heart of an area regarded as rather unsavoury for many decades, but which has recently undergone a renaissance. King's Cross is a relatively new name, and the village that stood here before the advent of the railway age was known as Battle Bridge. The latter name was most probably a corruption of Broad Ford Bridge, a long-demolished crossing point over the Fleet River. A monument to King George IV was erected near the crossroads here in 1830. While that monarch's general unpopularity ensured the structure only lasted until 1845, it did gave rise to the area's name. During its short stay the base of the King's memorial housed both a pub and police station.

During pre-history the area would have been heavily wooded and in 1690 the remains of a woolly mammoth was dug up near the site of the station. The Romans certainly had a military base named Brill near here, remembered in Brill Place to the west of St Pancras station. The most famous platform at King's Cross however is entirely fictional – platform 9 3/4 being the departure point for the Hogwarts' School train in JK Rowling's *Harry Potter* books. Despite its fictional status, the platform has been honoured with an official looking sign and has become a popular attraction in its own right.

The station was designed by Lewis Cubitt (1799-1883) and built between 1851-1852 on the site of the London Smallpox Hospital. It originally served as the London hub of the Great Northern Railway, and terminus of the East Coast Main Line. Largely forgotten today, the Cubitt brothers were probably responsible for developing more parts of London than any other family. Aside from Lewis,

Thomas Cubitt (1788-1855) built a number of squares in Bloomsbury and laid out much of Pimlico and Belgravia, whilst William Cubitt (1791-1863) built Cubitt Town on the Isle of Dogs.

The station has recently undergone a £550 million redevelopment. The dull 60s entrance has been taken down to reveal the Grade I listed Victorian façade, and a striking lattice-work roof covering an area equivalent to six Olympic swimming pools has been built over the western concourse. But the biggest transformation lies to the rear of the station, with nearly 70 acres of new buildings and roads laid out over what was once one of the seediest and most unwelcoming parts of the capital. More of this redevelopment will be seen nearer the end of the walk.

As you exit the station onto Euston Road look to the left where there is a triangular-shaped building dating from 1875 at the junction of Pentonville and Gray's Inn Roads. Nicknamed the ❷ 'Lighthouse', the purpose of the strange tower at the top has never been fully explained, although one theory is that it might have been an advertising gimmick for an oyster house, in the days when oysters were a cheap staple food for the poor. One London myth suggests a secret staircase leads down from the Lighthouse to an abandoned underground platform, apparently visited by squatters who once inhabited the building.

Continue along the Euston Road, originally known as the New Road when it was built in 1756 to allow cattle to reach Smithfield Market without having to travel through the congested centre of London. 'Euston' is named after a great local family of this era, the Fitzroys, whose titles include the Dukedom of Grafton and Earldom of Euston. The latter is derived from the family's country seat in Euston, Suffolk, where Euston Hall is today home to Henry FitzRoy, 12th Duke of Grafton. The peerage was created by Charles II for an illegitimate son, so the current Duke has links to the Royal family.

On the south side of Euston Road are a number of streets lined by dingy hotels, typical of the 'old' King's Cross. By total contrast on the north side is London's greatest railway station, the recently extended and modernised ❸ **St Pancras International**. The station's majestic 19th-century train shed spans 240 feet and is over 100 feet high and is a joy to experience on a Sunday morning with hardly anyone around, particularly when compared to the claustrophobic hell of Euston station a few hundred yards away to the west.

Designed by William Barlow, St Pancras station was built during the 1860s by the Midland Railway company on top of Agar Town – a slum area of 4,000 houses named after the early 19th-century landowner William Agar whose widow allowed developers to build on what were still open fields in the 1830s. The disappearance of

4

4

4

Agar Town to the railway was no great loss as the area was so poor it was described by Charles Dickens as a 'complete bog of mud filth.... The stench of a rainy morning is enough to knock down a bullock'.

The imposing red-brick Gothic-inspired façade of the ❹ **St Pancras Renaissance London Hotel** defines the station's street frontage on Euston Road. Originally the Midland Grand Hotel, it was designed by Sir George Gilbert Scott (1811-78), architect of dozens of churches and cathedrals around the world, although he is perhaps best known for the hotel and the Albert Memorial in Hyde Park. Constructed between 1868 and 1876 and boasting 250 rooms, the hotel was one of the greatest establishments of its day; however, in the early 20th century space constraints meant it was unable to compete with its newer rivals. In 1935 the hotel was converted for use as railway offices, but lay dormant from the late 1980s.

In recent years it has been used as a film location for blockbusters such as *Batman Begins*, *102 Dalmations* and the *Harry Potter* movies. Although it is perhaps best remembered as a backdrop to the Ealing comedy *The Lady Killers*.

Oscar Wilde (1854-1900), stayed briefly at the hotel in May 1895 after losing a libel action brought against Lord Queensberry – father of Wilde's lover Lord Alfred Douglas. Queensberry had publicly hounded Wilde over the relationship until the writer felt he had to take legal action. However, this back-fired as evidence of Wilde's love life was uncovered during the libel trial that would later result in his conviction for gross indecency, and subsequent imprisonment and social downfall. Queensberry was a violent, bitter man who sent his thugs to the hotel where Wilde was trying to remain anonymous. Under pressure from the gang, the hotel manager asked Wilde to leave. The playwright was forced to flee to his brother's house, his sibling later recalling that Wilde resembled a 'wounded stag'.

Both the railway station and the hotel were narrowly saved from demolition in the 1960s. The Poet Laureate Sir John Betjeman (1906-84) led the campaign to protect the site, just one of many he undertook in the 1960s and 70s as the first Secretary of the Victorian Society.

St Pancras – Victorian glass and iron train shed

Of St Pancras he wrote 'What [the Londoner] sees in his mind's eye is that cluster of towers and pinnacles seen from Pentonville Hill and outlined against a foggy sunset, and the great arc of Barlow's train shed gaping to devour incoming engines, and the sudden burst of exuberant Gothic of the hotel seen from gloomy Judd Street'.

If you walk inside the station you will see a **statue of Betjeman** gazing in wonder at WH Barlow's great Victorian glass and iron train shed, not far from a nine-metre-high bronze sculpture created by Paul Day and named *The Meeting Place*.

After many decades facing possible closure, St Pancras has got one over on its old rivals Euston and King's Cross by becoming London's international terminus, from which Eurostar trains depart for the continent.

Follow the map to walk along Bidborough Street, looking out for a classic old-style St Pancras pub, ❺ **the Dolphin**, on the left. You are skirting the back of Camden Town Hall, formerly known as the ❻ **St Pancras Town Hall**. On the left you will see a blue plaque remembering the renowned war artist Paul Nash (1889-1946) who lived in a flat on the street for many years. Follow the map to see the main entrance on Judd Street. It was during a cold spell in January 1959 that a small indoor Caribbean carnival was held here, organised by activist Claudia Jones. By the mid-1960s the carnival had moved outdoors to Notting Hill, and today the August bank holiday celebration attracts over a million people.

THE DOLPHIN

5

6

233

Contine along Euston Road, to find the ❼ **British Library** on your right. It was opened after many years of delay in 1997 and holds 25 million books. A controversial design by Colin St John Wilson, the reading room was likened by the then Prince Charles to the assembly hall of a secret police academy. Look out for Eduardo Paolozzi's bronze sculpture of Issac Newton, based on a William Blake print of 1795.

Take a small diversion down Duke's Road on the east side of St Pancras parish church. This (and adjoining ❽ **Woburn Walk**) contains a number of charming 18th and 19th-century houses. Numbers 1-9 Woburn Walk were the work of master-builder Thomas Cubitt and date from c.1822. The Irish poet W.B. Yeats lived at number 5 Woburn Place for nearly 25 years. On the left are the former headquarters of the ❾ **20th Middlesex (Artists') Rifle Volunteers Corps.** Opened in 1889 with the heads of Mars (god of war) and Minerva (goddess of wisdom) still look down from the Victorian façade.

The Volunteers was possibly the most unlikely force within the British army, comprising as it did of painters, musicians and others in creative professions. Its first commanders were the painters Henry Wyndham Phillips and Frederic Leighton. The unit served with distinction and their honours include eight Victoria Crosses. Today it continues as a territorial army unit (now known simply as The Artists Rifles) and was where the adventurer Bear Grylls received his military training.

Clearly D[...]ing

8 Woburn Walk

The magnificent ⑩ **St Pancras church** next door is also known as the 'New Church', after replacing the original parish church (seen later in the walk). Consecrated in 1822, St Pancras was built in a Greek revival style that was becoming fashionable in England. It was also the most expensive church built in London since St Paul's Cathedral arose from the ashes of the Great Fire.

Designed by William Inwood and his son Henry, the church was at the centre of a large parish that in the early 19th century stretched from Highgate to Oxford Street. Facing the busy traffic of Euston Road, the white Portland stone exterior is now smog-stained; however, when it was first built it looked out onto open fields.

The design is based on the Erectheum at the Acropolis, and is famous for its two sets of Coade stone caryatids, found on the north and south vestries. The caryatids are statues of female figures that take the place of pillars and here they guard the crypt that once housed 500 bodies. They were created by the sculptor Charles Rossi (1762-1839) who – having spent three years working on the caryatids in his studio – was shocked to find they were too tall to fit in their allotted positions at the church. He was forced to cut sections out of each midriff to ensure a correct fit – something thankfully not noticeable today.

The crypt was used as a makeshift bomb shelter during WWII, and today is used for various events including art exhibitions.

In the quiet churchyard on the south side (there is an entrance on Duke's Road – the main entrance to the church is on the west side), there is a memorial to victims of violence designed by Emily Young and placed there after the 7th July 2005 terrorist bombings in London. Young, one of the country's most acclaimed sculptors, is said to have been the inspiration for Syd Barrett's Pink Floyd song *See Emily Play*.

At the junction with Euston Road look across to see a remarkable red brick building – ⑪ **Elizabeth Garrett Anderson Hospital**. It was designed by the architect J.M. Brydon as a hospital for women and dates from 1890. In 1918 it was renamed after the pioneering female surgeon Elizabeth Garrett Anderson who was instrumental in its founding. In 1967 plans to close the hospital triggered a three-year staff occupation. The hospital survived here until January 2001 but has since moved and the building is now used by UNISON. The union still has a gallery within the building dedicated to the life and work of Garrett Anderson.

Cross over to Euston Station. When first opened in 1837 it was probably the greatest of the three stations established by the Victorians in this part of London, and was built for the London and Birmingham Railway line.

Samuel Sidney in his book *Rides on Railways* (1851) described Euston at the time as '...the greatest railway port in England, or indeed in the world....What London is to the world, Euston is to Great Britain'. Although the London and Birmingham Railway was the first mainline railway line to enter London, until 1845 locomotive engines still stopped at Chalk Farm station to the north and from there were detached and pulled by a long rope to Euston. This was partly because of a shortage of power but also to prevent scaring the local horse traffic.

The first Euston station was designed by Philip Hardwick, with Charles Fox responsible for the engine shed. Originally it had just two platforms and was famous for its vast Grand Hall and Hardwick's 72 ft high Euston Arch, which dominated the entrance to the station.

DUMFRIES.
DUNDEE.
EDINBURGH.
FLEETWOOD.
GLASGOW.
GREENOCK.
HALIFAX.
HEREFORD.
HUDDERSFIELD

12

Sadly the old station and Euston Arch were demolished in the 1960s and replaced by the bland and universally unloved shed seen today. The destruction is regarded by architectural historians as one of the greatest losses in recent London history. Today the only remnants of the old station still visible are the ⑫ **lodges** outside the main entrance.

⑬ **Euston Square** in front of the station was laid out on fields in around 1813. This was before the station had been built, and Euston Square then resembled one of the elegant squares of Bloomsbury that are still found to the south of Euston Road. Before it was built the fields around here were popular with Irish immigrants, who would gather to play at 'hurling to goals', a game using bat and ball.

Today the area is again experiencing great upheaval as the land surrounding Euston Station, including St James's Gardens, is sacrificed to make way for the terminus of the vast HS2 project whose costs and final delivery date are still a matter of speculation.

Continue along Euston Road and take an immediate right onto Melton Street. At the junction with Drummond Street you will pass the site of the Leslie Green designed Euston underground station that has been subsumed into the HS2 development in recent years.

As you walk along ⑭ **Drummond Street** you will see many 19th buildings. Some are listed, for example number 131 and 116 which date from c.1820 when this area was being developed for the first time. If you walked here in the 1890s you would pass carriage works, a saw mill, warehouses, and a smithy. Like many parts of inner city London, the Victorian past was much more industrial than today. There are also a number of mews streets.

Turn right up North Gower Street, passing no.200 looking for a ⑮ **plaque remembering Lord Pitt of Hampstead** (1913-1994). Born David Pitt in Grenada, he was a Labour party politician and the longest serving Black MP and only the second peer of African descent to sit in the House of Lords. This street also has fine early 19th

century houses. Carry on along the pedestrian path to reach Hampstead Road.

At the junction is a fine building with signage for the **16** **St Pancras Female Orphanage.** It was founded in 1776 and this building dates from 1904. Young female orphans in the parish were trained for a life in domestic service. In 1930 there were 46 girls between the ages of 4 and 12. The orphanage closed in 1945.

Continue along Hampstead Road passing tower blocks that look down onto the Euston railway lines below, you soon reach **17** **Mornington Crescent,** named after Richard Wellesley, Earl of Mornington and Governor-General of India. His successful career was overshadowed by his little brother, the Duke of Wellington.

Built from 1821, for the Southampton Estate, owned by the Fitzroy family mentioned earlier, who are associated with titles such as Earl of Euston, Duke of Grafton and Baron of of Southampton. The Georgian houses in the crescent originally stood surrounded by open fields, and it was only in the 20th century that the gardens within the crescent were built over. The east side facing Hampstead Road is dominated by London's most flamboyant factory design, originally the ⑱ **Carreras Black Cat Cigarette factory** (known as the Arcadia Works). It was designed in the 1920s in a highly unusual Egyptian style with bronze cats protecting the main entrance.

Walk along the crescent itself. This has always been an area popular with artists, and was the spiritual home of the influential collective of painters known as the Camden Town Group. Founded in 1911, it was led by Walter Sickert (1860-1942) who lived at ⑲ **number 6** (there is a blue plaque). Other members included Spencer Frederick Gore, Lucien Pissarro, Augustus John, Walter Bayes and Wyndham Lewis. While most did not live in Camden, they often congregated in Sickert's home and studio.

The group was named after Camden because Sickert claimed, according to Bayes, that 'the district had been so watered with his tears that something important must sooner or later spring from its soil'. Many of the Group's pictures include gritty depictions of ordinary life in London in the years preceding WWI.

Sickert has been the subject of several theories that he was – or was at least involved with – Jack the Ripper, the serial killer who killed at least five prostitutes in the East End in 1888.

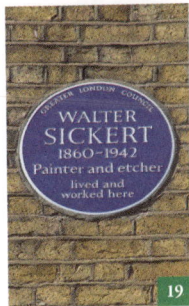

Sickert was undeniably fascinated by the Ripper myth, and even painted *Jack the Ripper's Bedroom* after his landlady at number

six told him of her strong suspicion that a veterinary student from Bournemouth, who had lodged in Sickert's room many years before, was the Ripper himself. Later Sickert produced a number of grisly works known as the *Camden Town Murder* paintings.

Continue round the crescent to reach **20 Mornington Crescent tube station**. It was opened in 1907 and later shut for several years before being beautifully restored and re-opened in 1998. The ceremony was attended by members of the panel of the Radio 4 show *I'm Sorry I Haven't a Clue*, which includes a long-running nonsense-game named 'Mornington Crescent'. The inside of the station contains a plaque in memory of former panel member and satirical cartoonist Willie Rushton.

Follow the map further into Camden along the busy Camden High Street. The area is named after the 18th-century landowner Charles Pratt, 1st Earl Camden (1714-94). Pratt took the name 'Camden' from Camden Place, his property in Chiselhurst, Kent, which, for its part, was named after its original occupant William Camden (1551-1623), the Elizabethan historian.

In the late 18th century the area largely still consisted of open fields and contained only two prominent buildings – the Old Mother Red Cap (today's World's End pub) and the Mother Black Cap (until 2015 the Black Cap pub). Both names are linked to an old London myth concerning a witch who once lived here.

During the 19th century the area became fully urbanised. It was popular with immigrant groups, particularly the Irish who dominated the area until the 1960s. During that decade the growth of further education saw an influx into Camden of students seeking cheap rental accommodation, attracted also by the many lively pubs that were still dominated by Irish folk music. Thus began the growth of Camden as the youth entertainment centre of north London, full of pubs, clubs, tattoo parlours and its famous street markets.

Follow the map up Pratt Street then left into Bayham Street, looking out for a ㉑ **Dicken's Plaque,** just above eye-level about 10 metres from the junction with Greenland Road. This marks where Charles Dickens lived as a young man in 1823. It was at this time that his father was confined to a debtors' prison.

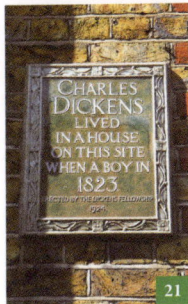

Look at the surviving ㉒ **19th-century houses** opposite to get an idea of what Dickens's home would have looked like. The house, demolished in 1910, is regarded as the inspiration for the Cratchit family's modest home in *A Christmas Carol* (1843). In the book a repentant Scrooge hires a small boy to buy a Christmas turkey 'twice the size of Tiny Tim' and take it to the Cratchit's house, telling the boy 'it's impossible to carry that to Camden Town....You must have a cab'.

Dickens clearly knew Camden well and in *Dombey and Son* (1848) described the devastation wrought on Staggs Gardens (most likely today's Parkway) by the construction of the Euston to Birmingham railway in 1836:

'The first shock of a great earthquake had, just at that period, rent the whole neighbourhood to its centre... Houses were knocked down; streets broken through and stopped; deep pits and trenches dug in the ground; enormous heaps of earth and clay thrown up... Everywhere were bridges that led nowhere; thoroughfares that were wholly impassable... In short, the yet unfinished and unopened Railroad was in progress'.

23

23

24

Turn left into Greenland Road with the ㉓ **World's End** public house on the right. Despite being packed most nights, the World's End is surprisingly civilised during the day. Inside there is a sign for the Mother Red Cap describing this as Camden's oldest drinking establishment.

Walk south down Camden High Street to find at no.171 the abandoned site of the cabaret venue called the Black Cap. In the late 70s and early 80s it was a favoured spot for the notorious serial killer Dennis Nilsen, who would find his victims there. The pub closed in 2015 but there is a campaign to reopen the legendary venue. Just a few doors down on the side of number 179 is a good example of a ㉔ **ghost sign for Boots the Chemist**.

Walk up Parkway, passing the ㉕ **ladies' lavatory** at the junction with Camden High Street. The first such lavatory in the country, it was installed in 1910 due to the efforts of George Bernard Shaw, the famous playwright and author, and less well known Camden councillor. Shaw's campaign involved years of fighting against the more prudish elements on the council who thought it improper for females to go to the lavatory anywhere other than in the privacy of their own homes.

Continue up Parkway past the renowned music venue the **Jazz Café** on the left that was founded in 1990. Shortly you reach the junction with Albert Street on the left. On the corner you will see the Spread Eagle public house, one of the favoured Camden haunts of Britpop's aristocracy in the early to mid-90s, particularly members of Blur and Oasis. Graham Coxon, guitarist with Blur, caused a stir when he made a nostalgic return to play a surprise gig in April 2009 – playing so loudly that some of the pub's light fittings fell down.

If you look north up Parkway you can also see the brightly-coloured Dublin Castle on the right hand side, for many years one of Camden's premier venues for up and coming bands. Madness, Blur, Coldplay, Supergrass, The Artic Monkeys, Amy Winehouse and countless other notable performers have played here, and many years ago a visitor might have even found Suggs or Winehouse standing behind the bar serving pints for the fun of it.

Leave Parkway by walking along to 26 **no.127 Albert Street** where in 1969 the film director and writer Bruce Robinson lived as a struggling actor with his eccentric house-mate Vivian MacKerrell. The experience inspired him to write and direct the cult film *Withnail and I* (1987). MacKerrell, the real-life inspiration for Withnail, was an unsuccessful actor who

died of throat cancer in 1995, not helped it is thought by his drinking of lighter fluid – a feat portrayed in the film. Today Albert Street is no longer the shabby road full of squats and a house here can set you back in excess of £3 million.

If you want to see where Noel Gallagher of Oasis wrote *Wonderwall* cross over Delancey Street into the other half of Albert Street (he lived at 88 in the early 90s until too many fans began to congregate outside). Otherwise head right along Delancey Street.

On the right hand side you will see a blue plaque outside number 54. The poet 27 **Dylan Thomas** (1914-53) lived here from 1951 to 1952 with his wife Caitlin. The couple used to argue bitterly, and their already irritated neighbours probably did not appreciate them parking their gypsy caravan outside. By this time the marriage was beyond repair, and the poet soon fled to America where he died of chronic alcohol poisoning the following year.

Continue on and if you need a stop but find Camden High Street and its surrounding streets a little frantic, then just ahead on the left is the 28 **Edinboro Castle** that first opened in 1839. This is a slightly more relaxed public house, which has a nice outside garden and offers a decent menu.

The railway line that runs underneath is a reminder of the 19th-century navvies (or 'navigators') who built it. These labourers often lived in Camden and were drawn from every part of Britain. Fights would often break out in the local pubs between the

King's Cross, St Pancras & Camden Walk

Scots, Irish, Welsh and English workers and it is widely believed that each nationality was encouraged to congregate in their own Camden pub. Hence the Edinboro Castle for the Scots, the Dublin Castle for the Irish, the Pembroke (or depending on which version of the story you hear, the Caernarvon) Castle for the Welsh and the Windsor Castle for the English. As some of these pubs were not trading until after the railway was built, this is almost certainly an urban myth.

Follow the map to reach ㉙ **Gloucester Crescent**, possibly the finest residential street in Camden and where houses can cost more than £6 million. The crescent has long been popular with artists and media types including the photographer David Bailey, playwright Michael Frayn and musician George Melly.

In 1974 the playwright and author Alan Bennett – who lived at number 23 – let an elderly eccentric named Miss Mary Shepherd move her van and belongings into his front yard. Bennett had become concerned about the way the old lady – who lived in the van – was being treated by passers-by on the street outside his house. What was supposed to be a temporary arrangement lasted for the

next 15 years, Bennett recalling 'one seldom was able to do her a good turn without some thoughts of strangulation'. After Miss Shepherd died he wrote a poignant story about her, later turned into the hit play and film *The Lady in the Van* with Dame Maggie Smith in the lead role.

Charles Dickens banished his long-suffering wife Catherine to ㉚ **number 70** Gloucester Crescent after they separated in the 1850s. While they remained married, Dickens was able to pursue a relationship with the actress Ellen Ternan. Catherine by contrast lived the

life of a recluse. Only her eldest son Charley chose to live with her, the other children hesitating to visit for fear of upsetting their domineering father. Catherine was not even invited to her daughter Kate's wedding in 1860.

Turn right down Inverness Street, looking out on the left for a single storey white building that was once home to **Sounds that Swing** – a rockabilly record shop where Bobby Gillespie of Primal Scream and Robert Plant of Led Zeppelin were said to be regulars.

Just ahead you reach the junction with Arlington Road, where you can see The Good Mixer public house on the corner. Turn left along Arlington Road (on the same side as the Good Mixer), and about a hundred yards up you will see a homeless hostel known as ❸❶ **Arlington House** at number 220. It was founded in 1905, and is the only surviving example of the Rowton Houses set up by the great Victorian philanthropist Lord Rowton (1838-1903) to help London's poor. In the 1930s a number of refugees from Stalin's purges in Russia stayed here as did George Orwell, who described it as 'one of the best lodging houses' in his book *Down*

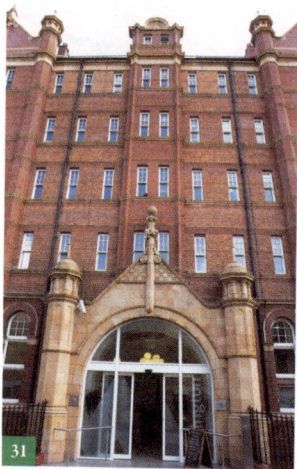

and Out in Paris and London (1933). Other residents have included Brendan Behan, and it is mentioned in songs by The Pogues and Madness.

It is best known for its large number of Irish residents, many of whom arrived in London after WWII to work on post-Blitz rebuilding projects and ending up staying here when the jobs dried up or they became too old to work. In the mid-1990s, when the Irish accounted for 8% of Camden's population, over 40% of the male residents of the hostel were from Ireland.

The poet Patrick Kavanagh (1904-67), from Co. Monaghan, stayed here in the 1930s and wrote in his autobiography, *The Green Fool* that 'Many Irish boys made Rowton House, Camden Town, first stop from Mayo. The soft voices of Mayo and Galway sounding in that gaunt, impersonal place fell like warm rain on the arid patches of my imagination'. In the 1980s the original Rowton company relinquished ownership and today it is run by the Novas Scarman Group.

Re-trace your steps to reach **32** **The Good Mixer** on the left – a classic trendy Camden pub where wannabee pop stars rub shoulders with students and the media types who work locally at places like MTV. In its heyday – in around 1993 – this was another favourite haunt of 'Britpop' stars from bands such as Blur, Pulp and Oasis; the latter's lead singer Liam Gallagher was eventually barred by the landlord because of his behaviour. In later years the 'be seen' pub in Camden became the Hawley Arms – found on Castlehaven Road off the High Street – which counted Kate Moss, Kelly Osbourne, and the late Amy Winehouse amongst the 'Hawley Arms Set'. Winehouse died tragically young on 23 July 2011 at her house at number 30 Camden Square, not far from here. Another high-profile star, Lily Allen, attended The Cavendish School that has an entrance on Arlington Road.

Continue down **33** **Inverness Street**, once famous as a fruit and vegetable market but now selling T-shirts and novelty gifts

34

34

36

to tourists. Turn left to follow the map up Camden High Street and through the heart of the vibrant **34** **Camden Market** that dominates the area. Although hard to imagine now, until the early 1970s the market was confined to Inverness Street.

Turn right into Buck Street where on the right is **35** **Camden deep-level air raid shelter**. This is one of two entrances and the shelter was one of several built in London during World War Two to protect civilians from German bombing raids. The shelter could hold 8,000 people.

Return to Camden, ahead is **36** **Camden Lock** on the Regent's Canal, and at this point you may wish to take some time to look around the sprawling market. The Hampstead Road Lock (on the west side of the bridge) is next to a basin that once served as a timber yard, but which is now decked over and forms part of the market.

The northern part of the market contains shops built into railway arches, the only visible sign of the Camden Catacombs that lie below and stretch down towards Euston station. The tunnels and vaults were used to stable horses involved in the early railways and later used by Gilbey's Gin Company for storage. Their route can be traced from the distinctive cast-iron grilles set at regular intervals into the road surface; originally the only source of light for the horses below. The network of tunnels includes an underground canal basin which can be seen from the canal just outside Camden Lock Market, close to Camden Lock itself.

CAMDEN LOCK

OPEN AS USUAL

OPTICIANS

GONE WITH THE WIND

£500

ARRIVA

34 Camden market

When finished, head under the bridge at Camden Lock. On your left you will see the vast copper edifice of **37** **Hawley Wharf** that was opened in 2020 and contains 178 apartments as well as shops and retail units. It is part of Camden Market but resembles an upmarket shopping area rather than the ramshackle stalls that once occupied the site. There are plenty of street food outlets here if you fancy a break.

From here head east on the towpath that runs alongside the Regent's Canal. The canal runs for nine miles between Paddington Basin and Limehouse in the East End. It was completed in 1820 with the great Regency architect John Nash one of the main driving forces behind the project.

The canal contains 40 bridges and 12 locks, and when originally built the towpaths were closed to the public. Horses would pull barges laden with heavy goods such as coal, timber and stone, and where there was no towpath available through a tunnel the boatmen would lie on their backs and use their legs to 'walk' along the tunnel ceiling in order to propel the barges through. The construction of the canal, together with the development of railway lines to Euston, did much to transform Camden from a rural backwater into a heavily-urbanised area by 1850.

As you walk along the towpath look out on the south side for the former offices of **38** **TV-AM**, the company that broadcast ITV's first breakfast television programme between 1983 and 1992. The familiar egg-cup symbols of TV-AM can still be seen on the outside of the building, which was originally designed by Terry Farrell.

Shortly you pass by a row of futuristic looking houses that lie at back of the **39** **Sainsbury's supermarket** on Camden Road. Completed in 1988, the houses were commissioned by Sainsbury's and designed by Sir Nicholas Grimshaw, winning a number of architectural awards. Grimshaw is also the architect of Waterloo International (now displaced by St Pancras as the Eurostar terminal).

Follow the canal for ten minutes or so. The fifth bridge after Camden Lock takes you under St Pancras Way, a road that follows the path of the 'hidden' River Fleet. Just before the bridge your will see on the opposite side **40** **two 19th century cottages** that were originally part of John Eeles Lawford's slate business and are now Grade II listed. The Constitution pub is accessed via steps at the bridge and has a garden overlooking the canal.

Continue along the canal on a long straight stretch before coming off at the next bridge onto Camley Street. Take the recently landscaped exit onto the road and then turn left until you see a gate that takes you into **41** **St Pancras Gardens**, which also contains St Pancras Old Church. The gardens stand beside the ominous-looking **42** **St Pancras Hospital** on the north side. The hospital buildings were originally used as a workhouse in the 19th century. An official report into the workhouse of 1868 noted the case of a three-year-old child who had 'fallen out of bed and injured its jaw, [and] was removed into the infirmary...[it] was greatly overcrowded, and as many as forty-two children had slept in the ward at one time. Ten days after having been admitted the injured child died from gangrene, which, according to the medical officer, might have been brought on through living in such an atmosphere'.

The gardens were opened in 1877 and were built over the former graveyards of St Giles-in-the-Fields and ㊸ **St Pancras Old Church**. The latter (on the south-east corner) is possibly the oldest church in London, said to have been founded in 314 AD. The Reverend Weldon Champneys, the church vicar between 1797 and 1810, claimed to have seen first-hand evidence of a 4th-century foundation among documents he had access to during a visit to the Vatican. This has not been verified since, but it is known that St Pancras was an early Christian martyr who was beheaded on the orders of Emperor Diocletian in 304 AD. It is also thought a Roman army camp once stood on the Brill, a site just to the west of here, so it is possible that early Christian soldiers based at the camp set up a place of worship dedicated to the then-recently executed martyr.

Whether or not the foundation was Roman, the church is certainly very old. The altar stone dates from the 6th century AD and its mar/ suggest it may have been used by St Augustine. There is therefore another theory that the church was founded during the time of St Augustine's visit to pagan England in 597 AD.

The medieval church was occupied in 1642 during the English Civil War by Parliamentarian troops. Eight years later it was described as standing '...in the fields remote from any houses in the said parish' and by the bank of the open River Fleet. This isolation meant that as its parish grew rapidly, particularly to the south, the old church was deemed inadequate. It was replaced in 1822 as parish church by the newly built St Pancras New Church on Euston Road visited earlier on. Old St Pancras was later rebuilt between 1847 and 1848, although you can still see some of the original Norman wall on the left-hand side of the main aisle.

In the mid-19th century the churchyard of Old St Pancras was badly damaged by the railway companies who were aggressively constructing their new lines through the area. This resulted in numerous complaints of insensitivity from the public who could see mangled corpses strewn around the freshly excavated ground. In the 1860s the poet and writer Thomas Hardy (1840-1928), then working for a firm of West End architects, was put in charge of the unpleasant task of organising the tidy-up of the burial ground.

Hardy was tormented by what he saw, particularly when he apparently discovered a freakish two-headed body of a man inside a coffin. The fledgling writer soon returned to the more pleasant environment of Dorset, but his work here was commemorated by the ㊹ **Hardy's Tree**, that stood to the north-east side of the church. The tree was ringed by old gravestones that were neatly stacked there under Hardy's supervision, and became enveloped over time by tree roots. In 2022 the remarkable tree fell in a storm and now the grave stones circle a vacant space. Hardy's wrote of his time here in the poem *The Levell'd Graveyard*:

'O passenger, pray list and catch
Our sighs and piteous groans
Half stifled in this jumbled patch
Of wretched memorial stones'

King's Cross, St Pancras & Camden Walk

The burial ground includes **45 Sir John Soane's monument** of 1816 to his wife Elizabeth, one of only two tombs in London with listed building status (the other is Karl Marx's tomb in Highgate Cemetery). It is said to have influenced Giles Gilbert Scott's 1924 design for the iconic 'K2' red telephone box. You can also see the plain tomb of noted Somers Town residents William Godwin (political philosopher, 1756-1836) and his wife Mary Wollstonecraft (an early feminist, 1759-97). Mary died giving birth to her daughter Mary Godwin (1797-1851), and it was while her daughter was visiting her mother's grave here that the Romantic poet Percy Bysshe Shelley (1792-1822) saw her by chance and instantly fell in love.

However, this was no fairy-tale romance as Shelley was already married. The couple had to endure being ostracised by London society before they could finally marry after the suicide of Shelley's first wife. In 1816 they went to Geneva to stay with their friend Lord Byron. The house guests, including Byron's doctor, John William Polidori (also buried here),

258

held a competition to write the best ghost story. Despite the presence of two literary greats – Byron and Shelley – it is Mary Shelley's *Frankenstein* and Polidori's *The Vampyre* that remain the best known products of the competition, both being regarded as key works in the development of the gothic horror novel.

The **46** **Burdett-Coutts memorial** sundial near the main western entrance to the park contains the names of notable people buried here, including John Mills, last surviving prisoner of the 'Black Hole of Calcutta', and Johann Christian Bach (1735-82), the composer and son of Johann Sebastian (known as the 'English Bach').

In July 1968 the Beatles – then at the height of their fame – came to the park one Sunday for a photo shoot by Don McCullin. They posed for photographs by the church and in the gardens, with excited locals crowding around the gates to watch the proceedings. Charles Dickens makes reference to Old St Pancras churchyard in *A Tale of Two Cities* (1859) as a place where the villain Jerry Cruncher liked to 'fish' – an old term

for body-snatching. The church was badly damaged by bombing during WWII and desecrated by Satanists in 1985, explaining why it is often closed.

To the west of the park is Somers Town – named after the Somers family that originally owned the land in the 18th century. Today it is a fairly unattractive area, with the grim reality of life there portrayed in Shane Meadows's film *Somers Town* (2008).

When finished at the park return through the gate to the road and turn right (passing under a bridge) to reach the **47 Camley Street Natural Park**. Standing on the site of a former coal drop, this is a pleasant two-acre wildlife park. It is open throughout the week and has a pleasant café with views across the canal.

Once finished at the nature park cross the canal on the new Somers Town Bridge that opened in 2022 and was designed by Moxon Architects. The bridge offers great views of the hulking Victorian gasholders erected in around 1880 by the Gas, Light and Coke Company. They have now been incorporated into the framework of modern apartments. From the other side of the bridge, head briefly to your left to get a view of **48 St Pancras Basin** where many canal boats are moored. The basin opened in 1870 and was originally used as a coal wharf. The old lock keeper's cottage is nearby.

From here, follow the map through the landscaped area surrounding the shopping complex known as Coal Drops Yard. It was designed by Thomas Heatherwick and

48 *St Pancras Basin*

50

51

51

opened in October 2018. As you continue look to the left to see the main thoroughfare with its unusual 'kissing roof' that connects the buildings on either side.

On your left you will soon see the Grade II listed ㊾ **Granary Building**, which is now home to the University of the Arts London, which includes Central Saint Martins – one of the country's finest art colleges. Former students include singer Jarvis Cocker, designer Jeff Banks, Clash member Mick Jones, and artists Lucian Freud, and Gilbert and George. The students contribute to the vibrancy of King's Cross as do the public fountains just outside in the recently created Granary Square. A great place to relax when the weather is fine.

Continue just past the college and exit the canal by the bridge under York Way. Follow the map passing by ㊿ **King's Place** just on the south side of the canal – housed within the distinctive 'wavy' building. This is a popular cultural centre that opened in 2008 and describes itself as a 'hub for music, art, dialogue and food' – this includes a café and restaurant if you need a break.

After this is an opportunity to visit the (51) **London Canal Museum** (open Wed-Sun 10am-4.30pm). Just follow the map to reach New Wharf Road. The museum is housed in a building that served in the 1850s as an ice warehouse and was owned by the millionaire Swiss-Italian entrepreneur Carlo Gatti (1817-1878). Gatti became the main ice trader in London during the 19th century – as well as running a number of music halls – and is credited with popularising ice cream in this country. At the museum you can also see inside a narrowboat cabin and learn about the history of London's canals as well as look out onto Battlebridge Basin.

If you do not want to visit the museum – or when you have finished – follow the map to enter 52 **King's Boulevard**. This is one of London's newest streets, one of many laid out as part of the redevelopment project. In the parallel avenue you can see the European HQ for Google. This is an impressive sign that King's Cross is at the centre of London's hi-tech, post-industrial future.

At the end of King's Boulevard look out on the right for the 53 **German Gymnasium**. A striking building that dates from the mid 1860s and was largely paid for by the German community who then formed the largest immigrant group in London. It was used by the German Gymnastics Society who practiced exercises including Indian club swinging and broadsword practice. It also had a large number of non-German members, attracted by the fashionable Germanic exercise regime.

The Charles Dicken's London Dictionary of 1888 noted that the society 'stands at the head of all institutions of its class... The thousand and seventy-three members who were on the roll in 1878 not only had the opportunity of thoroughly learning all that the German system of gymnastics has to teach, combined with fencing and boxing, but the privilege of joining a singing-class, a literary club, and an English dramatic club; a library of 2,500 volumes being also at their disposal'.

In 1866 the Gymnasium (or 'Die Turnhalle') hosted some of the indoor events organised by the National Olympic Games – a forerunner of the modern Olympic movement. It retained its original purpose right up to WWI when all things German fell out of favour, and the immigrant community that once supported the Gymnasium was reduced in size and influence. The building declined in the following decades, but has recently been restored to its former glory and is now a café and restaurant

Head south and follow the map back to King's Cross station and the end of the walk. ●

SHOP...

Camden Markets, NW1
Inverness Street, Camden
High Street, Camden Lock &
The Stables
Open: Thurs-Sun 10am-5pm
www.camdenmarket.com

VISIT...

British Library (see p.234)
96 Euston Road, NW1 2DB
www.bl.uk
Exhibitions, Bookshop,
Library, Café

Camley Street Nature Park
12 Camley Street, N1C 4PW
www.wildlondon.org.uk

King's Place (see p.262)
90 York Way, N1 9AG
www.kingsplace.co.uk
Exhibitions, concerts and café

London Canal Museum
12-13 New Wharf Road, N1 9RT
www.canalmuseum.org.uk

EAT, DRINK...

The Dolphin (see p.233)
47 Tonbridge St, WC1H 9DW
www.thedolphin-pub.com

World's End Pub
174 Camden High Street,
NW1 0NE
www.theworldsend.co.uk

Jazz Café
5 Parkway, NW1 7PG
www.thejazzcafelondon.com

Spread Eagle
141 Albert Street, NW1 7NB
www.spreadeaglecamden.co.uk

Edinboro Castle
57 Morning Terrace, NW1 7RU
www.edinborocastlepub.co.uk

The Good Mixer
30 Inverness Street, NW1 7HJ
www.thegoodmixer.com

Hawley Arms
2 Castlehaven Road, NW1 8QU
www.thehawleyarms.co.uk

The Constitution
42 St Pancras Way, NW1 0QT
www.conincamden.com

Searcys St Pancras,
Upper Concourse,
St Pancras Station, N1C 4QL
www.searcysstpancras.co.uk

Kensington Church Walk, see p.272

9 Kensington Walk

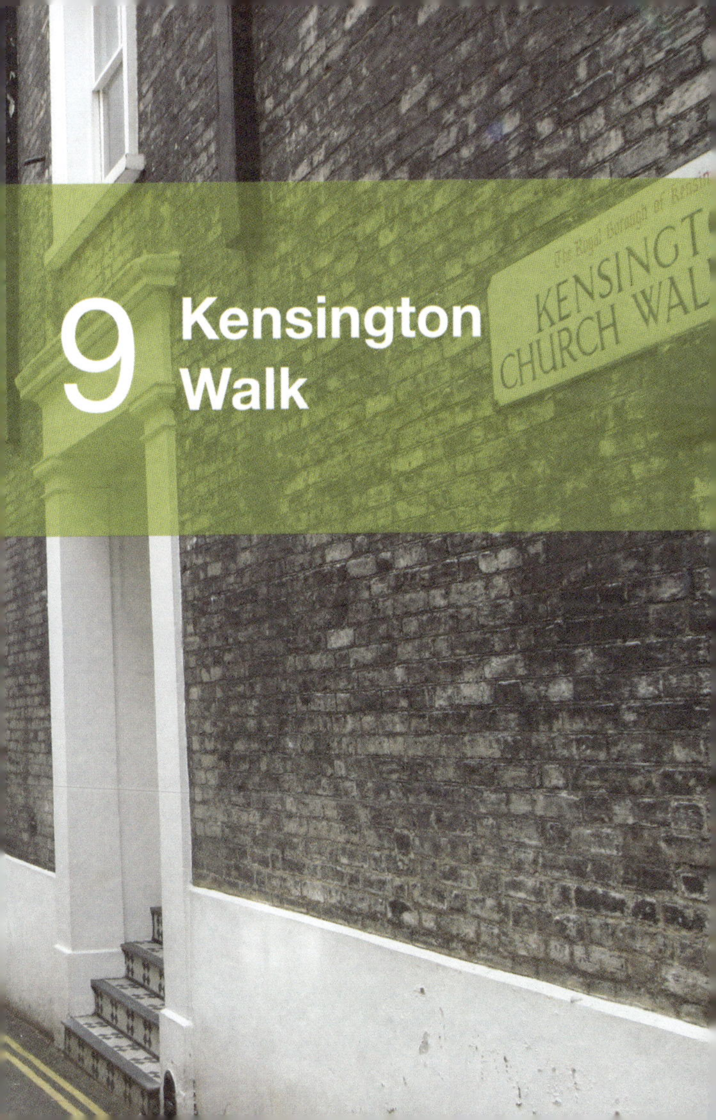

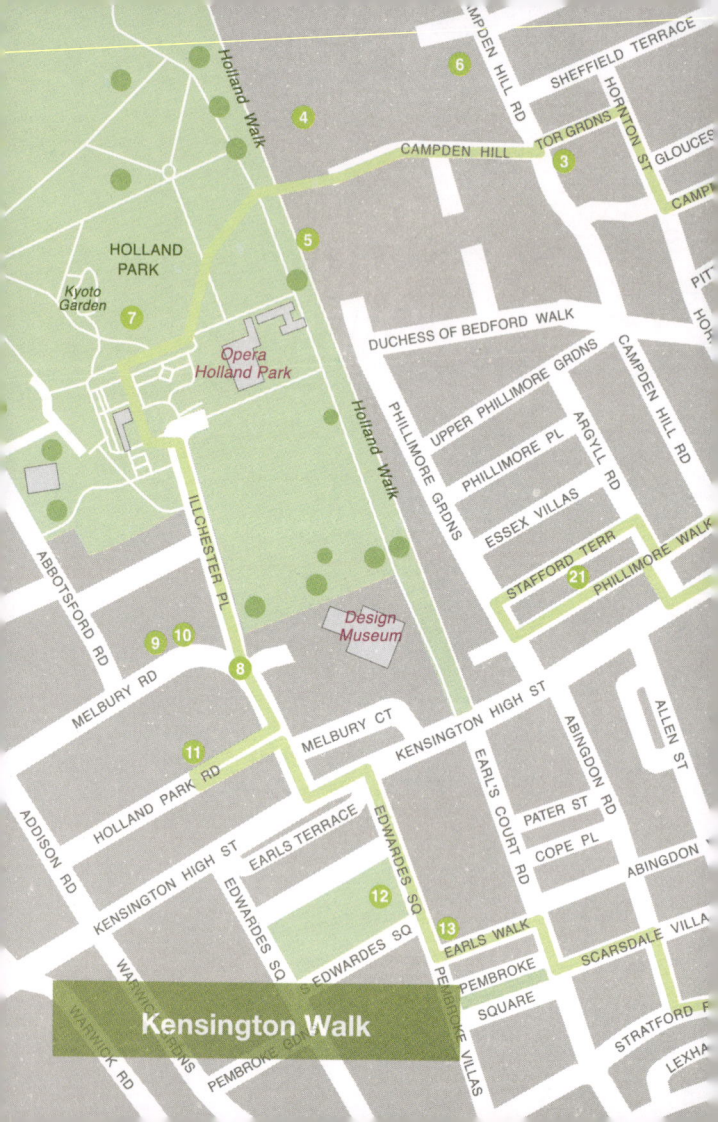

HOLLAND PARK

Kyoto Garden

Opera Holland Park

Holland Walk

Campden Hill Walk

CAMPDEN HILL RD

SHEFFIELD TERRACE

HORNTON ST

CAMPDEN HILL

TOR GRDNS

GLOUCES

CAMP

PIT

HOR

DUCHESS OF BEDFORD WALK

CAMPDEN HILL RD

UPPER PHILLIMORE GRDNS

PHILLIMORE GRDNS

PHILLIMORE PL

ARGYLL RD

ESSEX VILLAS

STAFFORD TERR

PHILLIMORE WALK

Holland Walk

ILLCHESTER PL

ABBOTSFORD RD

Design Museum

MELBURY RD

MELBURY CT

KENSINGTON HIGH ST

EARL'S COURT RD

ABINGDON RD

ALLEN ST

HOLLAND PARK RD

ADDISON RD

KENSINGTON HIGH ST

EARLS TERRACE

EDWARDES SQ

PATER ST

COPE PL

ABINGDON

EDWARDES SQ

EARLS WALK

SCARSDALE VILLA

WARWICK GARDENS

PEMBROKE GDNS

PEMBROKE VILLAS

EDWARDES SQ

PEMBROKE SQUARE

STRATFORD RD

LEXHA

WARWICK RD

Kensington Walk

1 St Mary Abbots
2 Kensington Church Walk
3 Ford Madox Ford
4 Holland Park School
5 Holland Walk
6 Thorpe Lodge
7 Holland Park
8 Melbury Road
9 Tower House
10 Sir Samuel Luke Fildes RA
11 Leighton House Museum
12 Edwardes Square
13 Scarsdale Tavern
14 Cornwall Gardens
15 Kensington Square
16 Number 18
17 Number 17
18 Convent of the Assumption
19 Number 16
20 Kensington Roof Gardens
   (now closed)
21 Sambourne House

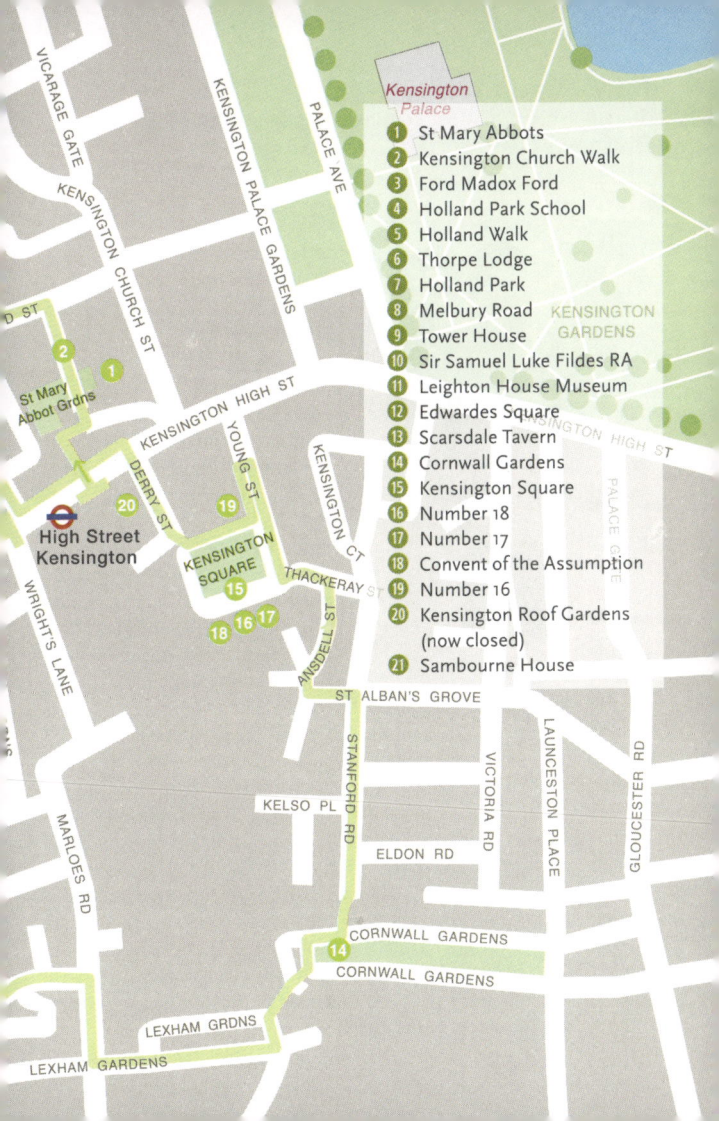

KENSINGTON
GARDENS

KENSINGTON HIGH ST

St Mary
Abbot Grdns

High Street
Kensington

KENSINGTON
SQUARE

St Alban's Grove

Kelso Pl

Eldon Rd

Cornwall Gardens

Cornwall Gardens

Lexham Grdns

Lexham Gardens

Kensington Walk

Start/finish: High Street Kensington underground station
Distance: 3.2 miles

From High Street Kensington underground station cross over the road and head up Kensington Church Walk. Dominating the view ahead of you is the soaring spire of ❶ **St Mary Abbots**, Kensington's parish church.

The current building dates from 1872 and is the work of the great Victorian architect, Sir George Gilbert Scott (1811-1878). The spire is 278 feet high, the tallest of any parish church in London. The garden in the church grounds is a quiet refuge from the crowds of 'High Street Ken' – one of the busiest thoroughfares in London.

The church stands on the site where Kensington originated as a village in the 8th century AD. The place name is possibly derived from a Saxon named Chenesit or Cynesinge who founded a settlement (or 'tun') in the area, the combination of these words becoming 'Kensington'. After the Norman Conquest the manor of Kensington was given to Aubrey de Vere. Later his son became very ill, but was cured by the Abbot of the Benedictine Abbey of St Mary at Abingdon. In gratitude, the de Veres bequeathed the church and around 270 acres to the Abbey which continued to own the land until Henry VIII's Dissolution of the Monasteries in the 1530s. In the churchyard look for the listed tomb of Elizabeth Johnstone dating from 1784 and designed by Sir John Soane, one of the greatest architects of his era

① St Mary Abbots

After visiting the church continue north up ❷ **Kensington Church Walk.** The poet Ezra Pound lived at number 10 between 1909-14. Follow the map, which leads you up to Campden Hill. Kensington is the neighbourhood of choice for many of the capital's wealthy inhabitants with some of the larger, elegant properties you pass costing well in excess of £10 million.

The reason for Kensington's popularity with London's wealthier classes is largely attributable to William III's chronic asthma. For the sake of his health, the King (1650-1702) decided to leave his Palace at Whitehall and live in rural Kensington. He bought Nottingham House in 1689 and began its transformation into Kensington Palace (which lies to the west of Kensington High Street). The King's courtiers flocked to the area, and developers soon began to build new townhouses and squares to keep up with demand. Within a few decades many of Kensington's orchards and fields had been built over, and by 1705 John Bowack described Kensington as having an 'abundance of shopkeepers and... artificers... which makes it appear rather like part of London, than a country village'. During the 19th century Kensington became part of London and between 1801 and 1901 its population grew from 8,500 to over 175,000. The monarchy resided at the palace until 1760, but Kensington remained a favourite of the royal family most recently being the residence of Diana, Princess of Wales.

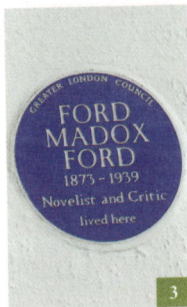

Walk along Tor Gardens to reach Campden Hill Road where on the left (number 80) is a blue plaque commemorating the controversial writer and journalist ❸ **Ford Madox Ford**. Not least of his controversies was the fact that he lived here with his lover Violet Hunt, when his wife refused to grant him a divorce. His novel *The Good Soldier* (1915) is still considered one of the greatest works of the 20th century.

Cross over Campden Hill Road and continue down Campden Hill past ❹ **Holland Park School** to meet ❺ **Holland Walk**, a lovely tree-lined path that runs from Notting Hill down to Kensington High Street. The School opened in 1958 and was London's first purpose-built comprehensive. Given its wealthy catchment area, it earned the reputation as the 'socialist Eton' in the 1960s after several high-profile figures such as Labour MP Tony Benn chose to send their children there. Past pupils include Oscar-winning actress Anjelica Huston and writer Polly Toynbee. A number of grand houses used to occupy the site of the school however today only the early 19th century ❻ **Thorpe Lodge** remains within the school grounds. This was once the home (from 1904 until his death in 1950) of Montagu Norman, for many years Governor of the Bank of England and a controversial character because of his alleged assistance to the Nazis before WWII.

Across Holland Walk you reach ⑦ **Holland Park**. This superb 54 acre park occupies the former grounds of Holland House, the latter largely destroyed during the Blitz. The old East Wing can still be seen, however, and part of it now serves as a youth hostel. The original Jacobean manor was known as Cope's Castle and was built around 1605 by Sir Walter Cope, a courtier to James I. His ghost is said to haunt the grounds.

When Cope died the house passed to his daughter Isabel, wife of Henry Rich, the 1st Earl of Holland. It was while the house was occupied by the 3rd Baron Holland of Holland (1773-1840), a major figure in Whig politics, that it became a glittering literary and political salon. The poet Lord Byron, Prime Minister Lord Palmerston, and writers such as Charles Dickens and Sir Walter Scott were regular visitors at the lavish gatherings held here.

The best features of the park are the Orangery, the Kyoto Garden and the excellent children's playgrounds. It is also home to the open-air Holland Park Theatre, which often hosts opera (see www.operahollandpark.com for concert details). The Park has a good café so you may wish to stop here for a break after the steep climb uphill.

Leave the park on the south side and walk down Ilchester Place passing the Design Museum. You soon reach **8 Melbury Road**, once the centre of an artists' colony called the *Holland Park Circle* during the 19th century. Stop at the junction to see two grand houses immediately on your right.

The Grade I listed **9 Tower House** is at number 29. It was built in 1877 in a 13th-century French gothic style by the eminent Gothic-revivalist William Burges, described as the greatest of the Victorian 'art-architects'. Burges built the house for his own use. In the 1960s it was bought by the actor Richard Harris who renovated it using the architect's original designs. In 1972 Harris sold the house to the Led Zeppelin legend Jimmy Page, who is said to have outbid David Bowie for the property.

The vast 47-room Woodland House next door (on the corner) was built for **10 Sir Samuel Luke Fildes RA** (1843-1927), a painter and illustrator who was commissioned by Charles Dickens to illustrate *The Mystery of Edwin Drood* (1870). The film director Michael Winner (1935-2013) grew up in the house, bought it from his parents in 1972 and lived there until his death. Regarded as one the best properties in Kensington, it was later purchased by pop star Robbie Williams. In a clash of rock versus pop, Williams and Jimmy Page have engaged in highly-publicised disputes over the Williams's changes to the house.

Continue down Melbury Road and turn right along Holland Park Road. At number 12 is **11 Leighton House Museum**, named after its original occupant the great Victorian painter and sculptor Frederic, Lord Leighton (1830-1896). Leighton was very widely travelled and this is reflected in the design of the interior, particularly the superb Arab Hall which was built to house his dazzling collection of tiles bought in the Middle East.

Leighton was knighted in 1878, and in 1896 became the first painter to be given a peerage – the day before he died. Given Leighton was unmarried, the Barony was extinguished on his death making it the shortest-lasting such honour in the history of the English peerage. The house is now a museum, preserving its spectacular interiors for posterity. It is open Wednesday to Monday (see p.283).

Retrace your steps to Melbury Road and continue south to reach High Street Kensington again. At this point you may wish to visit the former Commonwealth Institute building neglected and unused for many years, but since November 2016 the home of the Design Museum following its move from Shad Thames. The £80 million redevelopment of the site by architect John Pawson has preserved the Grade II listed exterior, but transformed the interior to provide a space worthy of a museum dedicated to design.

Follow the map and head down **12 Edwardes Square**. It covers 3.5 acres and was developed by Frenchman Louis Léon Changeur between 1811-1819. Changeur, as a Frenchman working in London during the height of the Napoleonic wars, had to endure cruel gossips who claimed he was building the Square to house the officers of Napoleon's army in the event of an invasion of England.

An Act of Parliament in 1819 regulated every function within the square, including the requirement that residents sweep outside their houses before 9am every morning or face a fine of 5 shillings. The writer GK Chesterton, author of the *Father Brown* detective stories and *The Napoleon of Notting Hill*, lived at number one in 1901.

11 *Leighton House*

13 Scarsdale Tavern

Head out of the square on the south-east corner past the ⑬ **Scarsdale Tavern**, one of the most atmospheric public houses in Kensington. The name is derived from the Derbyshire estate of the aristocratic Curzon family who owned Scarsdale House in Kensington. The family coat of arms is on the pub's sign.

Follow the map for a few minutes to reach Lexham Gardens. On the north-east corner (between numbers 44 and 48) is a small lane that leads you up to ⑭ **Cornwall Gardens**, typical of the huge white stuccoed mansion blocks that dominate parts of Kensington. Bear left around Cornwall Gardens and shortly head up a tiny lane to Stanford Road. Take a left at St Alban's Grove to walk up Ansdell Street then left again along village-like Thackeray Street to reach ⑮ **Kensington Square**.

This is probably the finest square in the area, and the oldest having been developed in the 1680s. Maps of London in the early 18th century show the square was still adjoined by extensive fields to the south. During this period it became a popular residence for courtiers after Kensington Palace became home to the Royal family.

The philosopher, political economist and MP John Stuart Mill (1806-1873) lived at ⑯ **number 18** between 1837 and 1851. It was here that one of literary history's great disasters happened when Mill's maid accidently used the only manuscript copy of Thomas Carlyle's book *The French Revolution, A History* – to make a fire. Carlyle (1795-1881) had left the manuscript with Mill for his comments, and had kept no research notes. Fortunately the rewritten work was arguably Carlyle's finest single achievement.

The composer Sir Charles Hubert Parry (1848-1918) lived next door at ⑰ **number 17**. Parry is probably best known for the choral

song *Jerusalem*, which is based on William Blake's 1804 poem *Milton*. The song was written by Parry in 1916 when morale in England was low due to the losses of WWI. Blake's poem had become popular after being included in a patriotic anthology of verse and Robert Bridges, the Poet Laureate, asked Parry to put the poem to music. The composer Vaughan Williams (1872-1958) used to come to this house for his music lessons as a boy.

On the south-west corner of the Square is the chapel of the ⑱ **Convent of the Assumption**, a religious order of nuns that has been based here since 1869 and has its origins in a French order founded in Paris in the 19th century. Hidden behind the convent is a large garden that is about the same size as the private garden at the centre of Kensington Square. Both gardens (like many in the area) are closed to the general public.

Walk around the square and head up Young Street. On the left is a Georgian house at ⑲ **number 16** that is now part of a private college but which was once home to the great Victorian writer William Makepeace Thackeray (1811-1863). He wrote part of his most famous work *Vanity Fair* (1848) while living here between 1846 and 1853. Thackeray walked past the house with a publisher after having moved away and remarked 'Down on your knees, you rogue, for here *Vanity Fair* was penned, and I will go down with you, for I have a high opinion of that little production myself'.

It was at this house that Charlotte Brontë came to dinner in May 1850 after having dedicated *Jane Eyre* to Thackeray. However, Thackeray became so bored with the conversation between his guests, who included Thomas Carlyle amongst their number, that he sneaked out and went to his club nearby instead.

Walk back to the Square and on the north-west corner head up Derry Street. Just on the left is the entrance to the **㉗ Kensington Roof Gardens,** one of London's most amazing open spaces. Described as an 'urban oasis in the heart of London', the Gardens stand 100ft above street level and on top of the old 'Derry and Toms' department store. The gardens were laid out in the mid-1930s and cover one-and-a-half acres, offering a fantastic view across London. The garden was Grade II listed in 1998 and remained open to the public until its closure in 2018. Unfortunately, at the time of writing there are no plans to reopen this rare rooftop garden.

20 Sambourne House

Head up Derry Street to reach Kensington High Street. Continue westwards and follow the map to reach Stafford Terrace. At number 18 is ㉑ **Sambourne House**. Built in the 1870s, this was home to the *Punch* cartoonist Edward Linley Sambourne (1844-1910) and his family from 1874. After Sambourne's death the house was left undisturbed by his family and came into the hands of Anne Messel, whose son Antony Armstrong-Jones married Princess Margaret in 1960 and was created Earl of Snowdon.

Anne helped found the Victorian Society and under its sponsorship the house was opened to public in 1980. The house is now run by the council with each room providing a fascinating insight into the life of a prosperous Victorian family. The highlight of any visit is Sambourne's studio with many of his cartoons, illustrations and photographs on display.

Follow the map back to Kensington High Street where the walk ends. ●

VISIT...

Design Museum (see p.276)
224-238 Kensington High Street, W8 6AG
www.designmuseum.org

Leighton House (see p.276)
12 Holland Park Road, W14 8LZ
www.rbkc.gov.uk/museums

Sambourne House
18 Stafford Terrace, W8 7BH
www.rbkc.gov.uk/museums

EAT, DRINK...

Holland Park Café
Holland Park, W8 6LU

Scarsdale Tavern (see p.279)
23a Edwardes Square, W8 6HE
www.scarsdaletavern.co.uk/

Café Le Monde
56 Earl's Court Road, W8 6EJ

The Orangery
Kensington Gardens, W8 4PX
ww.hrp.org.uk

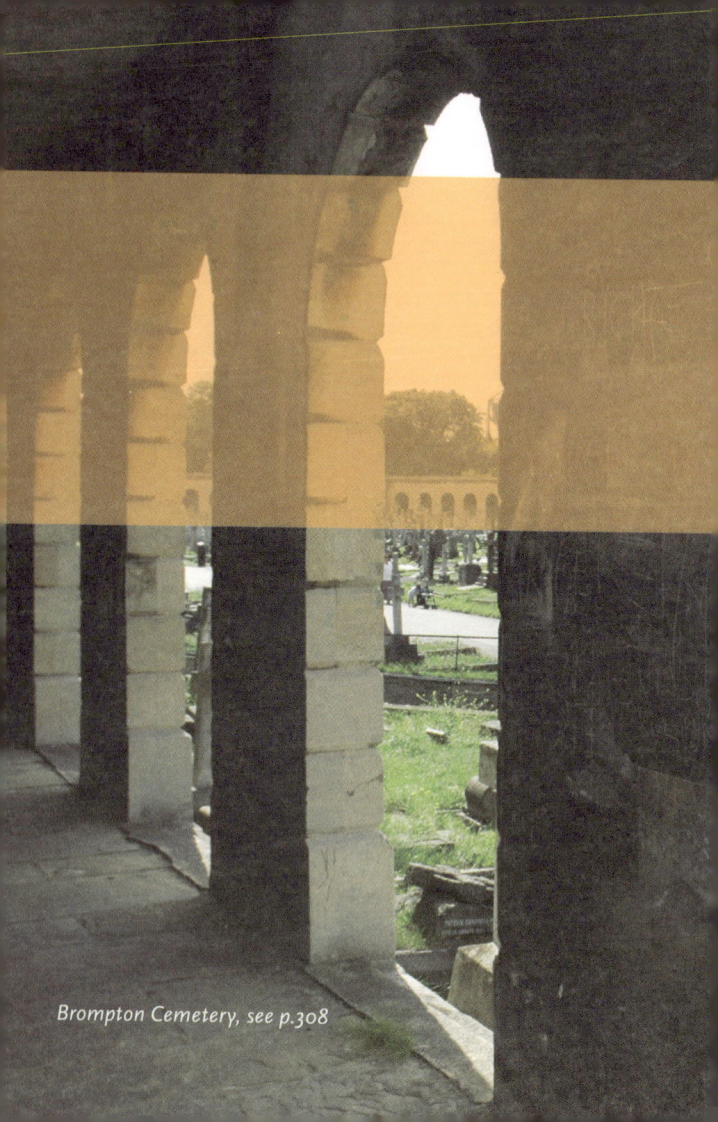
Brompton Cemetery, see p.308

10 Chelsea & Brompton Cemetery Walk

1 Sloane Square tube station
2 Royal Court Theatre
3 The Royal Hospital Chelsea
4 Ranelagh Gardens
5 Chillianwallah Memorial obelisk
6 Outlet of the Westbourne
7 Oscar Wilde residence
8 Chelsea Physic Garden
9 Number 3
10 Number 4
11 Number 10
12 Number 14
13 Number 16
14 Number 21
15 Henry VIII's plaque
16 Numbers 38 and 39
17 Number 48
18 Thomas Carlyle's House

19 Number 16
20 Number 50
21 Carlyle Mansions
22 Chelsea Old Church
23 Roper's Gardens
24 Crosby Moran Hall
25 Number 93
26 Numbers 96-100
27 Number 104
28 Numbers 118-119
29 Number 120
30 World's End Estate
31 Cremorne Gardens
32 Lot's Road Power Station
33 Brompton Cemetery
34 Number 488
35 Number 430
36 Moravian burial ground

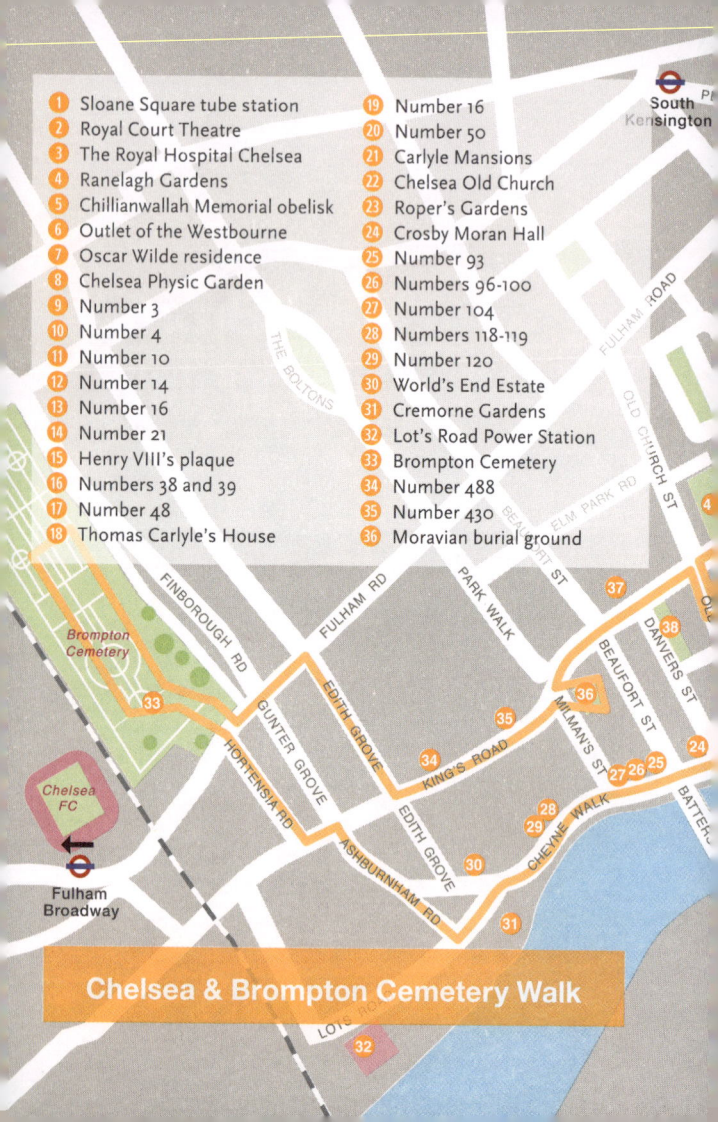

South Kensington

THE BOLTONS

FULHAM ROAD

OLD CHURCH ST

Brompton Cemetery

FINBOROUGH RD

FULHAM RD

PARK WALK

ELM PARK RD

BEAUFORT ST

DANVERS ST

37

38

GUNTER GROVE

EDITH GROVE

36

BEAUFORT ST

MILMAN'S ST

35

HORTENSIA RD

KING'S ROAD

34

27 26 25

24

Chelsea FC

28

29

CHEYNE WALK

BATTE

Fulham Broadway

ASHBURNHAM RD

EDITH GROVE

30

31

Chelsea & Brompton Cemetery Walk

LOTS RD

32

Map labels (streets and locations):

DRAYCOTT AVE
SLOANE AVE
CADOGAN ST
PAVILION RD
SLOANE ST
EATON GATE
Sloane Square
Sloane Square
BOURNE ST
IXWORTH PL
SLOANE AVE
DRAYCOTT PLACE
CULFORD GDNS
DRAYCOTT AVE
HOLBEIN PL
King's Road
LWR SLOANE ST
Saatchi Gallery
PIMLICO RD
CALE ST
ELYSTAN PL
GODFREY ST
MARKHAM ST
ROYAL AVE
FRANKLIN'S ROW
CHELSEA BRIDGE RD
St Luke's Gardens
BRITTEN ST
SMITH ST
Burton Court
London Gate
Royal Hospital Chelsea
Ranelagh Gardens
TEDWORTH SQ
FLOOD ST
ROYAL HOSPITAL ROAD
WEST RD
S ROAD
OAKLEY STREET
CHEYNE GDNS
Royal Hospital Road
THE ST
Embankment Gardens
EBE'Y ...
CHEYNE ROW
SWAN WALK
DILKE ST
CHELSEA EMBANKMENT
CHEYNE WLK
RIVER THAMES
BATTERSEA PARK

Legend:

- 37 Bluebird restaurant
- 38 Paultons Square
- 39 Old Rectory
- 40 Sound Techniques studio
- 41 Carlyle Square
- 42 Number 50
- 43 Turner Studios
- 44 Charles Rennie Mackintosh building
- 45 Numbers 213 and 215
- 46 Dovehouse Green
- 47 St Luke's Church
- 48 Numbers 232-42
- 49 Chelsea Old Town Hall
- 50 Chelsea Manor Studios
- 51 Number 127
- 52 The Pheasantry
- 53 Markham Square
- 54 Number 9
- 55 30 Wellington Square
- 56 Chelsea Drugstore
- 57 Royal Avenue
- 58 Cheltenham Terrace
- 59 Saatchi Gallery
- 60 Holy Trinity Sloane Square

Chelsea and Brompton Cemetery Walk

Start/Finish: Sloane Square underground station
Distance: 6.7 miles

The tour starts on the eastern edge of Chelsea at ① **Sloane Square tube station**. Before you exit the station look up to see a metal pipe running high above the platforms. Within this is contained the River Westbourne – one of London's 'lost' rivers – which has now been covered over and largely forgotten. The Westbourne originates in Hampstead and flows southwards near Kilburn through Maida Vale and into Hyde Park. It then continues under Knightsbridge and Chelsea before reaching the Thames (where its outflow can be seen later). If you could be transported back to 1750 and looked out over what is now Sloane Square, you would see the Westbourne flowing from north to south across the open fields, briefly going underneath what would become known as the King's Road. There also used to be a cricket pitch here.

Peter Llewelyn Davies (b.1897) – one of five brothers who inspired J.M Barrie to create his famous character Peter Pan – committed suicide by jumping in front of a train at this station on 5th April, 1960. Barrie first met the Llewelyn Davies boys by chance in Kensington Gardens in 1897 and soon became a family friend. After the boys' parents died Barrie became their guardian; however, his relationship with them became strained as they grew up and he left them nothing in his will. Peter Llewelyn Davies, given his first name, was most closely associated by the public with Peter Pan. However he grew to resent what he called Barrie's *'terrible masterpiece'*. He became an alcoholic and on the night he died he spent time drinking at the bar of the Royal Court Hotel (now Sloane Square Hotel) nearby.

Leave the station and enter Sloane Square – named after Sir Hans Sloane (1660-1753) who purchased the Manor of Chelsea in

1712. You will see on your right the ❷ **Royal Court Theatre**, which is one of the best theatres outside the West End and was where John Osborne's groundbreaking play *Look Back in Anger* was premiered in 1956.

Chelsea extends from the World's End in the west to Sloane Square in the east, and from the Thames north to the Fulham Road. Its name may have originated from Saxon times when there was a chalk wharf (or *cealchyoe*) situated near the river. For many centuries Chelsea remained an isolated fishing village located beside the Thames where Chelsea Old Church stands today. However, during the Tudor period it became a fashionable country retreat for London's wealthier classes, particularly after Sir Thomas More and Henry VIII built mansions here.

Chelsea became known as the 'the village of palaces', although the lack of road connections to London delayed the area's urbanisation. This changed in the 17th century when Charles II built the famous King's Road that allowed him to pass quickly through West London to reach

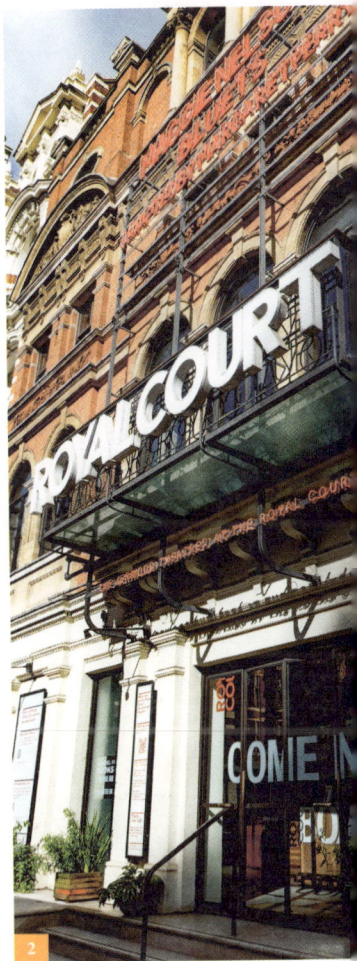

the countryside. Although it remained a private road until 1830, Chelsea was now connected to the rest of London and began to be developed for urban living.

Walk down Lower Sloane Street and then Royal Hospital Road to admire the impressive façade of ❸ **The Royal Hospital Chelsea**. One of London's finest buildings, it was founded by Charles II for his retired soldiers. The hospital was designed by Sir Christopher Wren and based upon the Hôtel des Invalides for French veterans in Paris. Wren also designed Greenwich Hospital which looked after veteran sailors for 170 years until 1869. According to tradition Nell Gwynn – the King's mistress – felt such sympathy for the destitute old soldiers and sailors she saw in London's streets that she persuaded Charles to sponsor the project.

❸ The Royal Hospital Chelsea

To be eligible as a Pensioner you must be a former non-commissioned officer or soldier in the British Army and aged over 65, with no dependants. On entering the hospital a Pensioner's army pension is swapped for board, lodging and clothes, and aside from obeying the hospital rules the men are free to come and go as they please. In 2009 women were permitted to join the ranks of the Chelsea Pensioners for the first time.

The hospital is only open to the public by guided tour when visitors can explore the three main courtyards including Figure Court with its famous gilded statue of Charles II dressed as a Roman emperor, that is the work of renowned Baroque sculptor, Grinling Gibbons. A tour also gives a chance to see the Great Hall, the museum and the chapel, as well as the outside grounds. Access is now only via the London Gate entrance (see p.321).

The hospital shop and museum are all accessed through London gate and are open daily, usually manned by one of the Pensioners who are a great source of information and anecdotes about life at the Hospital. In the grounds the batteries of cannon on display include some captured at Waterloo in 1815. There is also a memorial to the vicious battle between the British and the Sikhs at Chillianwallah in 1849. Since 1913 the RHS Chelsea Flower Show has been held annually on the South Grounds.

Regardless of whether you take the tour it is at the end of East Road that you access ④ **Ranelagh Gardens.** This quiet, almost forgotten park was the site of one of the capital's most famous pleasure gardens in the 18th century. Its central feature was the sadly now demolished rotunda, which could hold 600 people and was based upon the Pantheon in Rome. The entertainments on offer attracted the cream of London society and the rotunda was immortalised in a painting by Canaletto (now in The National Gallery of Art Washington DC, USA).

1849

5

Historian Edward Gibbon thought the gardens 'the most convenient place for courtships of every kind – the best market we have in England', while Horace Walpole remarked 'the floor is all of beaten princes ... you can't set your foot without treading on a Prince or a Duke of Cumberland'.

Wolfgang Amadeus Mozart (1756-91) played a charity concert here on 29 June 1764 during his short residence in London. The great romancer Giacomo Casanova (1725-1798) also lived in London during the 1760s, and recorded in his memoirs that he went to the gardens 'intending to amuse myself till midnight, and to find a beauty to my taste'.

After exploring the gardens retrace your steps along East Road, making sure to look out for the imposing ⑤ **Chillianwallah Memorial obelisk** dating from 1853. The Memorial commemorates the 1849 battle during the Second Sikh War. The granite obelisk lists the 251 soldiers of the 14th Light Regiment who lost their lives in the bloody battle. The casualties on both sides were much greater than commemorated here, and the battle was a major dent in the prestige of British forces in the Punjab.

Within the grounds of the hospital are interred the ashes of Britain's first female Prime Minister Margaret Thatcher (1925-2013). Her simple burial stone is a regular site of homage for Tory MPs seeking to claim her legacy.

Follow the map heading south on Chelsea Bridge Road and take a right onto Chelsea Embankment. When parallel with the Chillianwallah Memorial, cross over the busy road to reach the southern wall. Look over the wall and you will see the ⑥ **outlet of the Westbourne**. If the tide is out you can get a better view by using some stairs about 150 yards to the west.

293

Cross back onto the northern side of Chelsea Embankment and head westwards to begin an exploration of a small number of streets that have been inhabited by perhaps London's greatest concentration of artists, politicians and intellectuals over the centuries. The Chelsea Embankment was constructed by Joseph Bazalgette in 1874 and built upon land reclaimed from the river. It reduced the Thames to a regular width of about 700 feet.

By this time Chelsea's days as a fishing village were long over. During the 19th century Chelsea developed a bohemian reputation, attracting artists and intellectuals such as JM Whistler, JMW Turner, Oscar Wilde, Henry James, Mark Twain and Thomas Carlyle. Many of them were attracted by the reasonable rents and elegant buildings best illustrated by the early 18th-century Queen Anne houses of Cheyne Walk. Painters were also drawn to the clear light and splendid views over the Thames.

Head up Tite Street, whose most famous resident was ⑦ **Oscar Wilde**. The writer and poet lived in the tall but rather unassuming red-brick house at number 34. He lived here between

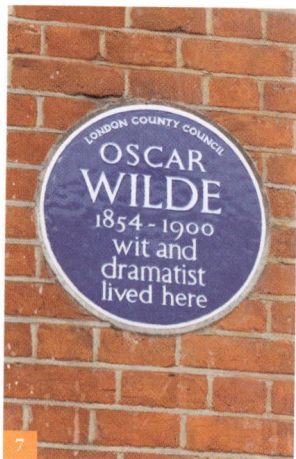

1884 and 1895 with his family and wrote much of his best work at the house, including *The Importance of Being Earnest* and *The Picture of Dorian Grey*. However, it was also a place that featured in his downfall: he met his future lover Lord Alfred Douglas – or 'Bosie' – at a dinner party here in 1884.

Bosie's father, the Marquess of Queensberry, was disgusted by the relationship. While it is well known that Queensberry left a calling card for Wilde at his club accusing the writer of being a *somdomite* [sic] – an act that provoked Wilde's libel action, which ultimately led to his downfall – the Marquess also came to Tite Street to confront Wilde. Wilde recalled in a letter to Lord Douglas how the Marquess stood 'in my library in Tite Street, waving his small hands in the air in epileptic fury'. Wilde was later imprisoned for gross indecency and forced to sell his house to help pay his legal costs. His trial judge was also a neighbour in Tite Street.

Other famous 19th-century residents in this street included painters Augustus John, John Singer Sargent and James McNeill Whistler. The latter lived briefly at number 35 (now demolished), but the costs of building it, combined with legal fees the artist incurred during a libel action against the Victorian critic John Ruskin, resulted in Whistler's bankruptcy in 1879 and he was forced to sell the property. Ruskin had reviewed Whistler's work – *Nocture in Black and Gold: The Falling Rocket* – which captured a firework display that took place in Crenmorne Gardens (seen later). The critic acidly remarked that he 'never expected to hear a coxcomb ask two hundred guineas for flinging a pot of paint in the public's face'.

Head back down Tite Street and right along Dilke Street, bearing left until you see the back wall of the ❽ **Chelsea Physic Garden** (main entrance on Royal Hospital Road). The second oldest botanical garden in Britain, it was established by the Worshipful Society of Apothecaries in 1673. In 1722 Sir Hans Sloane donated the freehold to the Company in return for a promise they would donate 2,000 dried plants annually to the Royal Society. A statue of Sloane stands in the middle of the garden. In addition to giving his name to various parts of London, he also found time to invent

milk chocolate and collect an impressive number of fine artefacts that would later form the basis of the original British Museum collection.

The Apothecaries were particularly interested in the science of botany for medicinal purposes – the word *'physic'* relates to the science of healing. The society founded the four-acre garden – closed to the public until 1983 – near the Thames as it offered fresh river air and good light. It contains 5,000 species of plant and includes the largest fruiting olive tree in Britain and the world's northernmost grapefruit growing outdoors. The pond rock garden dates from 1773 and is both the oldest rock garden open to the public in England, and one of the most unusual structures to attain Grade II listed status.

The Garden's greatest contribution to botany was its global seed exchange programme, which included sending the first cottonseed to Georgia in the USA. It is therefore partly responsible for starting America's long and often controversial association with the cotton fields. The programme was also responsible for the worldwide spread of the Madagascar Periwinkle, and India's huge tea industry can also trace part of its origins back to curator Robert Fortune's transport of Chinese tea plant seedlings to India in 1848. Today the garden is not just a museum, but continues to host research activities. Visiting times are from 11am-5pm, Sunday to Friday (www.chelseaphysicgarden.co.uk).

⑧ *Chelsea Physic Garden*

From the Garden continue westwards until you see the entrance to Cheyne Walk (pronounced *'chainey'*). Continue along Cheyne Walk, the epitome of Chelsea 'cool' where even flats built amongst the mainly 18th-century houses routinely sell for more than £10 million. It has also been home to a significant number of famous Londoners, from kings to painters, the most notable including the following:

9 **Number 3** – Rolling Stone Keith Richards between 1969-78, where he lived with Anita Pallenberg – actor John Barrymore also lived here. **10** **Number 4** – George Eliot, author of *Middlemarch* and *Mill on the Floss* lived here briefly before her death in 1880. At **11** **Number 10** politician and Prime Minister David Lloyd George lived, while at **Number 13** composer Ralph Vaughan Williams lived and wrote *Fantasia on a Theme by Thomas Tallis* and *The Lark Ascending*. **12** **Number 14** was where Bertrand Russell lived for two years from 1902 while writing *The Principles of Mathematics*. **13** **Number 16** – Dante Gabriel Rossetti, one of the most original poets and painters of the Victorian age lived here between 1862 and 1882 with a bizarre collection of exotic animals including a zebra and a kangaroo. Poet Algernon Swinburne lived here briefly amid the domestic chaos.

14 **Number 21** was inhabited at different times by painter James McNeill Whistler (who also lived at numbers 96 and 101). In 1871 he painted a picture of his mother – entitled *'Arrangement in Black and White'* – while living at number 96. Now one of the most famous paintings in the world, it can be found in the Musée d'Orsay in Paris. **Numbers 19-26** – site of Henry VIII's Manor House of 1536, later lived in by Sir Hans Sloane after he bought the Manor of Chelsea in 1712. It was finally demolished

in 1753 and the present houses built soon afterwards. Henry gave the house to his last wife Katherine Parr as a wedding present, and Elizabeth I lived here for a while. As a 14 year old, she allegedly had to fight off the advances of Parr's new husband Sir Thomas Seymour.

At the corner of Cheyne Walk and Cheyne Mews you can see a ⑮ **small plaque** that commemorates Henry's manor and describes how part of his former garden lies behind the end wall of the Mews, said to contain some mulberry trees planted by Elizabeth herself. **Number 27** – *Dracula* author Bram Stoker lived here in the 1880s. He wrote a book partly set in Cheyne Walk entitled *Miss Betty* (1898). ⑯ **Numbers 38 and 39** – was built in 1899 by Charles Robert Ashbee, an influential designer and leading figure within the Arts & Craft movement of the late 19th and early 20th century. ⑰ **Number 48** – home to Rolling Stone Mick Jagger between 1968 and 1978, and where the police mounted a famous drugs raid in 1969. Jagger lived here with Marianne Faithfull and later with his wife Bianca.

For an interesting detour follow the map north to ⑱ **Thomas Carlyle's House** at number 24 Cheyne Row. Now a National Trust property, this is probably the only chance most people will get to see inside a superb Chelsea house. Carlyle (1795-1881) is now a largely forgotten figure, but in the 19th century he was revered. A dour Scottish essayist, historian and satirist, he translated Goethe into English, and wrote the influential *The History of the French Revolution*.

The History was published despite the sole original manuscript being accidentally burnt by John Stuart Mill's maid, forcing Carlyle to start again from scratch as he had already destroyed his writing notes. The Scot lived here from 1834 until his death. His long-suffering wife Jane lived with him here for over 30 years, often struggling to cope with her famously difficult husband who once wrote in his journal of being 'strangely preoccupied by thoughts of life as a continual nightmare, of an awakening in hell, of a wife who bore devils'. He wrote to Jane when he first found the house, noting 'Chelsea is unfashionable; it was once the resort of the Court and the great, however, hence numerous old houses in it, at once cheap and excellent'. John Ruskin, Alfred Lord Tennyson and Charles Dickens were among the regular visitors here, Dickens remarking 'I would go at all times farther to see Carlyle than any man alive'. Throughout his entire residence Carlyle's rent remained at £35 per annum.

Today the museum shows the house as it would have appeared to Carlyle while he lived here from 1834 until his death, and contains many of his original possessions. The house is open by appointment every Wednesday from mid-March to the end of October, you can check dates and book your visit on the National Trust website.

After Carlyle's House continue along Cheyne Row, then Upper Cheyne Row until you reach Lawrence Street. Among the charming terrace houses you will see a blue plaque outside ⑲ **number 16**

commemorating this as the site of Chelsea's once famous 18th-century porcelain china industry that was founded by Huguenot Nicholas Sprimont. The current houses are built on the site of the now-demolished factories, and pieces of porcelain still turn up in local gardens. The industry was eventually moved to Derby and Chelsea's flirtation with hard artisan graft was over. The plaque also records that Tobias Smollett (1721-1771), author of *The Adventures of Peregrine Pickle* (1753), once lived here.

Continue down Lawrence Street to rejoin Cheyne Walk, passing the Cross Keys pub, on your right. Turn left to find **20** **Number 50** – now a brasserie and formerly the King's Head and Eight Bells public house. They were originally two separate pubs that merged in 1580. It was popular with a bohemian set in the 1950s, including (inevitably) poet Dylan Thomas. It was also allegedly the local for Henry VIII, who drank in the King's Head whilst his lesser courtiers had to make do with the Eight Bells. John le Carré's fictional spy George Smiley drank here.

Retrace your steps passing **21** **Carlyle Mansions** (situated between numbers 50 and 60). It was named after nearby resident Thomas Carlyle. Past residents have included Bond creator Ian Fleming, poet T.S. Eliot (who shared number 19 with noted literary editor John Hayward), and Henry James (number 21) who lived and died here in 1916. Fleming, with typical panache, wrote his first Bond book *Casino Royale* (1952) here on a gold-plated typewriter.

You will now come to ㉒ **Chelsea Old Church** (All Saints) on your right. The church is closely associated with one of London's few saints, Sir Thomas More (1478-1535). His now-demolished Beaufort House occupied a 34-acre site just to the west of the church, and was influential in establishing Chelsea as a place where the rich and well-connected aspired to live. More, who used to sing in the church choir and even rebuilt the south chapel for his own use, lived in Beaufort House from 1524 until his death. A sombre statue of him staring towards the Thames can be seen outside.

This saint, lawyer, statesman, philosopher and writer served as Lord Chancellor to Henry VIII. He initially assisted his king in the difficult break with Rome, but they later fell out and More was beheaded after being convicted of high treason. His last days of freedom were spent with his family at Beaufort House.

The church dates back to 1157, although was heavily rebuilt after extensive damage during the Blitz. More's south chapel survives, as does the tomb of his first wife. Poet and clergyman John Donne preached here in 1625, having fled the plague-infested City, and there is a memorial to writer Henry James whose funeral took place in the church in 1916. Sir Hans Sloane (see above) was buried here in 1753 and a monument to him can be found in the churchyard. It is also thought Henry VIII may have married Jane Seymour in the church in 1536 in advance of the state ceremony.

Outside the church are the small modern ㉓ **Roper's Gardens**, commemorating land given by More as a marriage gift to his

daughter Margaret and her husband William Roper. Margaret was a good daughter, and after her father's head had been displayed to the public on a long spike she bought it and preserved the grim relic in spices. It is said that More's head was buried alongside his daughter when she died aged only 39. Her husband William cemented More's reputation by writing the first biography of his famous father-in-law.

Continue west past Chelsea's oldest street, Old Church Street, until you see **24** **Crosby Moran Hall** on the right. This building has a very unusual history, incorporating a medieval Great Hall that was built for Sir John Crosby in 1466 as part of his mansion – Crosby Place – on Bishopsgate in the City. Crosby was a prominent City alderman and MP who was knighted in 1471 by Edward IV, and also served as Mayor of Calais. After his death Crosby Hall was occupied by Richard, Duke of Gloucester, who later became Richard III.

The Bishopsgate building was later owned by Sir Thomas More in the 1530s, a curious coincidence given that today the hall stands on the site of More's Chelsea mansion. Another coincidence is that William Shakespeare mentions Crosby Place three times in *Richard III*, most likely because of the tradition that Richard was

offered the crown there, and the playwright would have relied on More's own *History of Richard III* for the factual content of the play. In the early 1600s the Hall became the headquarters for the East India Company that would soon govern much of India.

The hall was moved to Chelsea in the early 20th century after the Bishopsgate mansion was demolished as part of a road-widening scheme. Today Crosby Hall – which More, Richard III and Shakespeare would all have known – is a private residence owned by insurance millionaire Christopher Moran. He is reported to have spent more than £25 million restoring the property.

Continue along Cheyne Row to 25 **Number 93** – where Elizabeth Gaskell, author of *Mary Barton* and *North and South*, was born.

26 **Numbers 96-100** – originally all part of Lindsey House, possibly the oldest house in Chelsea. It dates from 1674 and is named after one of its earlier owners, Robert 3rd Earl of Lindsey. In the early 19th century part of the house (now number 98) became home to engineers Sir Marc Brunel and son Isambard Kingdom Brunel. In 1966 an apartment within Lindsey House was owned by antiques dealer and socialite Christopher Gibbs, whose parties were attended by the wealthy bohemian Chelsea set, rock stars and counterculture leaders. In April 1966 perhaps the most unlikely and radical BBC programme ever was filmed here – free LSD (then still legal) was given out to a group of London counterculture figures and the results filmed.

Later that year the director Michelangelo Antonioni, perhaps inspired by the BBC programme, used the house for the wild party scene in the cult film *Blow Up*.

㉗ **Number 104** – home to writer and MP Hilaire Belloc, and also painter Walter Graves.

㉘ **Numbers 118-119** – where painter JMW Turner died in 1851, after living here largely anonymously for five years. Before he died, and at the height of his fame, hardly anyone knew that the resident calling himself 'Admiral Booth' was England's greatest living painter. He left thousands of his works to the nation and these are now housed in the Clore Gallery extension to the Tate Gallery. Ian Fleming also lived here with his mother Eve, from 1923 to 1936 and it is perhaps a surprise to discover that the creator of the ultra-macho 007 lived with his mother until his late twenties. Eve had a passionate affair with neighbour and painter Augustus John during the 1920s.

㉙ **Number 120** – home to Sylvia Pankhurst, women's rights campaigner.

Continue west passing the seven dispiriting towers of the ㉚ **World's End Estate** to your right. The Clash's Joe Strummer lived on the estate, where he wrote – *London Calling* – with its line 'London is drowning and I live by the river'. Look out for the village of houseboats on the Thames – each one typically costs more than £300,000 although some exceed £1 million. Floating celebrity residents have included Laurence Olivier, Nick Cave and Damien Hirst.

Leave Cheyne Walk to follow Lots Road on the left. By the Thames are the modern **31** **Cremorne Gardens** – originally part of pleasure gardens of the same name that occupied this site between 1843 and 1877 and immortalised in a number of paintings by Whistler. In 1861 a tightrope walker known as Madam Blondin walked between Battersea Bridge and Cremore Gardens watched by 20,000 people. The gardens extended from the river all the way north to King's Road – hard to imagine now given the garden's modest size, although you can at least see the vast gates that once stood on the King's Road entrance. Before the gardens were laid out, this area was public fields known as 'Common Lots', where cattle could graze.

Ahead looms the gigantic **32** **Lot's Road Power Station**. Opened in 1905, it was once the world's largest power station. It supplied electricity for the London Underground before closing in 2002. The site has been redeveloped for multi-million pound luxury apartments.

Walking towards the power station take a right at Ashburnham Road, walking north until you reach the King's Road. At this point you can visit the magnificent Brompton Cemetery or if you prefer a shorter route, you can continue east along King's Road to pick up the walk further along.

To visit Brompton Cemetery, follow the map up Hortensia Road to Fulham Road. Cross over and head east. On your left you will see the Cemetery's southern entrance.

Brompton Cemetery – a 40-acre site consecrated in 1840 and originally privately owned – is arguably central London's finest cemetery. The railway line that today runs along the western edge was built directly on the filled-in Kensington Canal. The cemetery is tremendously atmospheric and you can spend hours looking at the 35,000 monuments that date from the 19th and early 20th centuries. It is still occasionally used for burials to this day.

Notable people buried here include: **Samuel Baker** – founder of Sotheby's auction house. **Henry Cole** – founder of the Victoria and Albert Museum, the Royal Albert Hall and the Great Exhibition of 1851, and inventor of the Christmas card. **Samuel Cunard** – founder of the Cunard shipping line. **Lone Wolf** – Sioux Indian chief. **Henry Augustus Mears** – founder of Chelsea Football Club. **Emmeline Pankhurst** – suffragette. **John Snow** – anaesthesiologist and epidemiologist who demonstrated the link between cholera and infected water. **Sir Andrew Scot Waugh** – British army officer and surveyor who named the world's highest mountain after Sir George Everest. **John Wisden** –founder of the famous cricketers' almanac named after him. Brompton also contains the graves of thirteen holders of the Victorian Cross, and a number of Chelsea Pensioners.

Standing in the shadow of Chelsea football club at Stamford Bridge, the cemetery is full of birdsong and squirrels and is well worth a visit. Its unusual atmosphere inspired writer Beatrix Potter who lived nearby in Kensington in the 1860s. She often used to walk here and is believed to have used a number of names seen on gravestones for characters in her books, including Mr Nutkins, Mr McGregor, Jeremiah Fisher, Tommy Brock and Peter

33 Brompton Cemetery

Rabbett. The cemetery is open from 8:00 to 20:00 in the summer and 8:00 to 16:00 in the winter.

Leave the cemetery and follow the map to get back to King's Road, then head east. You will notice that the shops become increasingly more upmarket the further you go. Continue along King's Road, with the towers of the World's End estate on the right. On the north side almost opposite look out for ㉞ **number 488**. This was once home to one of London's – if not the world's – most influential fashion boutiques – Granny Takes a Trip. Opened in 1966, the boutique epitomised the Swinging Sixties.

During its heyday, the author Salman Rushdie lived above the boutique. When models were posing in front of the boutique during fashion shoots, he used to earn extra money by charging the photographers to take shots out of his bedroom window.

A decade later the original punks flocked to ㉟ **Number 430** on the left-hand side (look out for the distinctive clock at the front). This store was owned by fashion designer Vivienne Westwood, and is where she and Malcolm McLaren helped launch the British Punk movement when they opened the Let it Rock boutique in 1971. Relaunched as Sex in 1974, and renamed

Seditionaries two years later, the shop was where Johnny Rotten auditioned for the Sex Pistols and the Pretenders' Chrissie Hynde used to work.

Continue until you stop on the right-hand side at the junction with Milman's Street. Near the top of this street – through a small door in the wall – you reach one of London's strangest places: the ㊱ **Moravian burial ground and chapel** that is open on Fridays and Sundays (www. moravianchurchchelsea.com).

A Moravian church was established here on the site of the former stables of Sir Thomas More's Beaufort House, and around 400 people have been buried in the plot since 1751. The headstones are set flat in the earth and married men, women, and single men and women, are each confined to their own quarter. The Moravians believe strongly in equality in death, explaining why the gravestones are exactly the same size.

Continue eastwards along King's Road. You pass Beaufort Street, which stands on the old entrance road to Thomas More's Beaufort House. You then past the distinctive art deco frontage of the 37 **Bluebird restaurant** complex founded by Sir Terence Conran (1931-2020). This building dates from 1923 when the first occupant was the Bluebird Motor Company. Shortly on the right stop to look at 38 **Paultons Square** an excellent example of the kind of grand square developed in Chelsea during the 1830s. Notable past residents include writers Gavin Maxwell and Samuel Beckett, and artist Augustus John.

Soon you reach Old Church Street, which bisects King's Road. Just a short way down the southern part of Old Church Street you will find on the left-hand side, at number 56, the 39 **Old Rectory** which dates from the late 18th century. This was originally the rectory of St Luke's parish church, but today is a very desirable private residence This is partly on account of its 2.5 acre garden – one of the largest private gardens in central London.

Walk down Old Church Street to see at 46A (down a little alley) the location from 1965-76 of 🔟 **Sound Techniques studio**. Under producer Joe Boyd, one of the leading counterculture figures of the era, a number of bands recorded here including Nick Drake, Fairport Convention and Pink Floyd (who recorded the early singles *See Emily Play* and *Arnold Layne* here). Look out for the beautiful wall tiles on the outside of the building that depict the building's origins as a dairy in the early 19th century.

Head back to King's Road, and cross over along the northern part of Old Church Street. **Number 111** was where the Secret Intelligence Service (SIS) trained agents from Latvia, Lithuania and Estonia during WWII. Take the first left along Mallord Street. This was where AA Milne (1882-1956) wrote *Winnie the Pooh* (1926) while living at number 13. His son and inspiration for the book was Christopher Robin who was born in the house in 1920. Like Peter Llewelyn Davies, Christopher resented his association with a classic children's tale and remarked 'It seemed to me almost that my father had got where he was by climbing on my infant shoulders, that he had filched from me my good name and left me nothing but empty fame'.

You will have noticed that a large number of buildings in Chelsea are quite unusual and individualistic in their design – illustrative of the terrific confidence (and usually wealth) of its residents over the centuries. By way of example look out for the wall tiles at the start of Mallord Street, and the huge swans high up on the building as you walk back to connect with Old Church Street.

Follow the map from Old Church Street to enter **41** **Carlyle Square** – worth a walk around before continuing on along King's Road. You will also notice that nearly all the well-tended gardens within Chelsea's exclusive squares are for residents only. The next road on the left is Manresa Road where poet Dylan Thomas lived with his wife Caitlin from 1942 to 1944 and where their child Aeron was born. The block of flats they lived in has now been demolished.

Head down Glebe Place. This is worth a visit just to see the ostentatious Mediterranean baroque building at **42** **number 50** at the far end – built in the 1980s for the advertising pioneer Sir Frank Lowe. The street is full of distinctive buildings including **43** **Turner Studios** at numbers 68-70. **44** **Number 49** is the only building in London designed by Charles Rennie Mackintosh, who was living in Chelsea at the time after the failure of his architecture practice in Glasgow.

313

43

45

46

Back on King's Road, continue east and look out for ㊺ **numbers 213 and 215** on the right-hand side where, respectively, film director Carol Reed (*The Third Man*, *Oliver!*) and Thomas Arne (who wrote *Rule Britannia* in the 18th century) used to live. Judy Garland rented Carol Reed's house in 1960 and Arne's house was later occupied by actress Ellen Terry and after that by Peter Ustinov.

Garland's time at number 213 was possibly one of the last relatively happy periods in her life. Nine years later – a hopeless addict and her health in tatters – she married her fifth husband Micky Deans in the Chelsea Registry Office (see p.315). Just a few months later she died of an overdose at another house in Chelsea (4 Cadogan Lane).

On the north side look out for ㊻ **Dovehouse Green** and cross through it diagonally to the north-east corner. You are now in the heart of an enormously prosperous district, although in the 1860s this area was the site of the St Luke's Workhouse and burial ground. A number of old gravestones and monuments can be seen.

Continue along King's Road to reach Sydney Street and head north towards the spire of ㊼ **St Luke's Church** that dominates the skyline. Built in the 1820s, this was one of the first neo-Gothic Victorian churches to be built in England, and 2,500 people could sit within what remains the tallest nave of any London parish church. The size accounts for its nickname of 'Chelsea's Cathedral', and it was chosen by Charles Dickens as the place where he married 20-year-old local girl Catherine Hogarth in 1836. His best man Thomas Beard described the ceremony as 'a very quiet piece of business'. Film buffs might recognise the church from the Disney film *101 Dalmatians* (1996). It was used as the setting for the marriage of the two main characters played by Jeff Daniels and Joely Richardson. In the film the happy couple were soon joined by 100 dogs.

Return along Sydney Street to the junction with King's Road. The north-east corner **48** **numbers 232-42** was once the site of the Chelsea Palace of Varieties – a music hall that opened in 1903. It later become a studio owned by Granada and perhaps its finest moment came in 1959 when, shortly before her death, the great American singer Billie Holiday performed here on the 'Chelsea at Nine' programme singing classics such as *Porgy* and *Strange Fruit*.

On the south side you see the imposing frontage of **49** **Chelsea Old Town Hall**. Dating from the 1880s, this contains a library, two halls and on the eastern side, the Chelsea Registry Office. Look out for the drinking trough set into the wall – set up by the Metropolitan Drinking Fountain and Cattle Trough Association. The Association was founded in 1859 to provide public drinking water for humans and animals in the last few decades before motor traffic replaced horses and domestic water supply became the norm.

As mentioned earlier Judy Garland was married here in 1969, as were Roman Polanski and Sharon Tate (1968) and Mrs Wallis Simpson (1928). Both Garland and Tate died in tragic circumstances in 1969 – Garland after an overdose, while Tate was a victim of Charles Manson and his gang.

Continue east until reaching Flood Street on the right. It was at number 4 50 **Chelsea Manor Studios**, 1-11 Flood Street (on the right-hand side), that the Beatles' *Sgt. Pepper's Lonely Hearts Club Band* album cover was shot by photographer Michael Cooper on March 30, 1967. The 'fab four' stood patiently for three hours amongst a collage of life-size cardboard cut-outs of people the band admired. The design was the work of Pop artist Peter Blake, who only received a single payment for his iconic image. Margaret Thatcher and family lived at number 19 from 1967 until she entered Downing Street (the house was sold in 1985). Look out for more glazed wall tiles at the corner as you return to King's Road.

Continue east looking out for 51 **number 127** on the right-hand side. Until 2009 the Picasso Café was to be found here, opened in 1958 by the Barbieri family during the Italian coffee bar boom. It became a favourite over the next half century with generations of Chelsea residents and celebrities including members of the Rolling Stones, Anita Pallenberg, Eric Clapton, Bob Geldof, Gordon Ramsay and former Chelsea footballer Joe Cole. The author Martin Amis later recalled his youth 'mincing up and down King's Road in skin-tight velvet trousers and grimy silk scarves and haunting a coffee bar called the Picasso, and smoking hash, then £8 an ounce, and trying to pick up girls'.

After a short walk cross to the north side to visit 52 **the Pheasantry** at number 152. The building dates from 1769 and has had a variety of uses. In 1916 it was a ballet academy founded by the Russian ballerina Serafine Astafieva. Her pupils included Alicia Markova (discovered by Sergei Diaghilev when he visited), Anna Neagle and Margot Fonteyn. Later the Pheasantry Club and Restaurant was based here from 1932 to 1966, popular with stars such as Humphrey Bogart, Lauren Bacall, Dylan Thomas, Lucien Freud, Marc Chagall, Francis Bacon and Augustus John.

In the 60s, flats within the building were occupied by notable figures such as Germaine Greer, Clive James, Eric Clapton and Martin Sheer of the controversial *Oz* magazine. Clapton later recalled how he and George Harrison would take acid here while writing songs, and how he narrowly escaped a police drugs raid by escaping out of the back of the building. Sadly, the site is now occupied by a pizza restaurant.

After a short walk on the same side you pass 53 **Markham Square** on the left where PG Wodehouse (1881-1975) lived around 1900. On the eastern corner of the square and King's Road is number 138a, where Mary Quant's fashion boutique 'Bazaar' opened in 1955. Her signature hot pants and mini-skirts were an essential part of London's fashion scene at the time. The restaurant Alexander's was also located downstairs – frequented by Audrey Hepburn, Brigitte Bardot, Stanley Kubrick and Rex Harrison. Another iconic boutique from this era – Top Gear – was based nearby at number 135a.

Continue along King's Road. The next road up – and full of pretty pastel coloured houses – is Bywater Street and where John Le Carré's fictional George Smiley lived at 54 **number 9**. Two streets up on the same side is Anderson Street where Karl Marx and his family briefly lived at number four in 1849. They were soon evicted for rent arrears, the great political philosopher having to suffer the indignity of a crowd gathering to watch his family's possessions being dumped into the street by bailiffs.

Bywater Street

Opposite Bywater Street are Wellington Square and Royal Avenue. Visit the square first. While Ian Fleming never specifically gives an address for James Bond in his novels, the description in *Casino Royale* describes the secret agent living in a 'comfortable ground-floor flat in a converted Regency House in a square off King's Road'. John Pearson, who wrote a fictional yet authorised biography of Bond after Ian Fleming had died, placed the spy at 55 **30 Wellington Square**. Had Bond lived for real it would have been interesting to see how he would have got on with his neighbour Aleister Crowley, the Satanist, who once lived at 31 Wellington Square.

As you walk round to Royal Avenue you will see a branch of McDonalds on the corner. This stands on the site of the 56 **Chelsea Drugstore** – one of the very coolest places to be in the 'Swinging 60s'. Modelled on Le Drugstore on Boulevard St Germain in Paris, the London version offered visitors a selection of bars, food outlets, a chemist, a record store and boutiques and was open 16 hours a day, seven days a week. It also offered a 'flying squad' home delivery service featuring motorbikes and girls clad in purple catsuits. Unsurprisingly, traditional Chelsea residents detested the Drugstore but luckily for them its era, like many 60s fashions, was short-lived.

Scenes from Kubrick's controversial film *A Clockwork Orange* (1971) were filmed in the Drugstore. Mick Jagger included the lyric 'So I went to the Chelsea Drugstore to get your prescription filled' in the Stones 1969 song *You Can't Always Get What You Want*, and as he used to live nearby he would have known the place very well.

Enter 57 **Royal Avenue** and take in the fine view of the Royal Hospital to the south.

The avenue was laid out by Wren in 1682 and was supposed to be the first part of an intended route between the Royal Hospital and Kensington Palace. However after Charles II died, the project was abandoned.

Continue along King's Road where shortly on the right is 58 **Cheltenham Terrace**. From 1933 to 1935 Oswald Mosley's British Union of Fascists were based here in a now-demolished building named Black House. An extraordinary woman named Elinor Glyn (1864-1943) lived at number 39. A writer of romantic fiction, she had an affair with Lord Curzon, was present at the signing of the Treaty of Versailles, is credited with creating the term 'It girl' and spent several years in Hollywood as a scriptwriter.

Soon on the south side you reach a vast area that was formerly the Duke of York's Headquarters. In 2000 the area has been hugely re-developed, the most notable addition being the excellent 59 **Saatchi Gallery.** This occupies the main building that dates from 1801 and was originally home to the Royal Military Asylum and later became a military barracks. The site was sold by the Ministry of Defence to developers for £66 million in 2000.

Fight your way along the busy King's Road eastwards to reach

Sloane Square, passing Peter Jones which has served generations of Chelsea residents since 1877 (the current Grade II listed art deco building dates from the mid-1930s). If you have the energy you can visit the vast church of 60 **Holy Trinity Sloane Square**. The building was completed in 1890 and is a notable example of Arts & Crafts architecture. A major feature is the east window, designed by William Morris and Edward Burne-Jones. Otherwise, the walk ends in Sloane Square. ●

59 *Saatchi Gallery*

VISIT...

Royal Hospital Chelsea Museum
Royal Hospital Road, SW3 4SR
www.chelsea-pensioners.co.uk

Chelsea Physic Garden
66 Royal Hospital Road, SW3 4HS
www.chelseaphysicgarden.co.uk

National Army Museum
Royal Hospital Road, SW3 4HT
www.nam.ac.uk

Carlyle's House
24 Cheyne Row, SW3 5HL
www.nationaltrust.org.uk

Saatchi Gallery
Duke of York's HQ,
King's Rd, SW3 4RY
www.saatchi-gallery.co.uk

Brompton Cemetery
SW10 9UG
www.brompton-cemetery.org

SHOP...

Lot's Road Auctions
71 Lots Rd, SW10 0RN
www.lotsroad.com

EAT, DRINK...

Bluebird (see p.311)
350 King's Rd, SW3 5UU
www.bluebird-restaurant.co.uk

The Garden Museum, see p.334

Lambeth &
Vauxhall Walk

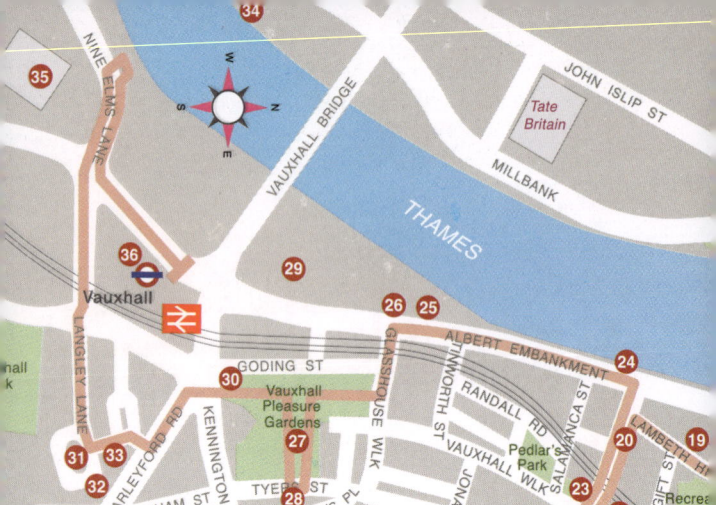

Map labels:

34 · 35 · NINE ELMS LANE · VAUXHALL BRIDGE · JOHN ISLIP ST · Tate Britain · MILLBANK · THAMES · 36 · Vauxhall · 29 · 26 · 25 · ALBERT EMBANKMENT · 24 · LANGLEY LANE · GODING ST · GRASSHOUSE WLK · TINWORTH ST · RANDALL RD · SALAMANCA ST · LAMBETH HI · HARLEYFORD RD · 30 · Vauxhall Pleasure Gardens · KENNINGTON LANE · VAUXHALL WLK · Pedlar's Park · 20 · 19 · 31 · 33 · 27 · Recrea Grou · 32 · DURHAM ST · TYERS ST · JONATHAN ST · 23 · WHITGIFT ST · 21 · 18 · ST OSWALD'S PL · 28 · TYERS ST · NEWPORT ST · BLACK PRINCE ROAD · LAMBETH WALK · 17 · VAUXHALL ST · The C · 22 · FITZALAN · ON S

Legend:

1. Lower Marsh
2. London Necropolis Station
3. Hercules Road
4. Centaur Street
5. Number One Centaur Street
6. Canterbury House
7. St Thomas' Hospital
8. Florence Nightingale Museum
9. Coade Lion
10. National Covid Memorial Wall
11. Lambeth Palace
12. Garden Museum
13. Archbishop's Park
14. The Marine Society
15. Juxon Street
16. Lambeth Walk
17. Newport Street Gallery
18. Old Paradise Gardens
19. The Windmill
20. Royal Doulton pottery company
21. Beaufoy Ragged School
22. Beaufoy Institute
23. Mosaics
24. Albert Embankment
25. Peninsula Heights
26. Tintagel House
27. Vauxhall Pleasure Gardens
28. Vauxhall City Farm
29. Secret Intelligence Service (MI6)
30. Royal Vauxhall Tavern
31. Bonnington Square
32. Harleyford Road Community Garden
33. Bonnington Café
34. Outflow of the Tyburn
35. New Covent Garden Market
36. Rowton House

Lambeth & Vauxhall Walk

HORSEFERRY RD

GREAT PETER ST

MILLBANK

PARLIAMENT SQUARE

PARLIAMENT ST

Westminster

Victoria Tower Gardens

Houses of Parliament

VICTORIA EMBANKMENT

THAMES

WESTMINSTER BRIDGE

Thames Path

Thames Path

London Eye

12

11

LAMBETH PALACE RD

10

9

Lambeth Palace Gardens

St Thomas' Hospital

7

Jubilee Gardens

BELVEDERE RD

8

13

Archbishop Park

ROYAL ST

UPPER MARSH

6

YORK ST

LAMBETH RD

14

CARLISLE LANE

5

LEAKE ST

COSSER ST

HERCULES RD

4

3

2

WESTMINSTER BRIDGE RD

1

Waterloo

ST WALK

KENNINGTON RD

Lambeth North

LOWER MARSH

CAB ROAD

SPUR RD

WATERLOO RD

LAMBETH RD

WESTMINSTER BRIDGE RD

BAYLIS RD

Waterloo Millennium Garden

CORNWALL RD

ROUPELL ST

Geraldine Mary Harmsworth Park

ST GEORGES RD

PEARMAN ST

MORLEY ST

WATERLOO RD

WEBBER ST

UFFORD ST

THE CUT

Imperial War museum

Lambeth & Vauxhall Walk
Start: Waterloo station
Finish: Vauxhall underground station
Distance 3.6 miles

Leave Waterloo station by the exit near platform one and follow the map along Cab Road and drop down along a pedestrian lane onto ❶ **Lower Marsh**. This street is named after the marsh that surrounded the original medieval thoroughfare, and today hosts a street market that began in the mid-19th century. Many of the buildings along the street also date from that century and it is now part of a conservation area.

Take a right along Lower Marsh and turn left on Westminster Bridge Road where at number 121 (on the other side of road) you can see the ornate former entrance to the now defunct ❷ **London Necropolis Station**. This unique railway service was operated by the London & South Western Railway and began transporting London's dead and their mourners 25 miles out to Brookwood Cemetery in Surrey in 1854.

The original terminus was based between York Street (now Leake Street) and Westminster Bridge Road. However, this was replaced by a larger building in the early 1900's while Waterloo station was being re-developed. The frontage at number 121 is all that remains of the second station.

Brookwood, once the world's largest cemetery, was created because of the problem of overcrowding in central London's old burial grounds. How the dead reached Brookwood depended on religious belief and class – there were different standards of train carriage according to what you could afford to pay, and at the cemetery end there was a north station for non-conformists and a south station for Anglicans. The original train service operated on a daily basis, but this was reduced to twice-weekly by the 1930s as other cemeteries around London were developed. The Necropolis Railway was closed after damage to the

line was inflicted by German bombing in 1941, and by 1948 the track had largely been removed. The north and south stations were dismantled over the following decades. Today, the only real remnants of London's strangest railway service are the frontage outside number 121 and the track bed of the railway that can still be followed through the grounds at Brookwood.

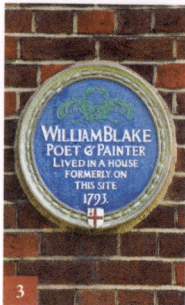

Follow the map passing Lambeth North tube station and head down ❸ **Hercules Road**. The poet and artist William Blake (1757-1827) lived in a house that once stood on the site of the modern flats at number 23 between 1793 and 1802 after moving here from Soho with his wife Catherine. Blake was robbed more than once whilst he was living here by thieves who haunted the surrounding marshes. The name Lambeth is itself derived from 'Loamhithe', an old English name for 'muddy landing place'.

Thomas Butts was one of Blake's patrons and a regular visitor to his house here. He once arrived to find the poet and his wife sitting naked in their garden enjoying the sun while reciting passages from *Paradise Lost*. Blake greeted his visitor with the cry 'Come in! It's only Adam and Eve you know!'. The Albion flour mill stood not far from here near Blackfriars Bridge, and was burnt down in 1791 – perhaps by angry workers whose jobs the mill was threatening. The burnt out shell of the mill would have been familiar to Blake as he travelled northwards, and it has been suggested this was the inspiration for the 'dark Satanic mills' depicted in Blake's famous poem *Milton*. The rubble-covered post-Blitz area around Hercules Road was used for most of the outdoor scenes in *Passport to Pimlico*, the charming Ealing comedy of 1949. In the film the residents of Pimlico (actually north of the Thames) find some historical documents suggesting their area of London is legally part of Burgundy in France and attempt to declare a state of independence.

Head down ❹ **Centaur Street**, looking out on the left for the striking modern house ❺ (**number 1**) just before the railway bridge.

Designed by Anglo-Dutch partnership de Rijke Marsh Morgan, it won a number of architectural awards, including RIBA London Building of the Year (1993). Continue walking under the railway bridge, along what initially appears to be a rather soulless stretch of road. However if you look on the walls, you will see mosaics depicting Blake's engravings and excerpts from his poems. This rather unexpected showcase of his work in a London tunnel is nevertheless in keeping with Blake's maverick spirit.

On the other side continue up Royal Street looking out for ❻ **Canterbury House** on the right-hand side. Now part of the many 20th-century housing estates that dominate this part of the borough, the building stands just to the south of the site of Canterbury Music Hall, one of the earliest and most important music halls in Victorian London. It was originally a public house, but impresario Charles Morton rebuilt it as a 700 seat venue in 1852. It was later rebuilt to host 1,500 people and rivalled the traditional theatres. Morton earned himself the nickname 'Father of the Halls' through his efforts, though he sold the venue in the 1860s to concentrate on other parts of his growing empire. It continued as a music hall although by WWI it was increasingly being used as a cinema. The building was damaged during the Blitz in 1942 and in the 1950s rebuilt as Canterbury House.

Cross Lambeth Palace Road to reach ❼ **St Thomas' Hospital**, named after Thomas à Becket. The hospital was founded in the 12th century in Southwark when it was originally part of the Priory of St Mary Overie. It was later re-founded by Edward VI on a secular basis after his father Henry VIII had dissolved the priory in the 1530s. The development of London Bridge station forced the hospital to move in 1862 and it re-opened here in the early 1870s.

Head right up Lambeth Palace Road looking out on the left-hand side for a sign to the **8** **Florence Nightingale Museum**, dedicated to the famous 'Lady with the Lamp'. Nightingale (1820-1910) came from a wealthy background, but provided help for the soldiers near to the battlefield during the Crimean War. She later establishing the first nursing school at St Thomas' in 1860.

Less well known is her Jamaican-born contemporary Mary Seacole (1805-1881). Seacole came from a modest background and despite her lack of funds and racial prejudice in Victorian Britain, was determined nurse wounded soldiers in the Crimea. Nightingale rejected her application, but she made her way to the war zone and established a valued team of nurses. Nightingale later dismissed Seacole as a 'woman of bad character' who kept a brothel ('a bad house') while in the Crimea. In 2016, after years of campaigning, a statute of Seacole was unveiled in the hospital gardens.

If you walk past the museum into the hospital grounds by the main entrance you can see a copy of a statue of Edward VI that was originally located within a gatehouse dating from 1682, and which stood in the original Southwark building. There are pleasant gardens to the east, often full of patients with their families enjoying the view across the Thames. One such patient was a thirteen-year-old Ray Davies who was later inspired to write *Waterloo Sunset*.

If you walk over to the north side of the hospital you get a great elevated view of the Palace of Westminster on the other side of the Thames. By tradition any commoner dying within the palace is normally recorded as having died at the hospital otherwise they would technically be eligible for a state funeral.

Follow the map to Westminster Bridge looking out for the ❾ **lion** made of Coade stone, an artificial ceramic that was famously weatherproof. It was invented by Mrs Eleanor Coade (1733-1821) and produced nearby until 1833 when cheaper alternatives forced the factory to shut down. Mrs Coade's stone was made to a recipe including ground fired ceramics, crushed flint, quartz, soda lime glass and Dorset clay and could theoretically be produced today, although its exact composition is still not known. The lion, originally coloured red, used to stand outside the Red Lion Brewery beside Hungerford Bridge and was moved here in 1966 after the Brewery was demolished.

When you reach the river, walk down steps to the Thames Path. Continue along the path following the Albert Embankment, created by the great engineer Sir Joseph Bazalgette between 1866 and 1869. This 500 metre stretch is now the site of the ❿ **National Covid Memorial Wall**. It began unofficially in March 2021 to remember those who died during the COVID-19 pandemic. The memorial is made from over 240,000 individually painted hearts, each representing a victim of the virus and often including a name and message inscribed by the grieving family.

About half way along you will be able to get a glimpse of the statue to Sir Robert Clayton behind the wall. Until 2022 you could have gained access to see the statue by the steps but this gate is now closed. Clayton rose from humble origins to

11 *Lambeth Palace*

become a successful merchant and Lord Mayor and helped finance the rebuilding of St Thomas' Hospital. Despite his undoubted achievements, Clayton was also involved in the slave-trade and his statue, by Grinling Gibbons', now faces an uncertain future.

From here you get a stunning view of Westminster and Millbank and eventually on the left you reach ⑪ **Lambeth Palace**, the official London home of the Archbishop of Canterbury since around 1200. London was once peppered with great religious palaces such as Lambeth, many situated close to Westminster so their priors and bishops could be close to the heart of the political process. Most disappeared or were severely diminished during Henry VIII's Dissolution of the 1530s, although Lambeth's prestigious connection to Canterbury ensured it was a unique survivor.

Stephen Langton is thought to have been the first Archbishop to live at Lambeth in the 13th century and the chapel named after him is the oldest surviving part of the palace complex. The distinctive red brick gatehouse visible from the street is known as Morton's Tower, and was built by Cardinal John Morton in around 1490. Saint Thomas More is thought to have lived in the Tower as a young man whilst working at Lambeth. At the rear of the palace is one of the oldest and largest private gardens in London. While the palace and gardens are generally closed to the public, guided tours are possible on certain dates (for further information visit the palace's website www.archbishopofcanterbury.org).

Just beside the palace is St Mary-at-Lambeth, the former parish church. It dates from 1377 and was restored by Philip Hardwick in the 1850s. Today it houses the **⑫ Garden Museum**, which is inspired by two of the country's greatest gardeners – John Tradescant the Elder (c.1570s-1638) and his son John the Younger (1608-1662). Both men worked for Charles I and other great figures of the aristocracy, and these connections ensured they had the opportunity to travel to countries such as America, Russia and Africa collecting plants and other curiosities. Many of the latter were housed by the Tradescants in the Musaeum Tradescantianum in Lambeth – more popularly known as 'The Ark' – which was the first public museum in the country. Among the odd items on display were a dragon, the hand of a mermaid, and the spurs of a Barbary pirate.

John the Younger married at St Mary's and signed over certain rights to the collection – when drunk – to the prominent lawyer, astrologer, alchemist and all-round bad egg Elias Ashmole (1617-1692). After John died, Ashmole continued his relentless campaign to acquire the collection by hounding John's widow Hester through legal proceedings but she resisted. Not long after she drowned in a pond in suspicious circumstances and Ashmole immediately took over the collection. It later formed the basis of the famous Ashmolean Museum in Oxford.

The Garden Museum contains a 17th-century style garden situated on the old church graveyard. Within it is the fantastically eccentric tomb of the Tradescant family, featuring some of the exotic places both Johns visited and a strange many-headed hydra. If you are interested in the Tradescants, they feature in two highly acclaimed historical novels by Philippa Gregory (*Earthly Joys* and *Virgin Earth*). She is also author of *The Other Boleyn Girl*, which in 2008 was made into a film.

Nearby is the family tomb of William Bligh (1754-1817), the inscription remembering his achievements as a navigator, warrior and the man who brought the breadfruit to the West Indies. It tactfully omits to mention his central part in the 'Mutiny on the Bounty', which took place in 1789 and made Bligh's name notorious even to this day. Bligh lived at number 100 Lambeth Road and was a parishioner here.

12

12

12

When leaving St Mary's follow the map along Lambeth Road, looking out on the left for ⑬ **Archbishop's Park**. The Park was opened in 1901 using part of the grounds of neighbouring Lambeth Palace.

Just before the railway bridge look out for the red-brick building which is home to ⑭ **The Marine Society & Sea Cadets Centre**. The Society is the oldest public maritime charity in the world, founded in 1756 with the original intention of providing recruits – mainly orphans or unemployed youths, for the Navy. Admiral Nelson served enthusiastically as a trustee, and by the time of the Battle of Trafalgar it has been estimated approximately 15% of the Navy's manpower was sourced through the Society. It therefore had an important part to play in the history of the British Empire. Today the Society continues to be involved with young seafarers through its association with the Sea Cadet movement.

On the right (before the bridge) head down Pratt Walk and follow this into ⑮ **Juxon Street**. This street is named after William Juxon, a clergyman who gave the last rites to Charles I and stood by him on the scaffold when the king was executed in 1649. Later, remembering this loyalty, Charles II made Juxon Archbishop of Canterbury, although he died shortly after at Lambeth in 1663. From Juxon Street you meet Lambeth Walk and turn right.

⑯ **Lambeth Walk** has long been famous as a bastion of working-class London, and retains some of that reputation to this day. It was immortalised in the song *The Lambeth Walk* which featured in the 1937 musical *Me and My Girl* – and inspired a jaunty 'Cockney' style dance that became a craze in England, America and elsewhere. It became so famous, and allegedly immoral, that it attracted official criticism from Germany's Nazi party. During WWII a British propaganda film edited footage of Hitler and other Nazis so it looked as if they were dancing *The Lambeth Walk*. Upon seeing the film the Nazi's own propagandist Joseph Goebbels ran from the screening room in a terrible fury.

Before WWII, Hitler's fascist ally – Mussolini – reacted rather differently, flying a female singer over from London to Italy to have her perform the song just for him.

Between the 1690s and 1755 Lambeth Walk (originally 'Three Coney Walk') was the site of Lambeth Wells, a pleasure palace offering music and other entertainment and as well as medicinal waters from two local wells. Nothing remains of this vibrant past and today Lambeth Walk is a fairly drab stretch of road, Hitler having exacted his revenge by bombing the old town to pieces during WWII.

Follow the map right down Old Paradise Street and you will soon pass the junction with Newport Street where stands the ⑰ **Newport Street Gallery**. The gallery is the brain child of artist Damien Hirst and is dedicated to his work and other contemporary artists in his considerable collection. If you have the time, the gallery is well worth exploring, not least to admire the work of achitects Caruso St John. Their imaginative conversion of a former theatre scenery workshop has received high praise since it opened in 2015 and won the Sterling Prize for architecture in 2016.

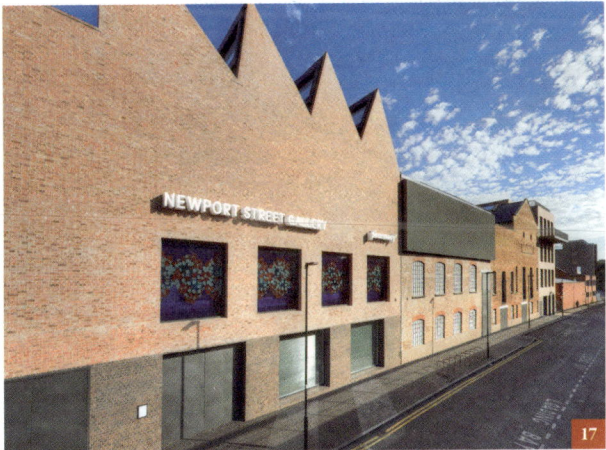

Continue down Old Paradise Street to reach the **18 Old Paradise Gardens**, on your left. This stands on a former burial site used between 1703 and 1853. Many of the old gravestones and cigar-shaped tombs are still visible, and a stone marks the spot of the 1825 guard house where the parish's drunk and disorderly were once confined until they sobered up. You will see in this vicinity classic examples of 20th-century London social housing, both pre and post WWII, with bikes hanging precariously from multi-storey flats and kids practicing Parkour on whatever ledges and walls they can find.

Continue along Old Paradise Street to reach Lambeth High Street and turn left. You pass by **19 The Windmill**, a rare example of a Victorian public house in this area, and whose name recalls the three windmills that once stood in this part of Lambeth.

Continue on to the junction with Black Prince Road. On the corner is an office block dating from 1878 that once served as the showroom, and one of the factories used by the **20 Royal Doulton pottery company** – one of the world's leading suppliers of ceramics and crystal. The unique façade is covered with elaborate terracotta carvings and Doulton tiles and if you look up you can just see the Doulton name spelt out. The company was founded in Lambeth in 1815 by John Doulton, and its headquarters remained nearby until 1956 when the business moved to its main pottery production centre in Staffordshire.

The Doulton business had a major influence on the area over the years it was based in Vauxhall, even having its own private dock (White Hart Dock – situated just over the wall at the junction of the Albert Embankment with Black Prince Road and Salamanca Street). As well as employing people in its pottery, it used many local artists trained at the Lambeth School of Art based nearby, which was founded in 1854 by William Gregory, vicar of St Mary the Less church.

To learn a little more about this area's social history, walk up Black Prince Road until reaching Newport Street and turn left. On the left you will see the building that was formerly the ㉑ **Beaufoy Ragged School**. This was opened in 1851 and sponsored by the Beaufoy family – who like the Doulton's – were an important local family and also great philanthropists. The Beaufoy's originally opened a gin distillery in the mid 18th century, later moving onto the manufacture of vinegar. The family eventually sold the business in the early 1930s.

The ragged schools formed a social and educational safety net for the poorest children, and this school could hold over 1,000 pupils. They were only educated on Sundays, as many of the children had full time jobs. There were several hundred ragged schools in England by the late Victorian age, however after the Education Act of 1870 introduced free state education, the ragged schools were taken over or closed. The building still has an educational role as home to the Beaconsfield Arts Gallery which has a pleasant café if you need a break.

Continue along Black Prince Road – named after Prince Edward, son of Edward III, who was famous for his black armour and who lived in Kennington Palace which stood not far from here. Shortly you reach on the right the junction with Tyers Street. The block of flats on the right stands on the site of Lambeth workhouse – another reminder of the great poverty in this area which remains a problem to this day.

Continue on a short way up Black Prince Road to reach the junction with Vauxhall Street. On the right is the superb former **22** **Beaufoy Institute** – founded in 1907 by the trustees of the ragged school, mentioned earlier, after they sold that building to a railway company. The façade is an excellent example of the terracotta tiles and mouldings characteristic of the then fashionable Arts & Crafts movement.

Re-trace your steps back to the Doulton building and look out for Tyers Street on the left. It is named after Jonathan Tyers (1702-1767), a crucial figure in the development of the Vauxhall Pleasure Gardens (dealt with in more detail later on in the walk). As you pass though the tunnel look out for the **23** **mosaics** of the Black Prince.

Continue past the Doulton Building to reach the **24** **Albert Embankment** that runs alongside the Thames. Vauxhall is part of the borough of Lambeth, the name originating from a 13th-century French mercenary known as Falkes de Brent. He acquired the name after using a scythe ('Falkes' in old French) to kill a man. He founded a house – or hall – on Lambeth marshes and Falkes Hall eventually became Foxhall and later Vauxhall.

The Frenchman's emblem was the griffin – adopted by Vauxhall Iron Works when founded in 1857 on Wandsworth Road nearby. This business became Vauxhall Motors, which moved to Luton in 1905. Now owned by Stellantis, Vauxhall cars still bear the griffin logo.

Continue along the Thames path. Ahead – and in direct contrast to the social housing already seen in Lambeth – is the exclusive **㉕ Peninsula Heights**. Formerly Alembic House, it was built in the 1960s and is perhaps best known for being the London home of the disgraced writer and former politician Jeffrey Archer. He lives in a penthouse overlooking the Thames that was previously occupied by 'Bond' composer John Barry and motor racing supremo Bernie Ecclestone. The penthouse contains Archer's art collection, and is where until December 2023, the fun-loving Tory hosted his famous annual 'shepherd's pie and Krug' parties. The building also features in the hit film *The Italian Job* (1969), with Michael Caine planning his robbery here.

Next door is **㉖ Tintagel House**, built in 1960 and occupied by the Metropolitan Police for fifty years. The radical anarchist group The Angry Brigade bombed the building in May 1971, releasing their '9th communiqué' the same day, which stated: 'The Angry Brigade is the man or woman sitting next to you. They have guns in their pockets and hatred in their minds. We are getting closer... Power to the People'. Now largely forgotten, the group exploded about 25 bombs between 1968 and 1971 although only one person was injured and nearly all damage was to property.

Cross over Albert Embankment into Glasshouse Walk – named after the huge glass works that once occupied a substantial area just to the south. The glass produced in Vauxhall was world-famous, beginning in the 1670s under the patronage of the Duke of Buckingham and lasting until the mid-19th century.

Walk through **㉗ Vauxhall Pleasure Gardens** which lie approximately on the site of pleasure gardens laid out in 1661 and originally named the New Spring Gardens. Jonathan Tyers, remembered in the street name mentioned above, bought the lease to the gardens in the 1730s and with the help of artists such as Hogarth, Hayman and Roubilliac transformed them into a hugely

profitable and innovative entertainment centre. People now had to pay to get in, but the delights on offer included pavilions, a rotunda, a raised orchestra platform, a hall of mirrors and 150 dining booths.

Visitors delighted in the orchestras, fireworks and candle-lit walks on offer. In 1749, 12,000 people attended a rehearsal of Handel's *Music for the Royal Fireworks*, and 60,000 people took part in a fancy dress celebration staged in 1786. In the 19th century balloon rides took place here, and in 1827 the Battle of Waterloo was re-enacted by 1,000 soldiers. In his novel *Vanity Fair* (1848), William Thackeray devotes a chapter to Vauxhall, with Becky Sharp visiting the gardens while trying to ensnare the hapless Joss Sedley.

The diarist Samuel Pepys (1633-1703) was a regular here and in May 1667 recorded how he went by 'water to Fox-hall [now Vauxhall], and there walked in Spring Garden. A great deal of company, and the weather and garden pleasant: that it is very pleasant and cheap going thither, for a man may go to spend what he will, or nothing, all is one. But to hear the nightingale and other birds, and here fiddles, and there a harp, and here a Jew's trump, and here laughing, and there fine people walking, is mighty divertising'.

An earlier visit in July 1665 was much less fun as it was during the height of the Great Plague. Pepys described how he travelled to 'the Spring garden; but I do not see one guest there, the town being so empty of any body to come thither. Only, while I was there, a poor woman come to scold with the master of the house that a kinswoman, I think, of hers, that was newly dead of the plague, might be buried in the church-yard..'.

By 1785 the site was known as Vauxhall Gardens – famous throughout the world for the quality of the entertainment on offer. The word 'Vauxhall' itself became a generic term to describe a pleasure garden. It is thought the name explains the origins of the Russian word for railway station – '*Vokzal*' – because the famous pleasure gardens, 'Vauxhall' at Pavlosk, was the destination of the first Russian railway line, which opened between that town and St Petersburg in 1837.

However, fashions change, and by 1860 London's three great pleasure gardens – Vauxhall, Marylebone and Ranelagh (in Chelsea) – had all closed. The Tyers family had continued to manage the Vauxhall Gardens well into the 19th Century, but the encroaching railway lines began to change the character of the area.

The gardens became scruffier and perhaps less appealing compared to the growing attraction of the new music hall and other entertainments that were borne of the Victorian age. Dickens, in his 1836 collection *Sketches by Boz*, wrote of how 'We walked about and met with disappointment at every turn'. The gardens were later built over and it was only after Blitz damage that the flattened area allowed the current Vauxhall Pleasure Gardens to be developed.

If you have time and have children with you, ㉘ **Vauxhall City Farm** on the south side of the Gardens is worth a visit (see p.347 for more information on visiting). There is also an excellent tea and cake shop – the Tea House Theatre – on the north side.

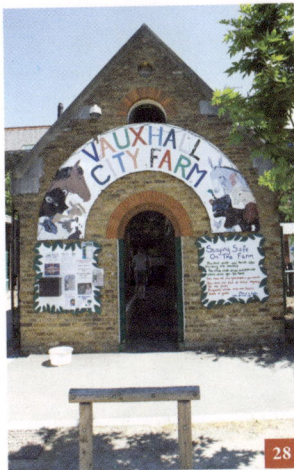

343

From the Gardens you can see the **29 Secret Intelligence Service (or MI6) headquarters** – designed by Terry Farrell – which opened in 1994. SIS had previously been located at Century House on Westminster Bridge Road. A walkway on the Thames Path leads around the building if you want a better look, and you may recognise the building from a number of films including the James Bond feature *The World is Not Enough* (1999). In September 2000 the building – which controversially cost over £250 million to complete – was hit by an anti-tank missile fired by a dissident Irish republican group. A hand-held rocket launcher was later found by the railway embankment near Vauxhall Pleasure Gardens.

Exit the Gardens on the south side, looking out on the right hand side for the **30 Royal Vauxhall Tavern** on Kennington Lane. The pub dates from 1862, and used to be a music hall. After WWII it became popular with the gay community, and in recent decades particularly known for the shows put on by drag artists, especially the late and great Paul O'Grady (aka Lily Savage). Vauxhall itself now rivals Soho as the centre of gay nightlife in London.

Follow the map down Harleyford Road and continue south along Vauxhall Grove to reach **31 Bonnington Square**. The sense of community spirit within the square is immediately obvious, and makes this one of the most unusual places in London. Much of the housing stock dates from the 1870s and was intended for railway workers. Many

properties are run by co-operative housing organisations, and heavily influenced by the squatting movement that was popular in the area in the 1970s and 80s. Together the residents have created the central 'Pleasure Garden' – one of the best community-run gardens in London. It is also open to the public, unlike so many of the gardens within the squares of West London.

Walk right round the square and on the north-east side a small alleyway leads into the ㉜ **Harleyford Road Community Garden** – another hidden gem. The vegetarian and community-run ㉝ **Bonnington Café** on Vauxhall Grove epitomises the Bonnington Square ethos and is well worth a visit. The co-operative rotates its cooks and you need to book ahead (see p.347 for more information).

From the square follow the map along Langley Lane and you soon reach Nine Elms Lane, then continue to the river bank alongside the Thames. There is a small garden and just before Vauxhall Bridge is the outflow of the River Effra, one of south London's 'lost' rivers that rises south of Crystal Palace. It flows through Norwood Cemetery and Dulwich, Herne Hill, Brockwell Park and Brixton before reaching the Thames. It was largely contained within the sewer system during the mid-19th century, and before then supplied fresh water to parts of south London such as Dulwich.

On the opposite bank of the Thames you can see the ㉞ **outflow of the Tyburn** – another hidden London river – which rises in South Hampstead and runs through central

London before reaching the Thames. The Tyburn sometimes leaks out into a tunnel at Victoria underground station and has to be pumped out for safety reasons.

Further to the west is ㉟ **New Covent Garden Market** – specialising in fruit, vegetables and flowers – which moved here from Covent Garden in early 1970s, where it had been based since the reign of Charles II.

From here re-trace your steps slightly and follow the map along Bondway. On the right look out for the massive Victorian building (numbers 1-9 Bondway) that was originally the first ㊱ **Rowton House** in London. Montagu William Lowry (1838-1903) – or Lord Rowton – was a philanthropist who helped London's homeless by setting up hostels. This one in Vauxhall opened in 1892 at the cost of £30,000 and eventually another five Rowton Houses were founded across London.

You are now beside Vauxhall underground and overland stations where this walk ends. ●

VISIT...

The Garden Museum (see p.334)
Lambeth Palace Road, SE1 7LB
www.gardenmuseum.co.uk

Vauxhall City Farm (see p.343)
165 Tyers Street, SE11 5HS
www.vauxhallcityfarm.org

Newport Street Gallery (see p.337)
Newport Street, SE11 6AJ
www.newportstreetgallery.com

SHOP...

Lower Marsh Market, SE1 7RG
www.wearewaterloo.co.uk

EAT, DRINK...

Tea House Theatre
139 Vauxhall Walk, SE11 5HL
www.teahousetheatre.co.uk

Bonnington Café
1 Vauxhall Grove, SW8 1TD
www.bonningtoncentre.org

The Garden Museum Café
Lambeth Palace Road, SE1 7LB
www.gardenmuseum.co.uk

St Saviour's Dock, see p.362

12 Bermondsey & Rotherhithe Walk

This is a map of the Bermondsey / London Bridge area showing numbered locations. Key streets and landmarks include:

HMS Belfast, Thames Path, ST KATHA, TOWER BRIDGE, London Bridge, City Hall, Potter's Fields Park, TOOLEY ST, SHAD THAMES, ST THOMAS ST, Guy's Hospital, WESTON ST, BERMONDSEY ST, CRUSIFIX LANE, GAINSFORD ST, SHAD THAMES, SNOWSFIELDS, GUY ST, CROSBY ST, Leathermarket Grdns, LEATHERMARKET ST, TANNER ST, TOOLEY ST, DRUID ST, JACOB, MILLWOLSELE, JAMAICA RD, LAMB WLK, TOWER BRIDGE RD, ROPEWALK, MALTBY ST, LONG LANE, ABBEY ST, NECKINGER, ENID ST, OLD JAM, GRANGE WALK, THE GRANGE, GRANGE RD, SPA R, Bermondsey Spa Gardens, SOUTH

1. Arthur's Mission building
2. Guinness Trust (1897)
3. Burial ground
4. London Leather Hide & Wool Exchange
5. Morocco Street
6. Number 78
7. Fashion & Textile Museum
8. White Cube
9. Christy & Co
10. St Mary Magdalen
11. Rectory
12. Time & Talents Settlement building
13. Graveyard of St Mary's
14. Old parish watch house
15. Bermondsey Square
16. Numbers 5-7
17. Bermondsey United Charity School
18. Grange Walk Infants School
19. Abbey Street Railway Bridge
20. Tommy Steele Plaque
21. New Concordia Wharf
22. St Saviour's Dock
23. Bermondsey Wall West
24. Barge gardens
25. Cherry Garden Pier

Bermondsey & Rotherhithe Walk

Wapping (⊖)

WAPPING HIGH ST

THAMES

Rotherhithe Tunnel

VAUGHAN WAY

...Y

...L WEST

...AMBERS ST

...OTT LIDGETT CRES

BEVINGTON ST

WILSON GROVE

MARIGOLD ST

WEST LANE

BERMONDSEY WALL EAST

CATHAY ST

King's Stairs Gardens

ST MARY CHURCH ST

SWAN ST

BRUNEL ROAD

ROTHERHITHE ST

Rotherhithe (⊖)

ALBION ST

NEPTUNE ST

MOODKEE ST

SURREY QUAYS RD

Canada Water (⊖)

DRUMMOND RD

SOUTHWARK PARK RD

JAMAICA RD

Bermondsey (⊖)

ST JAMES'S...

LOWER RD

SOUTHWARK PARK

HAWKSTONE RD

ROTHERHITHE NEW RD

...ARK RD

🔵 39 Cana.. Wat..

🔵 38

Map markers

25
26
27
28
29
30
31
32
33
34
35
36
37

Legend

26 14th century manor house
27 The Angel public house
28 Leaning tower
29 Rotherhithe Street
30 Mayflower public house
31 Brunel's Engine House
32 Grice's Grain Granary
33 St Mary Rotherhithe
34 St Mary Rotherhithe's Free School
35 Village Fire Station & Watch house
36 St Olave
37 Finnish church
38 Superintendent's Offices of Surrey Docks
39 Canada Water

Bermondsey & Rotherhithe Walk

Start: London Bridge station
Finish: Canada Water underground station
Distance 3.8 miles

From London Bridge station exit on the south side of the station to reach St Thomas Street. From here take a left and walk down past The Shard on your left until you reach Weston Street where you take a right.

Bermondsey is an up-and-coming area, combining grim estates with increasingly trendy areas such as Bermondsey Street. It is certainly not easy to imagine how this part of London looked in Saxon times when it was a largely desolate marshland punctuated by a few small islands.

Bermondsey's history really began when the Priory of St Saviour was established here by French monks of the Cluniac order in 1082, under the patronage of a wealthy Londoner named Alwinius Child. The priory drained the marshes and constructed river walls to stop the Thames from flooding the area and on the reclaimed land the monks built an extensive network of monastic buildings

as well as a farm that provided work for the locals. The priory became an abbey in its own right in 1399 and survived until Henry VIII's Dissolution of the Monasteries when the buildings were sold off, and later demolished in around 1540. The legacy of the old abbey, and Bermondsey's other great influences – the leather industries, and warehouses for the nearby docks – will be seen all along the walk.

As you walk down Weston Street take a small detour to the left down Snowsfields.

At the end is the ① **Arthur's Mission building (1865)**, which once housed a Victorian ragged school, and the splendid ② **Guinness Trust (1897)** flats opposite. They both serve as a reminder of Bermondsey's history as an area long blighted by social deprivation, and the efforts by Victorian philanthropists to improve the living conditions for those living in the slums. The Guinness Trust was founded in 1890 by Edward Cecil Guinness (1847-1927), great-grandson of the founder of the famous brewery, who injected £200,000 into the trust with the aim of providing housing for the destitute in Dublin and London. Today the trust continues his work, looking after around 4,000 properties across the capital.

Continue down Weston Street, in the shadow of the Shard skyscraper that stands 310 metres high (1,017 feet) and is one of the tallest buildings in Europe. It opened in 2013 and was designed by Renzo Piano, also responsible for the strikingly multi-coloured Central St Giles building near Oxford Street (see page 20), and perhaps best known for

4

4

5

his collaboration with Richard Rogers on the Pompidou Centre in Paris. On the right you pass a small park that in the 18th century served as the ❸ **burial ground** for Guy's Hospital. Further on, at the junction with Leathermarket Street, is the vast Victorian building that once housed the ❹ **London Leather Hide & Wool Exchange**, dating largely from 1879. The ornate reliefs by the entrance depict the processes of leatherworking including the buying and selling of hides, and the un-hairing and de-fleshing of the hide before it is hung up to dry.

From the Middle Ages Bermondsey was the principal place in London for the manufacture of leather goods, partly on account of a plentiful supply of water from the tidal Thames that was essential to the tanning process. The trading of leather hides also moved here in the 19th century from Leadenhall Market to the north, much of it taking place in the exchange. Bermondsey's location, well away from the City and more upmarket areas of London, meant it attracted industries that were generally unpleasant to live beside including tanneries that produced noxious smells and used dog faeces (called pure) to soften the leather.

By the end of the 18th century it was estimated that one third of all leather produced in the country was manufactured in Bermondsey, earning it the nickname 'the land of leather'. However, the reality of life here was captured in *Dicken's Dictionary of London* (1888), which described the area around the Exchange as being 'devoted entirely to skinners and tanners, and the air reeks with evil smells..', with the workers 'marked by many stains....and about them all seems to hang a scent of blood.' After WWII falling demand for leather goods and compulsory land purchases by the local council, helped drive out the industry from the area and the last tannery closed in 1997.

Continue along Leathermarket Street past a number of converted warehouses and tanneries, many with their original winching cranes still visible. The warehouses were used to store tanned hides, together with goods that had arrived from the Surrey Commercial Docks located in nearby Rotherhithe.

This street joins up with **5** **Morocco Street**, itself named after a type of leather once produced here. Much favoured as a book binding, 'Morocco' was made from goatskin which was dyed red and then tanned to bring up its characteristic bird's eye pattern. Ahead is Bermondsey Street, the most vibrant road in the area, and which was once the heart of

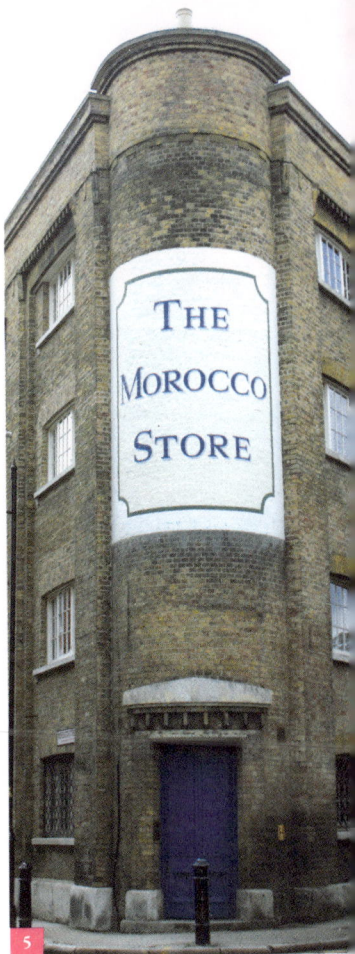

5

Bermondsey Village before it was swallowed by the rapid growth of London in the 18th century. Long before then Bermondsey Street had acted as a causeway for the medieval abbey across the surrounding marshes.

Head left to see a group of old houses on the left-hand side. The most notable building is **6** **number 78**, which dates from the late 17th century and features an oriel window and large well-lit attic above. Nearly opposite is the gaudily coloured **7** **Fashion and Textile Museum**. Founded by British designer Zandra Rhodes, the museum was designed by renowned Mexican architect Ricardo Legorreta and hosts regular fashion, textile and jewellery exhibitions (visit www.fashiontextilemuseum. org for details of forthcoming exhibitions).

Re-trace your steps and walk the other way down Bermondsey Street that now has many fashionable shops and cafés. You pass Tanner Street on the left, a reminder of the leather industry's historic importance to the area. The small park you can see stands on the site of St Olave's Union Workhouse. It was originally founded in the late 18th century and continued to be the last resort for the poor of the area until the start of the 20th century.

Continue down the street, looking out for the **8** **White Cube** gallery on the right-hand side. Owner Jay Jopling does not open

galleries just anywhere, and the choice of Bermondsey Street (the other is in St James) is official confirmation of this area as south London's coolest neighbourhood. Jopling made his name promoting the work of the so-called Young British Artists in the early 1990s including Tracey Emin and Damien Hurst. The gallery is a stunning modern space – a refashioning of a 1970s building by the architect Casper Mueller Kneer that was opened in 2012.

7 *Fashion and Textile Museum*

A little further along at number 169 and at the building just opposite once stood ⑨ **Christy & Co.** Founded in 1773, by the mid-19th century it was the largest hat and cap maker in the world and at its peak employed around 500 people. The phrase 'mad as a hatter' had a serious meaning in Bermondsey as the effects of the mercury and sulphuric acid on workers who used the chemicals to mould the hats often caused them to tremble and appear insane. The phrase was in fairly common use even before the appearance of the famous 'Hatter' character in Lewis Carroll's *Alice's Adventures in Wonderland* (1865). The company left Bermondsey in 1972, although it still survives today in Witney, Oxfordshire.

Ahead is the church of ⑩ **St Mary Magdalen**, the oldest building in Bermondsey, that was first recorded in 1290. The current building dates from 1680 although it incorporates a 15th century tower and parts were built in the 18th and 19th centuries. It retains its original ⑪ **rectory** alongside.

Beside the rectory at numbers 187-9 is the former ⑫ **Time & Talents Settlement building**. This charitable institution was founded in 1887 by a group of Christian ladies who wanted to help well-to-do girls use their 'Time and Talents' to help others. Based here from 1899 to 1962, the Settlement offered a clubroom for recreational activities such as basketwork and singing. In 1913 the group founded a hostel to house factory girls who were crowded out of their homes. Although its focus has changed somewhat, the charity is still going strong today, and is actively engaged in helping the disadvantaged of Bermondsey and Rotherhithe.

Just past the church on the left is the former **13** **graveyard of St Mary's**, now converted into a pleasant park. Among the tombs still found here is one for the Rolls family, who pioneered the luxury motor cars that still bare their name. By the entrance is the **14** **old parish watch house** dating from 1810 and used by the parish constables to guard against body-snatchers – otherwise known as resurrection men – attempting to steal the corpses of the recently interred. The building is now a smart café (see p.375).

At the time the watch house was built body-snatching was flourishing in the capital. This was because of the shortage of corpses available for dissection at the growing number of anatomy schools. Officially anatomists were only allowed to use the bodies of prisoners who had been sentenced to be executed and dissected. However, by the early 19th century only around fifty prisoners a year were being sentenced in this way,

and so the anatomists went to the resurrection men to fill the gap. The Anatomy Act of 1832 largely ended the trade allowing unclaimed bodies and those donated by relatives to be used for the study of anatomy.

Cross over Long Lane to continue down Bermondsey Street where on the left-hand side you will find the recently re-developed ⑮ **Bermondsey Square.** This was the site of the inner courtyard of Bermondsey Abbey that was founded in 11th century. After the abbey was demolished, it became the site of Bermondsey House, built by Sir Thomas Pope, founder of Trinity College, Oxford. Both great buildings are now long gone, and today the square hosts Bermondsey Market (officially the New Caledonian Market) early each Friday morning. The antiques market moved here from Islington in 1950 and until the 1990s benefited from the ancient law of 'marché ouvert' which meant stolen goods could be sold within the market between sunrise and sunset without anyone being able to later challenge a purchaser's legal title.

One great feature of the redeveloped square is that you can see the foundations of Bermondsey Abbey beneath a glass floor at number 11 (currently Lokma Restaurant).

Follow the map to enter **Grange Walk** which once formed part of the abbey complex between its eastern gatehouse and the monks' farm. In medieval times goods were transported from the abbey farm along the River Neckinger to St Saviour's Dock by the Thames (seen later on in the walk), however today the Neckinger is one of London's 'lost' rivers and flows underground. On the right-hand side of Grange Walk, at ⑯ **numbers 5-7**, can be seen some charming late 17th-century houses which incorporate part of the abbey gatehouse, the only other remnant of the abbey still visible.

Continue along Grange Walk looking out for two 19th-century school buildings that survive on the right-hand side – first the **⑰ Bermondsey United Charity School** dating from 1830, and later on the **⑱ Grange Walk Infants School** building from 1853. Head left up The Grange to reach Abbey Street.

At this point you can take a detour up Maltby Street and visit the bustling Maltby Street Market at Ropewalk. At weekends; stalls, shops, pop-up bars and eateries run along its length and under the neighbouring Victorian railway arches. At the end of Ropewalk turn left under the bridge, then right along Druid Street. Many independent food producers are based here and several open their doors to the public.

Continue along Abbey Street for a few minutes. You pass under a **⑲ Abbey Street Railway Bridge** and while doing so look out for the unusual supporting columns underneath. This bridge carried London's first railway – a pioneering venture that opened in 1836 and operated between Spa Road and Deptford, later extending to London Bridge and Greenwich. The original four-mile track was constructed across the meadows that still lay between Bermondsey and Rotherhithe.

Follow the map to cross Jamaica Road and walk down George Row. On the left look out for a **⑳ plaque** on the wall of Nickleby House marking the birthplace of Britain's first pop-star **Tommy Steele** (b.1937). On the left-hand side head down Jacob Street,

16

Ropewalk

19

21

22

bearing right at the end along Mill Street to follow the signs for St Saviour's Dock. You pass the massive buildings of ㉑ **New Concordia Wharf**, originally home to a 19th-century grain warehouse and later becoming the very first residential conversion in the Docklands. It is named after a prairie town near Kansas City, Missouri, whose imported grain was once stored here.

On the left, just before Mill Street bends round to the right to become Bermondsey Wall West, head up a small walkway that leads you to a footbridge running across the entrance to ㉒ **St Saviour's Dock**, also the site of the outlet of the River Neckinger. The river is believed to have been named after the 'devil's neckcloth' or hangman's noose used in past centuries here for the hanging of pirates and other criminals. This area was once part of a notorious slum named Jacob's Island, also nicknamed the 'Venice of Drains' on account of the noxious mud flats and streams that cut off the district from the rest of Bermondsey.

Jacob's Island was immortalised by Charles Dickens in *Oliver Twist* (1838), with the novel's chief villain Bill Sikes hiding out there before falling to his death in the mud-flats while trying to escape an angry mob. When describing the locality, Dickens writes of how there 'exists the filthiest, the strangest, the most extraordinary of the many localities that are hidden in London, wholly unknown, even by name, to the great mass of its inhabitants.... In Jacob's Island, the warehouses are roofless and empty; the

NEW CONCORDIA
·
WHARF

NEW CONCORDIA
·
WHARF

walls are crumbling down; the windows are windows no more... The houses have no owners; they are broken open, and entered upon by those who have the courage; and there they live, and there they die. They must have powerful motives for a secret residence, or be reduced to a destitute condition indeed, who seek a refuge in Jacob's Island'. Jacob's Island disappeared after its streams were filled in following a cholera epidemic in the mid-19th century, and the area is now very up-market with some flats in Concordia Wharf costing over £3 million.

Retrace your steps from the footbridge back onto Mill Street and continue along **23** **Bermondsey Wall West**, which runs parallel to the Thames. You will see on the left Tower Bridge Moorings with their **24** '**barge gardens**' – moored houseboats with fantastic gardens covering their decks. Despite this being a mooring site since the first half of the 19th century, in 2003 Southwark Council, after lobbying by residents of the nearby apartments, tried to evict the houseboats. A high profile and bitterly fought campaign by the boat residents resulted in the eviction plans being kicked out. The campaign was publicly supported by local resident and *Star Trek* actor Patrick Stewart who commented in 2004 that 'the converted wharf was once used to store goods, and now houses people. It makes sense for the historic moorings to now support a residential community'. This spot also offers the first panoramic view of the Thames with Tower Bridge and the City to the west and Canary Wharf to the east.

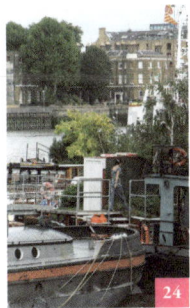

The path does not skirt the Thames continuously so follow the map inland to reach Chambers Street and then head down towards the river again via Loftie Street and Fountain Green Square.

Just ahead and overlooking the Thames is 25 **Cherry Garden Pier** where JMW Turner (1775-1851) sat to sketch the warship *Temeraire* as it was being towed to a breaker's yard in Rotherhithe. Turner's subsequent painting *The Fighting Temeraire* (1839) is today one of the best known paintings in the country, with its majestic depiction of the grand old warship – a veteran of Nelson's great victory over the French at Trafalgar in 1805 – on her final journey. In reality the *Temeraire* was badly damaged at Trafalgar and was later stripped of its masts and rigging before serving for many years as a prison ship. By the time Turner would have seen it the '*saucy Temeraire*', as she was known to her original crew, would have been a much-diminished sight so Turner clearly employed a great deal of artistic licence.

Samuel Pepys (1633-1703), the famous diarist, wrote of Bermondsey's rural charms when visiting a tavern that once stood here in 1667, recording that he 'took out my wife... and two of our mayds... over the water to the Jamaica House, where I never was before, and there the girls did run for wagers over the bowling-green; and there, with much pleasure, spent little, and so home'.

Continue east passing West Lane, the traditional parish boundary between Bermondsey and Rotherhithe. Ahead you will shortly see the historic Angel public house facing the Thames, and on the south side an area of open ground that contains the substantial foundations of a 26 **14th century manor house** built by Edward III (1312-1377). It is believed that Henry IV (1366-1413) later lived in the house in around 1412 while suffering from leprosy. A pottery factory and tobacco warehouse later occupied the site, and the medieval remains were only uncovered

during excavations in the mid-1980s. The Rotherhithe Mill Streams – one of London's 'lost rivers' – originated near here (around Southwark Park Road) and used to flow past the manor house.

27 **The Angel public house** dates from c.1837 but the original tavern dates back to the 15th century when it was owned by the monks of Bermondsey Abbey. The pub still contains trapdoors once used by smugglers trying to evade the landing charges on the Thames wharves. It also has fine views of the Thames and is a good place to stop for lunch.

Continue east past the Angel and on the same side, about 100 yards on, you will see an unusually thin, four storey building facing the Thames, known as the **28** '**leaning tower**'. For many years this served as the office for Braithwaite and Dean, a barge company. The barge workers – known as 'lighter men' – would come here to collect their wages. They performed a key role transporting goods from ships moored on the Thames back to the quays on the riverside. Their profession declined as London ceased to

be a global port during the 20th century, superseded by bigger docks such as Tilbury which were able to deal with the containerised cargoes introduced in the 1960s.

Continue east parallel to the Thames, through King Stairs Gardens, and shortly you reach the start of **29** **Rotherhithe Street**. What at first appears to be a rather quaint backstreet is in fact at two miles in length the longest street in London. We are now in Rotherhithe proper, although in Pepys's time it was known as Redriffe. The area has long been associated with the maritime industry and hundreds of docks, quays and wharves once lined this section of the Thames.

Many of the old, often timber-structured houses in this first stretch of Rotherhithe Street were favoured by the bohemian artistic set in the mid 20th century. However they were demolished in the 1960s, including one previously inhabited by the well-connected socialite and photographer Tony Armstrong-Jones (b.1930) – later the Earl of Snowdon after he married Princess Margaret. Snowdon recalled a night spent in his house being entertained at the piano by his friends Noel Coward and Marlene Dietrich. The poet Sir John Betjeman also lodged in Snowdon's house for a while, recalling how he put his bed 'to the river side of

the room and it was delicious to go to sleep to the solacing sounds of water'. Tasteful, but rather dull, modern flats now occupy this part of the street.

Continue heading eastwards and shortly you see the church of St Mary Rotherhithe on the right and the **30** **Mayflower public house** opposite. There's been a pub here since the 16th century, although it was rebuilt in 1780. It is a good place to stop for a break, and like the Angel offers panoramic views over the Thames. It is named after

Mayflower public house

the famous Rotherhithe-based ship that left from near here at the start of its epic journey in 1620 to take a group of religious non-conformists known as the Separatists to a new colony based at Plymouth, Massachusetts in America. Many of the Separatists – later known as the Pilgrim Fathers – joined the journey from the Netherlands where they had fled after suffering religious persecution in England.

Whilst their colony in America was not the first, it was ultimately the most successful. The captain of the *Mayflower* was Christopher Jones, a Rotherhithe resident who is buried in St Mary's. It is thought the ship was dismantled for its timber in Rotherhithe in around 1623, no doubt after being much battered on its gruelling voyage to America and back.

Continue past the Mayflower to see **31 Brunel's Engine House** on your right. In 1824 Marc Brunel (1769-1849), head of the most famous engineering family of the 19th century, began constructing the first tunnel in the world to be built under a navigable river. It ran between Rotherhithe and Wapping and was not completed until 1843, with the pump house playing a crucial role in preventing water from flooding the tunnel. However, the project was blighted by problems, including a collapse in which a number of workers died and Marc's son Isambard (1806-1859) almost drowned.

The tunnel was never successful financially, being only accessible on foot and full of squalid stalls selling their goods under gaslight. In 1865 it was taken over by a consortium of railway companies and now forms part of the East London Line. Today the Engine House contains the Brunel Museum, which is dedicated to the great engineering family and offers occasional floodlit tours of the tunnel (visit www. thebrunelmuseum.com for details).

Retrace your steps and walk down St Marychurch Street with St Mary's church on your right. On the left look out for the former 32 **Grice's Grain Granary** that dates from the late 18th century and is today home to **Sands Films**, a production company that is also a film studio and film costumer. Their picture research library is open to the public and contains a fascinating local history section.

Continue bearing right to reach the main entrance of 33 **St Mary Rotherhithe**. The church was built in 1715 and placed on plinths to prevent it being damaged by flooding from the Thames. It contains a number of memorials to the sailors and captains who lived and died in Rotherhithe, and some of the wood used inside was

salvaged from the *Temeraire*. Outside there is a memorial to the *Mayflower*, and the churchyard also contains the grave of Prince Lee Boo with the following inscription:

'To the memory of Prince Lee Boo, a Native of the Pelew or Palos Islands and Son to Abbe Thulle, Rupack or King of the Island Coo'roor'raa, who departed this Life on the 27 December 1784 aged 20 Years. This Stone is inscribed by the Honorable United East India Company as a Testimony of Esteem for the humane and kind Treatment afforded by his Father to the Crew of their Ship The Antelope [commanded by] Capt. Wilson which was wrecked off that Island on the Night of the 9th August 1783'.

The *Antelope* had been shipwrecked upon an island in what is today the Pacific Republic of Palau. The islanders helped Captain Henry Wilson and his crew to repair their ship, and their king persuaded Wilson to take his son Prince Lee Boo back to England to receive a Western education. The prince attended a Rotherhithe school and his exotic story generated a huge amount of interest. Sadly he died of smallpox six months after his arrival. His fellow islanders did not learn of his tragic end for many years. Today he remains a famous historical figure in Palau.

Near the graveyard is a building dating from 1797 that once housed 34 **St Mary Rotherhithe's Free School**. The school was founded in 1613 by two Elizabethan seafarers to teach the sons of their fellow sailors. The building still retains the figures of a boy and girl above the entrance. On the right past the old school you will pass the former 35 **village fire engine station** and **watch house**, both of which date from 1821 – the latter used to protect against body-snatchers who supplied Guy's Hospital. St Mary's Churchyard gardens lie behind the building and are worth a visit.

This immediate area seems like a location out of a period drama, but that feeling soon ends as you follow the road round to the left and continue ahead until you cross over the busy Brunel Road and the entrance to the Rotherhithe tunnel. The tunnel runs under the Thames and was opened in 1908. Just ahead facing onto Albion Street is the Norwegian church of 36 **St Olave,** and further along the same street at number 33 (beside the library) is the 37 **Finnish church**. Until 2013 there was also the Swedish Seaman's Church nearby.

The reason for these Scandinavian churches in this part of London lies just to the east, where the Surrey Commercial Docks once dominated the landscape. The docks in Rotherhithe originated with the

huge Howland Great Wet Dock, which was built in 1696 in unused marshland. During the 18th century this dock was used by Baltic whaling ships and re-named Greenland Dock. In 1865 it merged with Surrey Docks to form Surrey Commercial Docks.

A number of docks were created in this part of the Greenwich peninsula, many being named after the countries from where certain goods originated, such as Russia Dock, Canada Dock and Norway Dock. Britain was also a massive export market for the Scandinavian countries, and much of their timber would arrive at the Surrey Commercial Docks. During the 19th and early 20th centuries missions were opened near the docks to help stranded Scandinavian sailors, or those who had decided to settle here, and the Norwegian, Finnish and Swedish churches grew up to serve these new congregations.

The churches survive, but the Scandinavian sailors and their families have long since assimilated. The docks at Rotherhithe were shut down in the late 1970s, unable to compete with larger docks such as Felixstowe. Many of the docks were redeveloped, although Greenland and the Norway Dock still survive, as do Surrey Water and Canada Water.

Follow the map down Neptune Street into Moodkee Street and then bear right through St George's Field to reach Surrey Quays Road. Ahead is the former 38 **Superintendent's Offices of Surrey Docks** dating from 1887.

Continue along the road to cross Deal Porters Way, named after the athletic porters who worked on the docks. 'Deal' refers to the soft wood timber imported to the docks from North America. Just ahead lies 39 **Canada Water**, originally a dock but now a lake and wildlife reserve. Built in 1875-6, it became the main dock for the handling of Canadian produce.

Nearby is Canada Water underground station on the Jubilee Line where the walk ends. ●

Canada Water

SHOP...

Bermondsey Antiques Market
Bermondsey Square, SE1 3UN
Open: Friday 6am-2pm

Maltby Street Market (see p.361)
41 Maltby St, Ropewalk SE1 3PA
www.maltby.st

VISIT...

White Cube (see p.356)
144-52 Bermondsey St, SE1 3TQ
www.whitecube.com

Brunel Museum (see p.371)
Railway Avenue, SE16 4LF
www.thebrunelmuseum.com

**Fashion & Textile Museum
(see p.356)**
83 Bermondsey Street, SE1 3XF
www.fashiontextilemuseum.org

EAT, DRINK...

Fuckoffee
163-167 Bermondsey St, SE1 3UW

WatchHouse
199 Bermondsey St, SE1 3UW
www.watchhouse.com

The Angel (see p.367)
101 Bermondsey Wall East,
SE16 4NB

The Mayflower (see p.368)
117 Rotherhithe St, SE16 4NF
www.mayflowerpub.co.uk

About us:

Based in London, Metro is a small independent publishing company with a reputation for producing well-researched and beautifully-designed guides.

London's Hidden Walks Series

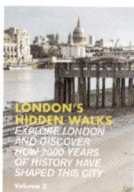

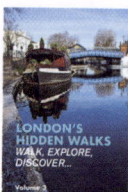

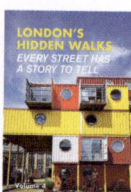

A wonderful way to explore this sometimes secretive city." Robert Elms, BBC London 94.9FM

To find out more about Metro and order our guides, take a look at our website:

www.metropublications.com

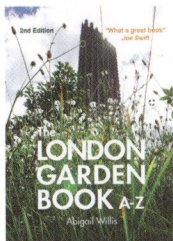

2nd Edition
"What a great book"
Joe Swift

The
LONDON
GARDEN
BOOK A-Z
Abigail Willis

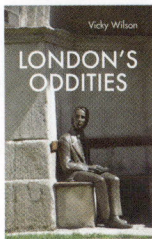

Vicky Wilson

LONDON'S
ODDITIES

LONDON
ARCHITECTURE
MARIANNE BUTLER

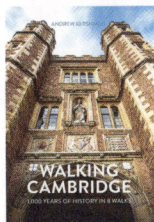

ANDREW KERSHMAN

WALKING
CAMBRIDGE
1,000 YEARS OF HISTORY IN 8 WALKS

ANDREW KERSHMAN

WALKING
BRIGHTON
& HOVE
1,000 YEARS OF HISTORY IN 8 WALKS

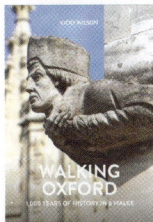

VICKY WILSON

WALKING
OXFORD
1,000 YEARS OF HISTORY IN 8 WALKS

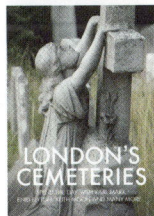

LONDON'S
CEMETERIES

STEPHEN MILLAR

LONDON'S
CITY CHURCHES

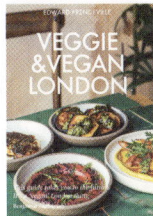

EDWARD FRENCH-LYLE

VEGGIE
& VEGAN
LONDON

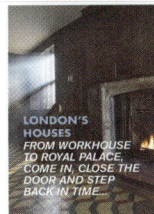

LONDON'S
HOUSES
FROM WORKHOUSE
TO ROYAL PALACE,
COME IN, CLOSE THE
DOOR AND STEP
BACK IN TIME...

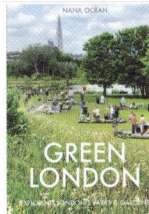

NANA OCRAN

GREEN
LONDON

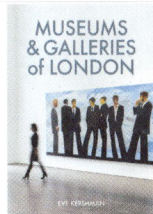

MUSEUMS
& GALLERIES
of LONDON

EYE KERSHMAN